ADVANCE PRAISE FOR

Datafied Childhoods: Data Practices and Imaginaries in Children's Lives

"What is it like to grow up with your every action tracked, analysed and potentially monetised? Today's children—the guinea pigs of the digital age—have no choice but to find out for themselves. But it is the wider economic and political interests of society that drive the processes of mediatization and datafication analysed in this ambitious and insightful book. Its conclusions should concern us all."

—Sonia Livingstone, London School of Economics;
Author of *Parenting for a Digital Future*

"Just as children experience all kinds of family and social backgrounds, their engagements with digital devices and data are diverse. In adopting a non-media-centric approach, this book does a wonderful job of revealing the diversity of datafied childhoods in all their nuances and complexities. Importantly, the authors acknowledge children's agency and the more-than-digital dimensions of their lives."

—Deborah Lupton, SHARP Professor, Centre for Social Research
in Health and the Social Policy Research Centre,
University of New South Wales, Sidney; Leader of the Vitalities Lab

"More than ever before, today's children are monitored and tracked across different digital platforms as they engage in education, play, and family life. In this thoughtful, child-centered volume, renowned childhood and family researchers Mascheroni and Siibak provide a comprehensive overview of international research on datafied childhood and parenting. Read this book to gain insights into how parents and children are navigating digital technologies, and to better understand the contemporary and future costs of a surveillance culture that is reshaping our families and our collective lives."

—Lynn Schofield Clark, University of Denver;
Author of *The Parent App: Understanding Families in a Digital Age*

Datafied Childhoods

Digital Formations

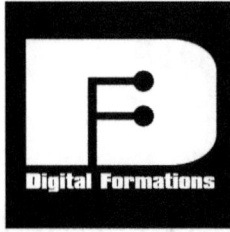

Steve Jones
General Editor

Vol. 124

The Digital Formations series is part of the Peter Lang Media and Communication list.
Every volume is peer reviewed and meets
the highest quality standards for content and production.

PETER LANG
New York • Bern • Berlin
Brussels • Vienna • Oxford • Warsaw

Giovanna Mascheroni and Andra Siibak

Datafied Childhoods

Data Practices and Imaginaries in Children's Lives

PETER LANG

New York • Bern • Berlin
Brussels • Vienna • Oxford • Warsaw

Library of Congress Cataloging-in-Publication Data

Names: Mascheroni, Giovanna, author. | Siibak, Andra, author.
Title: Datafied childhoods: data practices and imaginaries in children's
lives / Giovanna Mascheroni and Andra Siibak.
Description: New York: Peter Lang, 2021.
Series: Digital formations, vol. 124 | ISSN 1526-3169
Includes bibliographical references and index.
Identifiers: LCCN 2021027545 (print) | LCCN 2021027546 (ebook)
ISBN 978-1-4331-8314-0 (hardback) | ISBN 978-1-4331-8318-8 (paperback)
ISBN 978-1-4331-8315-7 (ebook pdf) | ISBN 978-1-4331-8316-4 (epub)
Subjects: LCSH: Internet and children. | Mass media and children. |
Internet of things.
Classification: LCC HQ784.I58 M37 2021 (print) | LCC HQ784.I58 (ebook) |
DDC 004.67/8083—dc23
LC record available at https://lccn.loc.gov/2021027545
LC ebook record available at https://lccn.loc.gov/2021027546
DOI 10.3726/b17460

Bibliographic information published by **Die Deutsche Nationalbibliothek**.
Die Deutsche Nationalbibliothek lists this publication in the
"DeutscheNationalbibliografie"; detailed bibliographic data are available
on the Internet at http://dnb.d-nb.de/.

To our daughters

CONTENTS

LIST OF TABLES

ACKNOWLEDGMENTS

The idea for this book emerged in November 2019, when Andra wrote an email to Giovanna inviting her to co-edit a volume on the datafication of childhood. Giovanna replied, suggesting that "the two of us could write the book, since we have both written extensively on children, families, and the internet, and, more recently, on children's data."

Following this email exchange and a Skype call, we enthusiastically embarked on this journey, and had the first draft of what is now Chapter 2 written by the end of December 2019. However, the journey to completing the book took much longer: life, work, and the COVID-19 pandemic in particular interfered with our passionate engagement with the datafication of children's (and families') lives.

We are therefore deeply grateful to our own families for their patience and support at times when everyday family life was complicated not only by the commitment that writing a book requires, but also by the restrictions implemented to contain the pandemic, and the complexities of balancing work with being home and parenting. Giovanna thanks her partner Massimiliano and her daughter Clara for tolerating weekends that she spent in front of a computer with a distracted mind, fully absorbed in this project—thanks for your love and understanding! Andra is deeply grateful to her partner and her daughters for their unconditional love, support, and understanding, and for her parents and sister for being the greatest safety net ever. Without the encouragement and support from you all, we would never have completed this project.

We would also like to thank the many friends and colleagues who helped us sharpen the ideas developed throughout the book through inspiring conversations, invitations to seminars, and day-to-day collaboration on common research projects. These include: Gaia Amadori, Piermarco Aroldi, Veronica Barassi, Göran Bolin, Davide Cino, Fausto Colombo, Nick Couldry, Ola Erstad, Catrin Finkenauer, Lelia Green, Leslie Haddon, Ellen Helsper, Andreas Hepp, Veronika Kalmus, Sonia Livingstone, Anu Masso, Tijana Milosevic, Maria Murumaa-Mengel, Jessica Piotrowski, Pille Pruulmann-Vengerfeldt, David Smahel, Julian Sefton-Green, Elisabeth Staksrud, Mariya Stoilova, Marit Sukk, Katrin Tiidenberg, Simone Tosoni, Lorenzo Zaffaroni, Bieke Zaman, and many more—sorry if we left anyone out. Thank you all!

We are very thankful to the series editor, Professor Steve Jones, for his recommendations and warm encouragement to develop our ideas into a book. We are also grateful to Dawn Rushen, who painstakingly edited our text and polished it from all the imperfections of non-native speakers. Formally, we note that the editing and proofreading were supported by Fondazione Cariplo, through the grant Ricerca Sociale 2019 for the DataChildFutures project.

In the book, we base our considerations on empirical evidence collected as part of the many research projects in which we have been involved since 2010 and earlier. We would therefore like to acknowledge the generosity of the families, children and parents alike, who let us into their homes and their lives.

This book is the outcome of a genuine and equal collaboration: we have shared each chapter, and we have learned a good deal from working with each other.

· 1 ·

INTRODUCTION

What This Book Is About

This book is about the multiple ways in which digital media, sensing networks of internet-connected objects, algorithms, and artificial intelligence (AI), are transforming the contexts in which children are growing up, as well as the practices in which children, families, and educators engage in their everyday life. By this, we do not mean to suggest that the latest technological developments alone are responsible for radical changes in childhood. Although the experience of being a child is undoubtedly changing, so, too, are parenting cultures, families, and education—in a word, society. While the children of today are still fundamentally children, and childhood has always been diverse, "children growing up today are among the first to be datafied *from birth*" (Children's Commissioner for England, 2018, p. 11; original emphasis). As homes, schools, and cities are increasingly equipped with smart technologies that collect data about the users and the environment, mundane everyday practices generate an incessant flow of data, while being simultaneously shaped by data. Therefore, as more of children's lives become digital, socialization, learning, development, self-expression, and social interaction are shaped by the very technological infrastructures and communication practices that support them. Childhoods and the media are changing in relation to each other, and in the context of broader social, political, technological, and economic transformations.

In this work, we argue that looking at datafication through the lens of children's and families' lives helps to avoid absolute and universalizing claims on the consequences and implications of data-driven business and governance models.

Our Approach

With this book we make the argument that the relationship between the changes in contemporary childhood and the changing media environment should be analyzed against the backdrop of broader social, political, technological, and economic transformations. Therefore, we make use of a child-centered perspective that recognizes children's active role in media socialization and in a surveillance culture, without neglecting the structuring force of social institutions—including the power of datafication and algorithmic governance—on childhood.

More specifically, we draw on the following assumptions, that will be discussed more thoroughly in Chapter 2 that follows. First, we theorize datafication as both a product and an intensifier of mediatization (Couldry & Hepp, 2017; Hepp, 2019)—an outcome of mediatization insofar as almost each and every social action and interaction is now mediatized and generates data traces, as well as objects of various kind being turned into media (Bunz & Meikle, 2018); but also as an accelerator of mediatization, since our everyday interactions and actions are increasingly reliant on the infrastructures of data and automation.

Second, in line with the "materialist phenomenology" (Couldry & Hepp, 2017, p. 5) that informs the social-constructivist theorization of mediatization, we adopt a "non-media-centric" approach. This means that our discussion of datafication assumes everyday life as the analytical entry point, aiming at foregrounding the practices through which digital media are put to use in social life, and the social consequences of data practices from the viewpoint of social actors. Relatedly, we also aim to emphasize how datafication is more than a data-driven business logic (Zuboff, 2019). Rather, it is a pervasive ideology (van Dijck, 2014) that has been normalized and interiorized in social imaginaries (Couldry & Mejias, 2019; Lyon, 2018), thus informing

and transforming social practices. On these bases, if we are to have a meaningful understanding of datafication, it is important to ground it "within the
frames of reference of ordinary people" (Lyon, 2018, p. 186). In the study of
the datafication of childhood, this approach translates into the attempt to
de-center data in order to look at the practices through which data are generated, consumed, and made sense of, in the diverse digital-material contexts
of children's lives. Accordingly, the book examines the datafication of early
childhood across differing life stages—the unborn, the baby, the toddler, the
preschooler, the primary school child, and the teen—and different life contexts: the home, the school, the peer network.

Understanding the contexts, actors, practices, media, and power relations
that give shape to the datafication of childhood is crucial if we want to avoid
both simplistic solutions and misplaced concerns. In fact, an everyday life,
non-media-centric approach to datafication is also a powerful antidote to the
resurgence of media power, and the displacement of media audiences by the
power of the data traces they leave behind (Livingstone, 2019). However, we
should not forget that "hopes and fears about media audiences have oscillated
over history, tightly linked to society's hopes and fears about the power of the
media and the uses to which they are put" (Livingstone, 2019, p. 170). As
much as audience studies have contributed to recalibrate problematic con-
ceptions of media audiences as powerless and vulnerable subjects, we believe
that empirical evidence on the situated data practices and imaginaries will
contribute to eradicate the essentialist generalizations that go to the detriment of a true understanding of the consequences of datafication for children. Conversely, contextualizing data into everyday life is vital if we want
to counter the ideology of *dataism* (van Dijck, 2014) and subvert the assumed
"normal" and inevitable character of datafication. As will be illustrated
throughout this book, there are reasons to believe that this is an opportune
moment, given current trajectories, to call into question the continued datafication of childhood at home, at school, and in a child's peer group, and to
imagine a different future in which data are repurposed for the social good and
best interests of children.

Overview of the Book

Chapter 2 that follows lays out our argument's foundations: the notions of
mediatization, datafication, surveillance capitalism, and a surveillance culture

within which the datafication of children's lives is contextualized. The chapter frames datafication as an outcome and an intensifier of mediatization, which has become naturalized and legitimized through citizens' interiorization of the culture of surveillance. Therefore, it examines how datafication—as the monitoring, tracking, and quantification of the environment and social practices into online quantified data—has emerged as a business model that is typical, at least initially, of social media and internet companies, but it has spread quickly within different social spheres, including family life, education, play, and so on. The pervasiveness of datafication cannot just be explained by its economic success as a source of profitable revenues. Instead, the normalization of datafication in a variety of everyday life contexts presupposes legitimizing ideologies and discourses that sustain a form of "data religion" or *dataism*—the belief in the validity of data and data-processing technologies, as well as in the predictive accuracy of algorithms for achieving various types of goals and resolving diverse social, political, and economic challenges. It is through the incorporation of technologies of data collection in a wide range of everyday life practices that the power of data and algorithms is actualized and performed. Therefore, we agree with scholars who understand datafication as an ensemble of data practices and data imaginaries that are appropriated, negotiated, enacted, and resisted at the level of everyday life, rather than an "a priori" condition.

Chapter 3 explores how children and young people are becoming increasingly entangled in human data assemblages, creating and shaping their data selves through various online and offline practices. A plethora of embodied technologies and mobile apps for fitness, health, and wellbeing provide young people with new opportunities for self-knowledge and self-presentation, inviting them to develop their own body, as well as self-projects, and to reach their self-improvement goals as part of the "quantified self movement." So, on the one hand, various gamified nudges these technologies are built on evoke a certain kind of agency, that of an active subject willing to succumb to self-governance while striving for self-realization and self-management. On the other hand, however, through the constant and willing self-surveillance and a series of gamified techniques that nudge the individual into self-discipline, such technologies turn users into docile bodies who need to adhere both to the standards set by the algorithms by which they are judged, as well as their peers who often act as markers of reference. Furthermore, despite the fact that the dataveillance economy is valorizing on the behavioral and biometric data generated through the use of such technologies, and is turning both self-trackers and biohackers into self-quantified commodities, the members of the younger generation seem to have adopted and accepted the idea of the human body as the greatest platform bound to generate value in this age of surveillance capitalism.

Chapter 4 provides an overview of the mediatized and datafied parenting practices present-day parents engage in. The mediatized performance of parenthood is often initiated during pregnancy, that is, by sharing the first ultrasound image on social media or through the use of pregnancy apps to monitor the fetus's development, leading to the datafication of the unborn. Such intimate surveillance continues after birth in the form of sharenting—that is, the (semi-)public sharing of family photographs and videos on social media—or through the use of parenting apps and wearables to monitor the infant's health, mood, or wellbeing, and later, in the use of parental controls or other tracking devices. Such mediatized parenting practices have also been called "caring dataveillance" to emphasize the entanglement of caring and dataveillance in the contemporary practices and imaginaries of "good parenting." However, once parenting practices become mediatized and increasingly reliant on technologies of caring and sharing, they are simultaneously imbued with a data-driven business logic called surveillance capitalism.

Chapter 5 explores the domestication of a variety of internet-connected devices in the homes and lives of families, and investigates how the boundaries between the home and the outside world, the private and the public, are being transformed. Indeed, the Internet of Things (IoTs), such as smart speakers or internet-connected appliances, turns the home into a datafied environment and family members into resources that provide data. The relations between family members and between social actors and the domestic environment are increasingly mediatized and data-driven. Yet, instead of arguing for the smart home as radical change, the chapter builds on previous studies of the role of the media in the domestic context—especially on the domestication of technology approach—to show how mediatization is constitutive of the very modern notion of home: the modern home emerged as a private, self-contained, autonomous space only because it was constitutively constructed as a relational space, dependent on overlapping interconnections with the outside world. At the same time, we acknowledge the specificity of the relationships between users and these new media objects. While the IoTs simulate interpersonal interactions and enter into a (scripted) communicative relationship with its users, their ability to automate processes and practices renders them increasingly opaque, and inaccessible to users. The chapter, then, focuses on the domestication of smart speakers by examining research on their incorporation into the domestic context, the most common practices initiated by adults or children, and the ways in which their presence is a source of conflict and negotiations in parent–child relationships.

Chapter 6 examines how a further agent of children's socialization—the peer network—is increasingly involved in forms, practices, and imaginaries of datafication. The peer group is a central part of children's socialization: it is through interactions with peers that children make sense of adults' cultures and produce their own. However, the process and practices that are shaped in interactions with the peer group—friendship, identity, and play—are now datafied. The notion of friendship itself is being reconfigured by algorithms that measure the frequency and visibility of contacts on social media as a proxy for intimacy, thus modeling friendship ties. The algorithms of (in)visibility also shape children's relations to their peers in unprecedented ways: while conforming to peer pressures and shared norms has always been an important part of negotiating self-identity in adolescence, the invisible work of algorithms makes such conventions more normative and binding, while the socialization to forms of self-tracking normalize a "quantified habitus." Children naturalize watching and being watched as a way of life, learn how to share mundane aspects of their daily lives, and how to measure and benchmark their bodies and activities against the backdrop of standard measures. The algorithms of social media also shape the ways in which children engage in and create their own digital cultures, with the rise of micro-microcelebrities on various platforms (YouTube, TikTok, Instagram, etc.). Play is also increasingly digital. Digital play is simultaneously a token for participation in peer interaction and an identity marker, as well as a further agent of datafication. The digitalization of peer cultures and relationships has intensified the datafication of childhood—indeed, it has been an essential resource during COVID-19 lockdowns, to compensate for lack of face-to-face interactions and physical play.

Chapter 7 goes on to describe how the datafication of the educational sector and increasing dataveillance of students is affecting millions of children on a daily basis. Although surveillance is deep-rooted and naturalized in the field of education, the growing predominance of the neoliberal logic that is inviting the schools and students to succumb to datafication in the name of better education has reached new heights. Much of these data-infused technological developments, such as facial recognition cameras, proctoring software, fingerprint scanners, learning analytics, or various attendance-tracking technologies, are dependent on students' biometric or behavioral data, and have not only started to transform the education sector, but also to change the learners', educators', and our own sociotechnical imaginaries of education. Students' data drain has accelerated and intensified even further during COVID-19, when educational systems all over the world have become dependent on the use of data-intensive edtech platforms capitalizing on the crisis.

Chapter 8 discusses the social consequences of datafication for children's futures. First, it engages with current examples of the inequalities and discrimination generated by datafication and the subsequent automation of decision-making and governance. Drawing on these examples, it shows how algorithmic social sorting affects children's access to education, health, job opportunities, credit, and so on. It argues that digital dossiers are therefore likely to impact profoundly not only on children's preferences and social relations, but more substantially, on their life chances too. Due to the biases in the data on which it is trained, algorithmic-automated governance results in allocative harm, exacerbating pre-existing social inequalities and vulnerabilities. Moreover, the chapter discusses the representational harms of datafication—namely, the impact of harmful stereotypes that are being reinforced through the regimes of algorithmic visibility. Furthermore, the novel social imaginary that legitimizes the social order of data colonialism is increasingly incorporated into identity projects as children are encouraged to use self-tracking applications and technologies by parents and/or teachers, and as algorithmic popularity base successful self-presentation on metrics such as number of "likes" or followers. The chapter, then, makes the argument that the social and political consequences of datafication extend beyond privacy issues to the sociocultural transformation of the very conditions under which citizenship is enacted: in fact, social media logic reshapes citizens' engagement. While the evidence regarding the existence of filter bubbles and echo chambers is disputed, the evidence around the resulting political polarization and fragmentation is less contested. What is under threat is citizens' public connection, that is, the feeling of belonging to a collectivity and the basic civic orientation to social and political issues as problems that affect every member of that given community. Finally, the chapter discusses the limitations of current regulations that protect children's rights to privacy, often to the detriment of other rights. However, it concludes that the recent General Comment 25 adopted by the United Nations (UN) Committee on the Rights of the Child, that extends children's rights to the digital environment, is an important recognition that children's rights apply online as much as offline. Here we see the seeds of an alternative discourse on datafication, that does not legitimize the imperative of data collection to the detriment of children's individual and social rights.

References

Bunz, M., & Meikle, G. (2018). *The Internet of Things*. Polity.

Children's Commissioner for England (2018). *Who knows what about me? A Children's Commissioner report into the collection and sharing of children's data*. www.childrenscommissioner.gov.uk/wp-content/uploads/2018/11/who-knows-what-about-me.pdf

Couldry, N., & Hepp, A. (2017). *The mediated construction of reality*. Polity.

Couldry, N., & Mejias, U. A. (2019). *The costs of connection: How data is colonizing human life and appropriating it for capitalism*. Stanford University Press.

Hepp, A. (2019). *Deep mediatization*. Routledge.

Livingstone, S. (2019). Audiences in an age of datafication: Critical questions for media research. *Television & New Media*, 20(2), 170–183. https://doi.org/10.1177/1527476418811118

Lyon, D. (2018). *The culture of surveillance: Watching as a way of life*. Polity.

van Dijck, J. (2014). Datafication, dataism and dataveillance: Big data between scientific paradigm and ideology. *Surveillance and Society*, 12(2), 197–208. https://doi.org/10.24908/ss.v12i2.4776

Zuboff, S. (2019). *The age of surveillance capitalism: The fight for a human future at the new frontier of power*. Profile Books.

· 2 ·

THE DATAFICATION OF EVERYTHING

Collecting Data From and About Children

"We are all now datafied—but children growing up today are among the first to be datafied *from birth*" (Children's Commissioner for England, 2018, p. 11; original emphasis). It is with these words that a report issued by the Children's Commissioner for England in November 2018 aimed to draw public attention to the massive collection of data from and about children, urging action from researchers, policy-makers, educators, and parents by pointing towards the problematic consequences of such an unprecedented and pervasive datafication of childhood. While the social, cultural, and political consequences of datafication have been addressed by a growing body of research in the area of critical data studies, surveillance studies, media studies, and digital sociology, the datafication of childhood has been relatively under-investigated, some notable exceptions notwithstanding (see, for example, Barassi, 2020; Lupton & Williamson, 2017; Montgomery, 2015; Siibak, 2019). This is surprising when compared to the vast amount of studies focused on other risky consequences of children's internet use, such as cyberbullying, sexual and violent content, excessive internet use, and screen time.[1]

Furthermore, the paucity of empirical evidence on the datafication of childhood so far available seems in contrast to the current age of "deep mediatization" (Couldry & Hepp, 2017; Hepp, 2019), when digital media have come to permeate all contexts of socialization—first and foremost the home—and are implicated in many of the everyday practices in which children engage. The internet has, in fact, become "a taken-for-granted means for being and doing" (Hine, 2015, p. 8), the medium through which even younger children, at least in Europe and North America, engage with the world (Livingstone, Mascheroni, & Staskrud, 2018). Touchscreen mobile media like tablets and smartphones slip easily into the routines and regimes of everyday life, and are now largely accessible to young children: recent research has shown that 95% of children in the U.S. aged 8 or younger have access to a smartphone at home and 78% to a tablet (Rideout, 2017). Likewise, 58% of 3- to 4-year-old children and 76% of 5- to 15-year-olds in the UK use a tablet at home (Ofcom, 2018; see also Marsh et al., 2018). Touchscreens offer intuitive and haptic forms of engagement such as tapping, swiping, and dragging (Broekman, 2018; Holloway, Green, & Livingstone, 2013), enabling young children's autonomous engagement with online content. As a consequence, not only are children online at an increasingly younger age, but they also generate an unprecedented, ongoing flow of personal and behavioral data that are being harvested, analyzed, manipulated, and commodified. It is estimated that the average child is exposed to up to 2 million online trackers per year, which collect around 5 million data points (Harris, 2017).

Children today do not encounter automated data collection and algorithmic calculation systems only as a result of their direct engagement with digital media; data about them is generated and shared by parents and other family members, and increasingly, by a number of internet-connected devices at home and at school. The datafication of childhood, then, is further expanded by two simultaneous and interdependent developments: namely, the mediatization of parenthood (Damkjær, 2018) and the domestication of Internet of Things (IoTs) devices.

New parents are increasingly performing their transition to parenthood through online communicative acts, that is, by sharing the first ultrasound image on social media (Leaver, 2015, 2017; Tiidenberg & Baym, 2017). A growing number of mothers are using pregnancy apps to monitor the development of their fetus and to track their own health parameters (Barassi, 2017; Bert et al., 2016; Lupton & Pedersen, 2016; Thomas & Lupton, 2016; Tripp et al., 2014). In this way, data about and around the child are generated from early gestation. Since the early days of the internet, pregnant women have turned to online discussion forums and websites (Das, 2020; Lupton, Pedersen, & Thomas, 2016) or "mommy blogs" (Morrison, 2011; Orton-Johnson, 2017) to find emotional support and information about pregnancy and childrearing. Men are also turning to the internet, to social media in particular, to "learn how to be a good father" (Ammari & Schoenebeck, 2015) and about a "caring fatherhood" practice, gaining support from online socialization (that is, communicating with other fathers for encouragement, confirmation, and advice; see Eriksson & Salzmann-Erikson, 2013). The mediatized performance of parenthood continues after birth, whether in the form of sharenting—the (semi-) public sharing of family photos and videos on social media (Autenrieth, 2018; Blum-Ross & Livingstone, 2017; Damkjær, 2018; Lazard et al., 2019; Lipu & Siibak, 2019; Siibak & Traks, 2019), or through the use of parenting apps and wearables to monitor infants' health and track sleeping or feeding patterns (Mascheroni & Holloway, 2019b; Nelson, 2008). Mediatized parenting practices (Mascheroni, Ponte, & Jorge, 2018), such as those briefly outlined, have been labeled "intimate surveillance" (Leaver, 2015, 2017) or "caring dataveillance" (Lupton, 2020) to emphasize the entanglement of caring and dataveillance (surveillance by means of digital data and datafication) in the contemporary practices and imaginaries of "good parenting." However, once parenting practices become mediatized and increasingly reliant on technologies of caring and sharing, they become simultaneously imbued with the very data-driven business logic that Zuboff (2015, 2019) calls "surveillance capitalism." We shall return to this later. Consequently, the small acts of intimate surveillance constitute children "as data which simultaneously provide reassurances about their well-being to parents while being aggregated and analyzed as elements of big data sets" (Leaver, 2017, p. 8). Once collected, turned into data, and aggregated, data about children and their behavior cease to be contextualized within the parent–child relationship of care, and become measurable, quantifiable, benchmarkable units of analysis, and sources of economic value in particular.

It is in the broader sociocultural context of caring dataveillance, mediatized parenting, and surveillance capitalism that numerous IoTs are designed and marketed for the child and the family. IoTs are objects and devices integrated into the digital infrastructures of the internet and equipped with different kinds of sensors, so that they can track users' behavior and personal data (including biometrical data); monitor the surrounding environment and react to various physical inputs (sounds, images, touch, movements, temperature, etc.); interact with users in real time on a personalized basis; and generate information (data) that is circulated through digital networks and feeds into profiling and predictive analytics. In a word, sensors and connectivity turn physical objects into "media—that is: means of communication and data production" (Hepp, 2019; p. 42) that "mediate what has not been mediated before" (Bunz & Meikle, 2018, p. 18). IoTs for children or accessible to children include wearable technologies such as socks, anklets, onesies, and smart dummies for the monitoring of babies' health; the Internet of Toys (Mascheroni & Holloway, 2019a), consisting of robots, talking pets and dolls, smart building blocks, etc.; smart watches to track children's whereabouts; and virtual home assistants and other domestic internet-connected appliances. Thanks to their monitoring capabilities and their networked connectivity, such objects refashion our homes into "datafied environments" (Hintz, Dencik, & Wahl-Jorgensen, 2017, p. 732) that allow for the nearly ubiquitous quantification of everyday life.

If we consider the quantification and commodification of children's data, the datafication of childhood does not differ from the datafication of (nearly) everything. Datafication can be defined as the massive and systematic monitoring, recording, and transformation of social actors' everyday practices online and offline—including aspects of the world not previously datafied and measured, such as friendship ties and emotions—"into online quantified data, thus allowing for real-time tracking and predictive analysis" (van Dijck, 2014, p. 198). The massive datafication of virtually everything originated as a business model. Indeed, the mechanisms of data extraction, manipulation, and monetization fulfill the logic of surveillance capitalism, which "aims to predict and modify human behavior as a means to produce revenue and market control" (Zuboff, 2015, p. 75).

However, the consequences of datafication extend beyond the market. Datafication as a business logic is legitimized through discourse and imaginaries. As van Dijck clearly outlined in her 2014 contribution, datafication is premised on the belief that human behavior—and increasingly, emotions (McStay, 2018)—can be monitored, quantified, predicted, and ultimately molded. The profitable appropriation and manipulation of data rests on a process of abstraction of the messiness of everyday life into abstract categories. Indeed, data is nothing but "the material produced by abstracting the world into categories, measures and other representational forms ... that constitute the building blocks from which information and knowledge are created" (Kitchin, 2014, p. 1). By means of automated predictive analytics, children, like adults, are temporarily classified and identified with "measurable types"—namely, dynamic "data templates" to which users are temporarily assigned based on the correspondence of their personal and behavioral data with pre-identified algorithmic models (Cheney-Lippold, 2017). The process of algorithmic identification means that online "a child 'is' according to what they do" (Willson, 2018, p.13). Or, more precisely, a child "is" according to how closely their data stacks up to pre-existing categories of children. Children are categorized according to the data they themselves (and their parents or carers) produce.

Data extraction and algorithmic classifications are not only used to construct different profiles of (children) consumers and to deliver targeted advertising or ad hoc personalized services and content; they are also employed as a means of data-driven governance, to regulate access to resources and services. Datafication may, in fact, generate opportunities for personalized learning, social inclusion, and civic and political empowerment, but it may equally result in discrimination, exclusion, and marginalization, especially if monopolized by a few corporations, as is the case in the current "platform society" (van Dijck, Poell, & de Waal, 2018). Concern is rising about the short- and long-term consequences of the datafication of children's lives. Back in 2015, Kathryn Montgomery had already contended that the continuous flow of data generated by and about children would form "'digital dossiers' that could follow young people into adulthood, affecting their access to education, employment, healthcare, and financial services" (2015, p. 268). Algorithmic classifications regulate and govern children's position in society by shaping the directions and futures that become available to them, thus potentially producing new forms of discrimination and inequality. Algorithmic social sorting, then, is likely to impact profoundly not only on children's preferences, social relations, and life chances, but also on children's rights (Livingstone & Third, 2017; Lupton & Williamson, 2017; Montgomery, 2015; Willson, 2018), and the very foundations of citizenship—including social imaginaries—are being transformed (Hintz et al., 2018; Isin & Ruppert, 2015; Mascheroni, 2018).

While adults—especially those who are already vulnerable and disadvantaged (Eubanks, 2018; Gangadharan, 2017; Marwick & boyd, 2018)—are equally affected by the predictive privacy harms (Crawford & Schultz, 2014) generated by algorithmic governance, throughout this book we make the argument that the consequences for children can be even more serious. Not only may children experience limited civic, social, and political rights in the future, on the basis of the data collected by and about them since they are born—or even since gestation—but children themselves are increasingly embedded within big data epistemologies, and socialized to being calculated and simultaneously, calculate themselves (Lupton & Williamson, 2017). Since early childhood, children learn how to share mundane aspects of their daily lives, and how to measure and benchmark their bodies and activities against the backdrop of standard measures. What are the consequences of growing up in datafied environments, amidst mundane data practices, and being socialized to what we might call a "quantified habitus" (Mascheroni, 2018)? What are the meanings of such data practices for parents, teachers, and children themselves? How is datafication being normalized in the context of children's everyday life? What are the tools, contexts, and relations that sustain children's datafication? These are some of the issues we will address throughout this book.

In this chapter, we provide the theoretical coordinates that will help us disentangle the social consequences of the datafication of childhood and family life, and which build the foundations of our interpretive framework. Our starting point is the assumption that datafication cannot be simply interpreted as the surveillance and monitoring of citizens/consumers through the use of data. Rather, we understand datafication as (1) an outcome and an intensifier of mediatization (Couldry & Hepp, 2017; Hepp, 2019); (2) which has become naturalized in both citizens' imaginaries and practices through a culture of surveillance (Lyon, 2018; van Dijck, 2014); (3) to the point that it is colonizing each and every life space (Couldry & Mejias, 2019).

Datafication as an Outcome and Intensifier of Deep Mediatization

The first building block of our theoretical framework is represented by the understanding of datafication as both an outcome and an intensifier of deep mediatization—an outcome of mediatization insofar as almost each and every social action and interaction is now mediatized and generates data traces, but also an accelerator of mediatization—as algorithmic-based automations increasingly characterize and structure the everyday opportunities for interaction and agency, digital media are more and more embedded into the texture of users' everyday lives, as well as institutional and corporate processes.

Before discussing the importance of looking at the datafication of childhood through the lens of mediatization in more depth, we need to position our book within a specific tradition of mediatization research, and clarify the concept of mediatization itself. Our approach to datafication builds on the social-constructivist perspective in the mediatization discourse (Hepp, 2013, 2019), which is interested in critically analyzing the interrelation between changes in media and communication on the one hand, and changes in culture and society on the other, from the viewpoint of human actors. The social-constructivist tradition of mediatization assumes that, despite its increasing complexity, "the social world remains something accessible to interpretation and understanding by human actors" (Couldry & Hepp, 2017, p. 5), thus emphasizing the practices of meaning-making through which digital media— and also, increasingly, data (Lupton, 2019) and algorithms (Bucher, 2018)— are appropriated and rendered meaningful in the context of everyday life. Within such a phenomenological perspective, mediatization can be conceived of as a sensitizing concept (Lunt & Livingstone, 2015, drawing on Blumer, 1954), which calls for an analysis of the interrelation between media change and social change as part of the daily communicative practices that form the basis for the social construction of everyday life. The notion of mediatization, however, is not characterized by a narrow focus on the micro-dimensions of the social world—or by neglecting the materiality of media and their infra-structures, as we will discuss later. By contrast, mediatization addresses and "describes the higher-order process of transformation and change across society that result from mediation going on at every level of interaction" (Couldry & Hepp, 2017, p. 35). In other words, the social-constructivist tradition in mediatization research assumes the everyday as the starting point for a comprehensive understanding of broader social, cultural, political, and economic transformations that are interwoven with changes in the media environment.

Mediatization, then, refers to the increasing entanglement of the social world with mediated processes of communication, with digital media and their infrastructures. As Couldry and Hepp argue, "the social world is not just mediated but mediatized: that is, changed in its dynamics and structure by the role the media continuously (and recursively) play in its construction" (2017, p. 15). It would be misleading to conclude that, according to mediatization research, every social domain and every social practice is now necessarily mediated. Rather, what Couldry and Hepp (2017) aim to highlight is, first and foremost, how the media have become "'environmental', being embedded in and significantly constitutive of today's practices, relationships and institutions" (Livingstone & Blum-Ross, 2017, p. 67). Not only are digital media saturating more and more social domains, producing a shift in balance between face-to-face and mediated interaction, but also, and more importantly, digital media have become both resources and reference points for human agency, even when we are not directly using any media to sustain social practices. Non-mediated interaction increasingly presupposes and depends on digitally mediated processes of communication and technological infrastructures: "the point is not that the face to face becomes less important but that in order to sustain its primacy (e.g. family meals) we now require continuous mediated coordination" (Hepp, 2019, p. 29).

The second point that Couldry and Hepp's definition emphasizes is the notion of recursive transformation (Hepp, 2019, p. 109). In computer science, recursivity means that the "rules are reapplied to the entity that generated them" (Couldry & Hepp, 2017, p. 217). When the social world becomes "sustained in and through media and their infrastructures" (Couldry & Hepp, 2017, p. 15), and many social practices become entangled with algorithmic-based media, the recursivity of social change deepens, and the complexity of the social world itself increases. Indeed, mediatization has both quantitative—the pervasiveness of digital media—and qualitative dimensions—the social and cultural consequences of media's saturation of everyday life (Hepp, 2019). The growing pervasiveness of digital media, the increasing interdependence of media and their infrastructures, along with the complex layering of mediated and non-mediated communication processes is what characterizes the current stage of radical mediatization or "deep mediatization" (Couldry & Hepp, 2017; Hepp, 2019). Deep mediatization, then, refers to a more profound, fine-grained saturation of everyday life with digital media, and simultaneously, to a deeper interdependence and interconnectedness of the technological infrastructures and social structures on which media practices depend.

Couldry and Hepp (2017) hypothesize that datafication represents a further wave of deep mediatization, characterized by a deeper interdependence between the media practices in which individuals, groups, and organizations engage, and infrastructures of communication based on the collection and processing of data. In his latest book, Andreas Hepp (2019) instead includes datafication among the five current trends of deep mediatization—along with the differentiation in the vast range of media available; the increasing connectivity enabled by the growing interconnectedness of such media; the omnipresence of media in every sphere of the social world; and the accelerated pace of technological innovation. As a quantitative trend characteristic of deep mediatization, datafication depends on the transformation of media into software-based, automated processes (Hepp, 2019).

The complex entanglement of algorithms, artificial intelligence (AI), and data traces, however, is precisely what motivates our understanding of datafication as simultaneously a consequence of deep mediatization—its more emblematic product—and a force molding the speed, reach, and pervasiveness of deep mediatization—an intensifier and accelerator. The more everyday life becomes mediatized, the more it is datafied, that is, turned into data that are subject to both symbolic and economic valorization. Vice versa, the more data traces generated in the context of everyday life become valuable resources in surveillance capitalism, the more users are encouraged, or pushed, to mediatize increasing portions of their everyday practices.

Irrespective of how we theorize the relationship between mediatization and datafication, the notion of mediatization provides a useful heuristic for the study of the everyday embedding of algorithms and data in children's lives. Taking the view that all the dimensions of the social are now constituted through digital media and their infrastructures translates into relevant epistemological and methodological standpoints. Namely, mediatization research assumes a "non-media-centric" approach that foregrounds the practices through which media are put into use in social life, and the social consequences of such media practices (Couldry, 2012). In the study of the datafication of childhood, this means to de-center data to look at the practices through which data are generated, consumed, and made sense of, in the diverse digital-material contexts of family life. A non-media-centric and non-data-centric approach to datafication recognizes that data traces are deeply entangled with situated social practices, and that the digital is an embedded, embodied, and everyday experience (Hine, 2015). Rather than assuming datafication as an a priori, universal condition of contemporary childhood and parenthood, we believe it is vital to "acknowledge that datafication is experienced and called into question at the level of the everyday" (Kennedy & Bates, 2017, p. 704). Therefore, we argue for the need to understand the relationship between changing media and changing childhood as it unfolds in the everyday practices and experiences of children, their families, and their communities.

A non-media-centric perspective, then, fits well with two further epistemological approaches that inspired our work; namely, the understanding of media as a socially situated environment of practice, and the epistemology of the everyday as the site where the social is made, remade, and unmade. On the first side, a non-media-centric approach to datafication is consistent with the notion of the media as "polymedia" (Madianou & Miller, 2012), that is, an environment of practice that is socially and culturally situated. Instead of focusing on discrete technologies, a non-media-centric and non-data-centric approach considers the datafied, media-saturated environment in which children and their families navigate in order to accomplish various everyday practices as a whole, looking at the relationships between the different digital media within such an environment of practice, between people and technology, and "among people through and 'in' media" (Madianou, 2015, p. 2). This also implies a shift from media-centric notions of the affordances of digital media (see, for example, boyd, 2010) to the non-media-centric concept of "affordances-in-practice" (Costa, 2018), which indicates "the process that mediates between the functionalities of a technological artifact and their enactment in situated social practices" (Berriman & Mascheroni, 2019, p. 802).

Second, the social-constructivist tradition within the mediatization debate adheres to epistemologies of the everyday that acknowledge the mundane but transformative potential of everyday life practices (Bakardjieva, 2011; de Certeau, 1984). Scholars in media and communication or data studies have already warned against essentialist and deterministic accounts of datafication, calling for the need to contextualize data traces within the everyday life contexts in which people generate, use, and make sense of data, and acknowledging the ambivalence of data practices as both empowering and alienating (Breiter & Hepp, 2018; Couldry & Hepp, 2017; Kennedy, Poell, & van Dijck, 2015; Lupton, 2020; Pink et al., 2017). More recently, a few empirical studies have started to approach the datafication of parenting and childhood in the context of everyday life, showing how the messiness, uncertainty, and taken for grantedness of everyday life generates complex entanglements of data and practices in family life (Mascheroni, 2020). For example, Lupton's (2020) work on how women are using apps during pregnancy and the early years of motherhood shows how dataveillance conducted in the context of caring relationships can be experienced by women as empowering and as an expression of love. Without neglecting how caring dataveillance is being constructed as a normal and normative part of being a "good" mother, she points to the diverse agential capacities that are implicated in the practices of dataveillance. Similarly, Thornham (2019, p. 179) argues that the "datalogical construction" of motherhood through apps silences the lived experiences of mothers—their emotions, anxieties, and everyday frustrations—as a potential threat to "a clean and simple, 'scientific' and atomized metric." However, while the metrics of the datalogical health discipline maternal bodies and practices, this is not without resistance and critique: for the mothers in Thornham's study, these data practices are not taken for granted and unreflective. Rather, parenting apps seem to encourage a process of reflexivity that makes them meaningful to mothers. In her research project on the impacts of big data on family life, Barassi shows how "children are being profiled on the basis of highly contradictory, inaccurate and imprecise data traces" (2018, p. 174), with parents failing to record systematically each and every behavior or pattern. Ultimately, systematic tracking of a child's behavior and health data fit poorly with the messy world of real families. Therefore, algorithmic calculations and predictions based on such erroneous and unsystematic data collection practices are necessarily untruthful and deceptive. Autenrieth (2018), Damkjær (2018), and Siibak and Traks (2019) equally show how parents appropriate, negotiate, and even resist sharenting by avoiding sharing photos, or by inventing new photo practices that minimize children's data.

The concept of mediatization adds to the epistemologies of the everyday by emphasizing the role of digital media and their infrastructures in constituting the social. Moreover, the social-constructivist approach to mediatization advances a materialist phenomenology (Couldry & Hepp, 2017) that simultaneously accounts for the symbolic and material aspects of everyday practices. More precisely, a materialist phenomenology recognizes the materiality of the digital—the materiality of the media, their underlying infrastructures, but also the materiality of algorithms and data—and the complex entanglements of the digital, the material, and the social that constitute social practices. However, as discussed above, it still conceives of the social world as constructed, at least in part, through communication and interpretation. In so doing, it rejects radical ontological posthuman or more-than-human approaches that assume no ontological distinction between human and non-human actors. Rather, it looks at the relations between humans and technology as situated enactments of the affordances—and the agency—of machines.

Datafication as a Cultural Phenomenon: The Culture of Surveillance

The reference to cultural materialism within the social-constructivist tradition of mediatization also constitutes a building block of our analysis of datafication under a further respect, as it frames the materiality of digital media as an integral part of their institutionalization. The institutionalization of media and mediatized communicative practices is a process through which digital media and their infrastructures acquire social legitimation and become part of the reciprocal expectations that govern social interactions: they are normalized and taken for granted as a "normal," constitutive component of social action and interaction. As Couldry and Hepp write, "'naturalization' is often an aspect of such materiality: certain forms and material aspects of media use, over time, have come to be so basic to everyday action that they seem 'natural'" (2017, p. 32).

In other words, the materialization of the media not only translates into the material presence of the media and its infrastructures, but also into their legitimate presence among "the norms and beliefs about 'how things are'" (Couldry and Hepp, 2017, p. 32). Institutionalization and materialization go hand in hand. What we want to emphasize here is that the mediatization and datafication of many everyday life practices now constitute for many a taken-for-granted experience and a precondition for social action and interaction. To put it more precisely, on the one hand, datafication has social and political consequences only on condition that the devices, platforms, and infrastructures that enable the quantification of almost every behavior and emotion become so meaningful and interwoven into people's everyday practices that they are eventually perceived as inevitable. On the other hand, through their institutionalization and materialization the media that support datafication become a "norm:" opting out of mediatized forms of interaction is less and less an option when digital media become (constructed as) inseparable from sociality. Therefore, it is through the process of naturalization of digital media in both its symbolic and material dimensions that datafication itself is normalized.

As already highlighted, the extension of the surveillance business logic of massive data extraction and algorithmic classifications from the consumer realm to other social contexts and spheres (the workplace and the labor market, the home and the relations of care, the school and education, health, etc.), has been possible only through its social legitimation and normalization through big data epistemologies. It is on the basis of an ideological and epistemological apparatus that automated data processing sits at the heart of the new regimes of algorithmic governmentality (Cheney-Lippold, 2017; Hintz et al., 2018), that is, the use of data and predictive analytics to regulate access to resources. Datafication would not have become so pervasive and so taken for granted if it weren't accompanied by a legitimizing ideology called "dataism" (van Dijck, 2014). Dataism presupposes, first, the unconditional belief that everything can be quantified and turned into data; and second, that big data constitute objective, more accurate, and impartial means of knowledge that can effectively supplement or replace human knowledge and judgment—by nature subjective, inaccurate, and partial. Moreover, a further assumption on which the ideology of dataism builds is represented by the belief that "a self-evident relationship between people and data" exists (van Dijck, 2014, p. 199). It is the positioning of data as truthful representations of individuals and social life that ensure their social legitimation as a one-size-fits-all solution for a variety of social problems (boyd & Crawford, 2012), as well as a means for personal empowerment (Lupton, 2016): from issues of national security, to the prediction of climate change or epidemics, to more effective management of welfare systems, to the improvement of one's productivity or sleep quality, big data seem to offer a panacea for each and every social problem. Finally, a fundamental ideological ground of dataism is trust in the (corporate or institutional) agents that collect, store, and process data. To put it simply, datafication enthusiasts endorse an understanding of online quantified "data as natural traces and of platforms as neutral facilitators" (van Dijck, 2014, p. 199). An example of dataism is provided by Thornham (2019), whose study of the datalogical perinatal care shows how midwives and physicists are inclined to trust digital data collected by apps and monitors more than the supposedly inaccurate subjective experiences of mothers.

The ideology of dataism is further elaborated on by Couldry and Mejias in their recent book (2019) where they discuss four narratives that, combined, provide the grounds for the social legitimation of datafication and its uncontested acceptance. First, there is the imperative of connectivity, "the requirement to connect here and now" (Couldry & Mejias, 2019, p. 16), which presents as natural, and even compulsory, the technologically mediated connections between individuals, groups, organizations, things, and processes. Then they discuss the ideology of datafication defined, as previously in van Dijck (2014), as the firm belief that everything must be quantified and translated into data in order to ensure its monetization. What makes datafication "attractive" (Couldry & Mejias, 2019, p. 16) to consumers is the commercial discourse of personalization, the promise of personalized services and content in return for individuals' acceptance of continuous data collection. Further, the myth of inevitability presents the technological infrastructures of connectivity and data extraction as inevitable, a progress that cannot be stopped, but will ultimately benefit all.

The ideological components of dataism shape user practices and give rise to a novel social imaginary, that is, to a "common understanding that makes possible common practices and a widely shared sense of legitimacy" (Taylor, 2004, p. 23). The emergence of such a datafied imaginary—or, more precisely, a culture that binds together imaginaries and practices—is what, according to Lyon (2018), distinguishes contemporary surveillance from both the surveillance state characteristic of modernity and the surveillance society of the last few decades. Rather, we now observe a shift from surveillance as "an institutional aspect of modernity or a technologically enhanced mode of social discipline or control" (Lyon, 2018, p. 9) to a culture of surveillance that reconfigures the repertoire of everyday practices and informs the shared beliefs about how things are and should be. Lyon emphasizes the mutual shaping of (data) practices and (datafication) imaginaries. Indeed, explicitly drawing on Taylor's (2004) theorization of social imaginary, Lyon defines surveillance imaginaries as:

> . . . shared understandings about certain aspects of visibility in daily life, and in social relationships, expectations and normative commitments. They provide a capacity to act, to engage in, and to legitimate surveillance *practices*. In turn, surveillance practices help to carry surveillance imaginaries and to contribute to their reproduction. (Lyon, 2018, p. 41; original emphasis)

Lyon identifies five features of the contemporary surveillance culture that mark the distinction between contemporary surveillance and modern surveillance. Although these features are inextricably intertwined, we can try to isolate, analytically, each of these molding forces.

First and foremost, the culture of surveillance is participatory. Being surveilled has become a "natural" experience as much as surveilling others: it has been incorporated into the shared frame of reference that orients our actions and interactions, and it has, therefore, become embedded into our daily practices. As a result, surveillance ceases to be exclusively something that impinges on citizens' lives, and becomes "something that everyday citizens comply with—willingly and wittingly or not—negotiate, resist, engage with and, in novel ways, even initiate and desire" (Lyon, 2018, p. 9). Watching and being watched has become "a way of life" (Lyon, 2018), consisting not only of a set of socially legitimized practices of surveillance and self-surveillance, but also of imaginaries of transparency and openness (Isin & Ruppert, 2015; van Dijck, 2014) that render data sharing desirable and normative. The practice of social surveillance in which social media users engage (Marwick, 2012), or the practice of self-tracking (Lupton, 2016; Neff & Nafus, 2016), are exemplary of how dataveillance relies on users' voluntary engagement. As prior research has shown, and as we shall see throughout this book, parents often initiate practices of "intimate surveillance" (Leaver, 2015, 2017) and "caring dataveillance" (Lupton, 2020) that involve the monitoring of babies through technologies—and a further set of practices based on the data thus collected—with the aim of governing a new situation, protecting their children, and performing a "good parent." Participation in the dataveillance of their babies is premised on emerging social expectations and shared norms around parenthood—a moral epistemology through which parents are encouraged to (1) conform to a normative pattern of digital parenting, whereby tracking babies and children is socially constructed as "the" norm of good parenting; (2) trust the data that parenting apps or wearable devices, used to track the baby/child, gives back as objective, accurate, and reliable, contrary to mothers' and fathers' "defective" and "deceptive" knowledge; and (3) act on such data-based knowledge, in order to ensure the baby/child's health, wellbeing, and development. Leaver (2017, p. 8) has noted that we have reached a point in society where "unplugged parenting is likely to be increasingly positioned as both irresponsible and aberrant." As the practices of intimate surveillance and caring dataveillance show, datafication now forms for many parents the "general background of everyday life" (Couldry & Hepp, 2017, p. 124), and shapes expectations around childrearing and understandings of "the ideal child" (Willson, 2018, p. 8). The moral imperative mobilized in mediatized parenting practices is not dissimilar to the rhetoric of control that characterizes self-tracking as a cultural practice (Lupton, 2016). Indeed, in both practices, the (self-)knowledge resulting from the use of monitoring technologies provides the basis for agency—whether the goal is to achieve self-improvement and self-management, as in self-tracking, or to conform to the expected levels of parental care and grow healthy and smart kids, as in the practice of intimate surveillance.

Second, surveillance is inextricably bound up with datafication: it depends on the continuous data collection through sensors and data trackers, as well as on algorithmic predictions and classifications. By this, we mean to point once more to the fact that datafication and dataveillance cannot be understood outside the deep mediatization of social life. Surveillance has become institutionalized, normalized, and materialized mostly through the domestication of digital media and their infrastructures into almost any sphere of the social. Not only do digital media and their infrastructures provide the backbone for an increasing array of everyday practices; the very mediatization of everyday practices is precisely what favors the normalization of dataveillance within contemporary social imaginaries. It is because digital media become a natural part of how we interact with each other that data practices become desirable and socially legitimated.

Third, surveillance has become a taken-for-granted, normalized condition. The domestication of surveillance, Lyon argues (2018), accounts not only for the proliferation of surveillance technologies, but also for citizens' participation in dataveillance, and their adherence to the principles of dataism (van Dijck, 2014). Not only have citizens become inure to surveillance—what Hintz et al. (2018) call "surveillance realism;" once surveillance is incorporated as a taken-for-granted component of our social ecology, expectations, and imaginaries, then citizens are willing to comply with it, although at times negotiating and resisting surveillance strategies in their everyday tactics (Lyon, 2018, p. 44). In other words, citizens incorporate what Lyon (2018, p. 47) calls a "surveillant habitus." Likewise, Couldry and Yu (2018) point to the naturalization of datafication and surveillance through discourses and routine practices that turn surveillance into a natural component of our societies, and construct data as a neutral means of governing the complexity of the social.

Fourth, dataveillance is imbricated with gamification. Drawing on Ellerbrok's (2011) study of facial recognition in the context of photo tagging on Facebook, Lyon argues that the playfulness of the practices of dataveillance that occur on social media contributes to the technological expansion and social legitimization of surveillance in public spaces and in a variety of social contexts. Similarly, Whitson argues that gamification—that is, the application of playful frameworks to non-play practices—is a "public legitimation tool" (2013, p. 164) through which technologies of surveillance such as self-tracking apps become normalized.

Finally, Lyon's theorization places emphasis on the situated and contingent nature of surveillance culture. Surveillance cultures are varied, plural, and complex. Citizens are not "involved or implicated in the same way" in surveillance culture (Lyon, 2018, p. 9). Along with, or against, dataism (van Dijck, 2014), emergent and alternative understandings can emerge within a surveillance culture (Lyon, 2018). For example, recent ethnographic research has challenged the notion of social surveillance as an intrinsic feature of social media platforms: rather, the affordance of visibility has been shown to be specific to given cultural practices of use in a situated environment (Costa, 2018).

The data practices in which citizens engage, and their meanings, cannot be predetermined outside of the situated "affordances-in-practice" of diverse technologies of surveillances. Moreover, data, and the digital environment that sustains datafication, are embedded in the everyday life of individuals—children and families included—and made sense of through embodied, affective, and sensory experiences (Kennedy & Bates, 2017; Kennedy et al., 2015; Lupton, 2020; Pink et al., 2017).

To conclude, surveillance and critical data studies show that, if we are to have a meaningful understanding of datafication, it is important to ground it "within the frames of reference of ordinary people" (Lyon, 2018, p. 186) in different cultural settings, and investigate how mundane activities—including parenting practices, children's play, family communication, etc.—are affected by and, in turn, affect surveillance imaginaries. It is at the level of the everyday that we can observe not only how surveillance culture is domesticated and normalized, but also how a critique of surveillance and dataism may arise (Lyon, 2018).

Datafication as the Colonization of Everyday Life

We would like to conclude our review of different approaches to datafication with a focus on Couldry and Mejias' book *The costs of connection* (2019), as it provides a fruitful yet original combination of the linear interpretation of datafication as essentially a business-driven process, with a phenomenological account of datafication as a complex phenomenon, driven by an economic logic but experienced, made meaningful, adopted, adapted, and resisted in the diverse contexts of everyday life. Their main argument, that dataism has pervaded relations, emotions, and culture, leading to the emergence of a new, "data's colonized subject," has remarkable implications for how we think of the consequences of growing up amidst data imaginaries and practices.

Couldry and Mejias (2019) use the concept of data colonialism to advance their unique contribution to the theorization of datafication. Data colonialism is the contemporary evolution of capitalism, one that relies on the appropriation of potentially every layer of human experience as a profitable source of data. This is not dissimilar to surveillance capitalism, one might argue. The differences exist, however, and have to do with a more systematic understanding of the inextricable implication of digital media and human lives as an economic but also, fundamentally, a social and cultural process, in which capitalism and mediatization converge.

Couldry and Mejias (2019) define data colonialism as a global process of conversion of human life into data that can be extracted and exploited by capitalism, just as historical colonialism spoiled natural resources and manual labor. The current phase of capitalism, then, may not yet represent a new mode of production, but certainly radicalizes the process of alienation that Marx identified as typical of the power relations of industrial capitalism. While workers were alienated from the product of their work, now humans are alienated from their own lives, which become annexed to capitalism and are reduced to raw materials for capitalist production. Under certain respects, the annexation of human experiences, actions, and interactions to capitalism through continuous and pervasive dataveillance is just the current version of capitalism's strategy to establish a social order that guarantees the maximization of profit and the concentration of power and wealth in the hands of the few. But what is appropriated and extracted today are no longer physical (human or natural) resources. Instead, "human life, and particularly human social life, is increasingly being constructed so that it generates data from which profit can be extracted" (Couldry & Mejias, 2019, p. 7). It is indeed a form of colonialism because it is gradually reducing the social spaces that are not yet datafied, that are not yet subjected to constant monitoring and algorithmic predictions.

As this quote suggests, the colonization of human life would not be possible without a simultaneous colonization of social imaginaries that normalize the social construction of everyday life as a resource for capitalism. Indeed, the extraction of data from everyday life is operationalized, but also legitimated through data relations, namely, new types of social relations that are sustained by the technologies of data collection and analysis and that are enabled by "data as a potential commodity" (Couldry & Mejias, 2019, p. 27). When humans are pushed to participate into data relations as the natural and inevitable form of (mediatized) connectedness, the very appropriation of personal, behavioral, and emotional data ends up being constructed as "natural." As we have seen, the perceived "naturalness" of data relations is a crucial precondition for citizens' participation in surveillance culture: as Lyon puts it (2018), being watched and watching others has become a way of life. Similarly, Couldry and Mejias point to how surveillance becomes interiorized, and therefore accepted and even desired, in a process of an "inverse panopticon effect":

If the panopticon effect relied on our inability to tell exactly when we were being watched, so that we behaved all the time as though we were, the 'inverse panopticon effect' of pervasive data surveillance relies on us knowing that we are being watched all the time but lapsing into behaving as though we are not, thus naturalising acceptance of a world in which surveillance and continuous tracking operate unnoted in the background. (Couldry & Mejias, 2019, p. 100)

The result is a deeper, more effective interiorization of the disciplinary gaze into the very affective relationships that make our everyday lives meaningful.

Further, the colonization of human life by process and imaginaries of data extraction has profound consequences at the epistemological level, redefining both what we know and how we know the world. Data define the very boundaries of social knowledge: what we are able to know, but also, more significantly, what it is worth knowing about our social world is what can be abstracted into, and represented through, data. Two particular mechanisms of power distribution, and of discrimination, are connected to the definition of epistemological boundaries through data abstraction and classification, as we shall discuss in more depth later, in Chapter 8. The first concerns (in) visibility as a form of power: if what can be known about the social world is exclusively what can be digitally monitored and quantified, what is not represented by data is not only invisible, but also excluded, as it does not belong to the social world. The second refers to the relation of human and automated knowledge: when knowledge is produced through the algorithmic classification of social actions, interactions, and processes abstracted into data, a new relationship between human actors and artifacts emerges, that Couldry and Hepp (2017, pp. 131–132) call "tool reversibility," to indicate how users themselves are being used (in order to produce classifications and knowledge) by the data-based, internet-connected tools embedded in their everyday lives.

This leads us back to one of the main questions this book aims to address, that is, what are the consequences of growing up in a world in which social interaction is increasingly lived in datafied environments and shaped by algorithmic classifications and predictions? Such consequences, we argue, are both the effect of the discriminations embedded in automated social sorting and of the socialization to surveillance culture. The combined force of surveillance imaginaries and practices embeds children in ever-intensifying networks of surveillance, through which they "become 'calculable persons' who are the subject of calculations performed by others (and by other digital things)" (Lupton & Williamson, 2017, p. 787). Being under constant intimate and corporate surveillance, children learn to think about their bodies and behavior as quantifiable measures, and how to be watched while watching others. As Lupton and Williamson put it:

> These calculating children are both calculated and metricized as data traces, but also encouraged to calculate about themselves through encountering their own data. (2017, p. 787)

Children as Active Agents

In this chapter, we have outlined our theoretical framework, which builds on and integrates a set of conceptual tools elaborated within mediatization research, critical data studies, and surveillance studies. The result is an understanding of datafication as a complex process molded by intersecting forces: deep mediatization, surveillance capitalism, and surveillance culture. More precisely, we propose to frame datafication as simultaneously an outcome and an intensifier of mediatization, which has become naturalized and normalized through a culture of surveillance, and which is gradually pervading and reconfiguring every social space.

What makes such a framework particularly apt to the study of children's data practices and children's datafication? We believe that all these epistemologies—mediatization research's call for non-media-centric media studies, surveillance studies' emphasis on the practices of appropriation, negotiation, and resistance through which humans participate in surveillance culture, and critical data studies' acknowledgment that datafication is variously experienced, made sense of, and acted on the contexts of everyday life (Kennedy & Bates, 2017; Kennedy et al., 2015; Lupton, 2020; Pink et al., 2017)—fit well with a child-centered approach, which recognizes children as participants of social and cultural change without neglecting the constraining nature of social structure (Corsaro, 2012, 2017).

In assuming a child-centered approach we draw on the new sociology of childhood. Recognizing children as active and knowing social actors, the study of childhood has contributed to advance and rethink the notion of socialization. Traditional understandings of "development solely as the individual child's internalization of adult skills and knowledge" (Corsaro, Molinari, & Brown Rosier, 2002, p. 324), that is, as a one-way top-down process, have been criticized for failing to acknowledge the complexity of the social. While recognizing that children develop individually, the sociology of childhood emphasizes socialization as a social accomplishment in which children participate not only by imitating and internalizing culture, but also by making sense of, reproducing, and reinventing it (James, 2013). In so doing, children simultaneously participate in two cultures: the adults' and their own peer cultures: "in attempting to make sense of the adult world, children come to collectively produce their own peer worlds and cultures" (Corsaro, 2017, p. 23). Corsaro defines the embedding of individual development in the collective production of cultures as "interpretive reproduction," whereby "interpretive" is used to "suggest the innovative and creative aspects of children's participation in society," while "reproduction" conveys "the idea that children do not simply internalize society and culture, but they actively contribute to cultural production and change" (Corsaro, 2012, p. 489). Interpretive reproduction, therefore, is "made up of three types of collective action: (1) children's creative appropriation of information and knowledge from the adults' world; (2) children's production and participation in a series of peer cultures; and (3) children's contribution to the reproduction and extension of the adult culture" (Corsaro, 2017, p. 44).

Following the child-centered approach to socialization, children's individual agency has been partly overstated (Hammersley, 2017; James, 2013; Paus-Hasebrink, 2018). However, the notion of interpretive reproduction does not ignore the structuring consequences of social institutions on the processes of being and becoming children (James, 2013). Indeed, Corsaro writes that childhood is exposed to and structured by the same societal forces as adulthood, and contends that the notion of interpretive reproduction "imply that children are—in their very participation in society—constrained by the existing social structure and by processes of social reproduction" (Corsaro, 2012, p. 489). The socialization of children takes place at the interplay of children's creative appropriation of adults' culture and active participation in society on the one hand, and the constraining nature of social reproduction on the other. The equal emphasis on agency and structure leads childhood studies to account for the role of power relations, social inequalities, and cross-cultural variations in shaping children's socialization.

Therefore, we agree with Pugh (2014), that the main achievement of the new sociology of childhood has been to reposition children at the center of social research and sociological theorization. In so doing, the new sociology of childhood has moved beyond the "ghettoization of children" and the confinement of childhood as "a site upon which existing theory is only applied" (Pugh, 2014, p. 72). Rather, acknowledging children as active, competent social actors, and childhood as diverse and varied, can lead to important theoretical contributions, since it helps researchers ask new questions, challenge prejudices, and overcome theoretical impasses. As for our field of investigation, we firmly believe that analyzing datafication from the viewpoint of children as both "subjects of data"—actors participating in data practices—and "objects of data" (Ruppert, Isin, & Bigo, 2017, p.3)—about whom data is produced by parents, family, educators, institutions, and corporations—would contribute to a better understanding of the datafication of nearly everything. This book, therefore, assumes a child-centered perspective that recognizes children's active role in media socialization and in surveillance culture, without neglecting the structuring force of social institutions—including the power of algorithmic governance and dataism—on childhood. On the contrary, it recognizes that changes in contemporary childhoods and the changing media environment that they and their families navigate should be analyzed against the backdrop of broader social, political, technological, and economic transformations.

Note

1 We do not mean to suggest that datafication is an internet risk comparable to other content, contact, or conduct risks, as it is a wider social, cultural, and political dynamic that pervades every social domain. Simply, we argue that the datafication of childhood has received relatively little attention compared to the datafication of adult consumers and citizens, but also compared with the study of other potentially risky consequences of children's engagement with the internet and digital media. For recent data on children's exposure to online risks, we refer to the EU Kids Online's latest comparative report (Smahel et al., 2020).

References

Ammari, T., & Schoenebeck, S. (2015). Understanding and supporting fathers and fatherhood on social media sites. In *Proceedings of the 33rd Annual ACM Conference on Human Factors in Computing Systems* (pp. 1905–1914). ACM Press.

Autenrieth, U. (2018). Family photography in a networked age. Anti-sharenting as a reaction to risk assessment and behaviour adaption. In G. Mascheroni, C. Ponte, & A. Jorge (Eds.), *Digital parenting: The challenges for families in the digital age* (pp. 219–231). Nordicom.

Bakardjieva, M. (2011). The internet in everyday life: Exploring the tenets and contributions of diverse approaches. In M. Consalvo & C. Ess (Eds.), *The handbook of internet studies* (pp. 59–82). Wiley Blackwell.

Barassi, V. (2017). BabyVeillance? Expecting parents, online surveillance and the cultural specificity of pregnancy apps. *Social Media + Society*, 3(2). https://doi.org/10.1177/2056305117707188

Barassi, V. (2018). The child as datafied citizen: Critical questions on data justice in family life. In G. Mascheroni, C. Ponte, & A. Jorge (Eds.), *Digital parenting: The challenges for families in the digital age* (pp. 169–177). Nordicom.

Barassi, V. (2020). *Child | Data | Citizen. How tech-companies are profiling us from before birth.* The MIT Press.

Berriman, L., & Mascheroni, G. (2019). Exploring the affordances of smart toys and connected play in practice. *New Media & Society*, 21(4), 797–814.

Bert, F., Passi, S., Scaioli, G., Gualano, M. R., & Siliquini, R. (2016). There comes a baby! What should I do? Smartphones' pregnancy-related applications: A web-based overview. *Health Informatics Journal*, 22(3), 608–617.

Blumer, H. (1954). What is wrong with social theory? *American Sociological Review*, 19(1), 3–10.

Blum-Ross, A., & Livingstone, S. (2017). "Sharenting," parent blogging and the boundaries of the digital self. *Popular Communication*, 15(2), 110–125.

boyd, D. (2010). Social network sites as networked publics: Affordances, dynamics, and implications. In Z. Papacharissi (Ed.), *A networked self* (pp. 47–66). Routledge.

boyd, D., & Crawford, K. (2012). Critical questions for big data: Provocations for a cultural, technological, and scholarly phenomenon. *Information, Communication & Society*, 15(5), 662–679.

Breiter, A., & Hepp, A. (2018). The complexity of datafication: Putting digital traces in context. In A. Hepp, A. Breiter, & U. Hasebrink (Eds.), *Communicative figurations: Transforming communications in times of deep mediatization* (pp. 387–405). Palgrave Macmillan.

Broekman, F. L. (2018). Tap in, swipe through, pinch out: Understanding the role of context, content and child in apps for children. PhD thesis, Amsterdam School of Communication Research. https://dare.uva.nl/search?identifier=29d39cf8-ae7d-4c52-99d1-10e0e4dcbb65

Bucher, T. (2018). *If . . .then: Algorithmic power and politics.* Oxford University Press.

Bunz, M., & Meikle, G. (2018). *The Internet of Things.* Polity.

Cheney-Lippold, J. (2017). *We are data: Algorithms and the making of our digital selves.* New York University Press.

Children's Commissioner for England (2018). *Who knows what about me? A Children's Commissioner report into the collection and sharing of children's data.* www.childrenscommissioner.gov.uk/wp-content/uploads/2018/11/who-knows-what-about-me.pdf

Corsaro, W. A. (2012). Interpretive reproduction in children's role play. *American Journal of Play*, 4(4), 488–504.

Corsaro, W. A. (2017). *The sociology of childhood* (5th ed.). SAGE Publications Ltd.

Corsaro, W. A., Molinary, L., & Brown Rosier, K. (2002). Zena and Carlotta: Transition narratives and early education in the United States and Italy. *Human Development*, 45(5), 323–348.

Costa, E. (2018). Affordances-in-practice: An ethnographic critique of social media logic and context collapse. *New Media & Society*, 20(10). https://doi.org/10.1177/1461444818756290

Couldry, N. (2012). *Media, society, world: Social theory and digital media practice.* Polity.

Couldry, N., & Hepp, A. (2017). *The mediated construction of reality.* Polity.

Couldry, N., & Mejias, U. A. (2019). *The costs of connection: How data is colonizing human life and appropriating it for capitalism.* Stanford University Press.

Couldry, N., & Yu, J. (2018). Deconstructing datafication's brave new world. *New Media & Society, 20*(12). https://doi.org/10.1177/1461444818775968

Crawford, K., & Schultz, J. (2014). Big data and due process: Toward a framework to redress predictive privacy harms. *Boston College Law Review, 55*(1), 93–128.

Damkjær, M. S. (2018). Sharenting = good parenting? Four parental approaches to sharenting on Facebook. In G. Mascheroni, C. Ponte, & A. Jorge (Eds.), *Digital parenting: The challenges for families in the digital age* (pp. 209–218). Nordicom.

Das, R. (2020). *Early motherhood in digital societies: Ideals, anxieties and ties of the perinatal.* Routledge.

de Certeau, M. (1984). *The practice of everyday life.* University of California Press.

Ellerbrok, A. (2011). Playful biometrics: Controversial technology through the lens of play. *The Sociological Quarterly, 52*(4), 528–547.

Eriksson, H., & Salzman-Erikson, M. (2013). Supporting a caring fatherhood in cyberspace—An analysis of communication about caring within an online forum for fathers. *Scandinavian Journal of Caring Sciences, 27*(1), 63–69.

Eubanks, V. (2018). *Automating inequality: How high-tech tools profile, police and punish the poor.* St Martin's Press.

Gangadharan, S. P. (2017). The downside of digital inclusion: Expectations and experiences of privacy and surveillance among marginal internet users. *New Media & Society, 19*(4), 597–615.

Hammersley, M. (2017). Childhood studies: A sustainable paradigm? *Childhood, 24*(1), 113–127.

Harris, R. (2017). 72M data points collected on children in spite of COPPA. *App Developer Magazine,* December 27. https://appdevelopermagazine.com/5769/2017/12/27/72m-data-points-collected-on-children-in-spite-of-coppa/

Hepp, A. (2013). The communicative figurations of mediatized worlds: Mediatization research in times of the "mediation of everything." *European Journal of Communication, 28*(6), 615–629.

Hepp, A. (2019). *Deep mediatization.* Routledge.

Hine, C. (2015). *Ethnography for the internet: Embedded, embodied and everyday.* Bloomsbury.

Hintz, A., Dencik, L., & Wahl-Jorgensen, K. (2017). Digital Citizenship and Surveillance Society-Introduction. *International Journal of Communication,* (11), 731-739. https://doi.org/1932–8036/20170005

Hintz, A., Dencik, L., & Wahl-Jorgensen, K. (2018). *Digital citizenship in a datafied society.* Polity.

Holloway, D., Green, L., & Livingstone, S. (2013). *Zero to eight. Young children and their internet use.* EU Kids Online, London School of Economics and Political Science. eprints.lse.ac.uk/52630/1/Zero_to_eight.pdf

Isin, E., & Ruppert, E. (2015). *Being digital citizens.* Rowman & Littlefield.

James, A. (2013). *Socialising children.* Palgrave Macmillan.

Kennedy, H., & Bates, J. (2017). Data power in material contexts: Introduction. *Television & New Media*, 18(8), 701–705.

Kennedy, H., Poell, T., & van Dijck, J. (2015). Data and agency. *Big Data & Society*, 2(2), 1–7.

Kitchin, R. (2014). *The data revolution: Big data, open data, data infrastructures and their consequences*. SAGE Publications Ltd.

Lazard, L., Capdevila, R., Dann, C., Locke, A., & Roper, S. (2019). Sharenting: Pride, affect and the day-to-day politics of digital mothering. *Social and Personality Psychology Compass*, 13(4), e12443.

Leaver, T. (2015). Born digital? Presence, privacy, and intimate surveillance. In J. Hartley & W. Qu (Eds.), *Re-orientation: Translingual transcultural transmedia. Studies in narrative, language, identity, and knowledge* (pp. 149–160). Fudan University Press.

Leaver, T. (2017). Intimate surveillance: Normalizing parental monitoring and mediation of infants online. *Social Media + Society*, 3(2), 1–10.

Lipu, M., & Siibak, A. (2019). "Take it down!" Estonian parents' and pre-teens' opinions and experiences with sharenting. *Media International Australia*, 170(1), 57–67.

Livingstone, S., & Blum-Ross, A. (2017). Researching children and childhood in the digital age. In P. Christensen & A. James (Eds.), *Research with children: Perspectives and practices* (pp. 54–70). Routledge.

Livingstone, S., Mascheroni, G., & Staksrud, E. (2018). European research on children's internet use: Assessing the past and anticipating the future. *New Media & Society*, 20(3), 1103–1122.

Livingstone, S., & Third, A. (2017). Children and young people's rights in the digital age: An emerging agenda. *New Media & Society*, 19(5), 657–670.

Lunt, P., & Livingstone, S. (2015). Is "mediatization" the new paradigm for our field? A commentary on Deacon and Stanyer (2014, 2015) and Hepp, Harvard and Lundby (2015). *Media, Culture & Society*, 38(3), 462–470.

Lupton, D. (2016). *The quantified self*. Polity.

Lupton, D. (2019). *Data selves: More-than-human perspectives*. Polity.

Lupton, D. (2020). Caring dataveillance: Women's use of apps to monitor pregnancy and children. In L. Green, D. Holloway, K. Stevenson, L. Haddon, & T. Leaver (Eds.), *The Routledge companion to digital media and children* (pp. 393–402). Routledge.

Lupton, D., & Pedersen, S. (2016). An Australian survey of women's use of pregnancy and parenting apps. *Women and Birth*, 29(4), 368–375.

Lupton, D., Pedersen, S., & Thomas, G. M. (2016). Parenting and digital media: From the early web to contemporary digital society. *Sociology Compass*, 10(8), 730–743.

Lupton, D., & Williamson, B. (2017). The datafied child: The dataveillance of children and implications for their rights. *New Media & Society*, 19(5), 780–794.

Lyon, D. (2018). *The culture of surveillance: Watching as a way of life*. Polity.

Madianou, M. (2015). Polymedia and ethnography: Understanding the social in social media. *Social Media + Society*, 1(1). https://doi.org/10.1177/2056305115578675

Madianou, M., & Miller, D. (2012). Polymedia: Towards a new theory of digital media in interpersonal communication. *International Journal of Cultural Studies*, 16(2), 169–187.

Marsh, J., Plowman, L., Yamada-Rice, D., Bishop, J., Lahmar, J., & Scott, F. (2018). Play and creativity in young children's use of apps. *British Journal of Educational Technology, 49*(5), 870–882.

Marwick, A. E. (2012). The public domain: Social surveillance in everyday life. *Surveillance & Society, 9*(4), 378–393.

Marwick, A. E., & boyd, D. (2018). Understanding privacy at the margins. *International Journal of Communication, 12*, 1157–1165.

Mascheroni, G. (2018). Researching datafied children as data citizens. *Journal of Children and Media, 12*(4), 517–523. https://doi.org/10.1080/17482798.2018.1521677

Mascheroni, G. (2020). Datafied childhoods: Contextualising datafication in everyday life. *Current Sociology, 68*(6), 798–813. https://doi.org/10.1177/0011392118807534

Mascheroni, G., & Holloway, D. (2019a). Introducing the Internet of Toys. In G. Mascheroni & D. Holloway (Eds.), *The Internet of Toys: Practices, affordances and the political economy of children's smart play* (pp. 1–22). Palgrave.

Mascheroni, G., & Holloway, D. (2019b). The quantified child: Discourses and practices of dataveillance in different life stages. In O. Erstad, R. Flewitt, B. Kümmerling-Meibauer, & I. S. Pires Pereira (Eds.), *The Routledge handbook of digital literacies in early childhood* (pp. 354–365). Routledge.

Mascheroni, G., Ponte, C., & Jorge, A. (2018). Introduction. In G. Mascheroni, C. Ponte, & A. Jorge (Eds.), *Digital parenting: The challenges for families in the digital age* (pp. 9–16). Nordicom.

McStay, A. (2018). *Emotional AI: The rise of empathic media.* SAGE Publications Ltd.

Montgomery, K. (2015). Children's media culture in a big data world. *Journal of Children and Media, 9*(2), 266–271.

Morrison, A. (2011). "Suffused by feeling and affect": The intimate public of personal mommy blogging. *Biography, 34*(1), 37–55.

Neff, G., & Nafus, D. (2016). *Self-tracking.* The MIT Press.

Nelson, M. (2008). Watching children: Describing the use of baby monitors on Epinions.com. *Journal of Family Issues, 29*(4), 516–538. http://dx.doi.org/10.1177/0192513X07310319

Ofcom (2018). *Children and parents: Media use and attitudes report.* www.ofcom.org.uk/__data/assets/pdf_file/0024/134907/children-and-parents-media-use-and-attitudes-2018.pdf

Orton-Johnson, K. (2017). Mummy blogs and representations of motherhood: "Bad mummies" and their readers. *Social Media + Society, 3*(2). https://doi.org/10.1177/2056305117707186

Paus-Hasebrink, I. (2018). The role of media within young people's socialization: A theoretical approach. *Communications, 44*(4). https://doi.org/10.1515/commun-2018-2016

Pink, S., Sumartojo, S., Lupton, D., & Heyes La Bond, C. (2017). Mundane data: The routines, contingencies and accomplishments of digital living. *Big Data & Society, 4*(1). https://doi.org/10.1177/2053951717700924

Pugh, A. (2014). The theoretical costs of ignoring childhood: Rethinking independence, insecurity, and inequality. *Theory & Society, 43*(1), 71–89.

Rideout, V. (2017). *The common sense census: Media use by kids age zero to eight.* Common Sense Media. www.commonsensemedia.org/research/the-common-sense-census-media-use-by-kids-age-zero-to-eight-2017

Ruppert, E., Isin, E., & Bigo, D. (2017). Data politics. *Big Data & Society*, 4(2), 1–7. https://doi. org/10.1177/2053951717717749

Siibak, A. (2019). Digital parenting and the datafied child. In T. Burns & F. Gottschalk (Eds.), *Educating 21st century children: Emotional well-being in the digital age*. OECD Publishing. https://doi.org/10.1787/313a9b21-en

Siibak, A., & Traks, K. (2019). The dark sides of sharenting. *Catalan Journal of Communication & Cultural Studies*, 11(1), 115–121.

Taylor, C. (2004). *Modern social imaginaries*. Duke University Press.

Thomas, G. M., & Lupton, D. (2016). Threats and thrills: Pregnancy apps, risk and consumption. *Health, Risk & Society*, 17(7–8), 495–509.

Thornham, H. (2019). Algorithmic vulnerabilities and the datalogical: Early motherhood and tracking-as-care regimes. *Convergence*, 25(2), 171–185.

Tiidenberg, K., & Baym, N. K. (2017). Learn it, buy it, work it: Intensive pregnancy on Instagram. *Social Media + Society*, 3(1). https://doi.org/10.1177/2056305116685108

Tripp, N., Hainey, K., Liu, A., et al. (2014). An emerging model of maternity care: Smartphone, midwife, doctor? *Women and Birth: Journal of the Australian College of Midwives*, 27(1), 64–67.

van Dijck, J. (2014). Datafication, dataism and dataveillance: Big data between scientific paradigm and ideology. *Surveillance and Society*, 12(2), 197–208. https://doi.org/10.24908/ ss.v12i2.4776

van Dijck, J., Poell, T., & de Waal, M. (2018). *The platform society: Public values in a connective world*. Oxford University Press.

Whitson, J. R. (2013). Gaming the quantified self. *Surveillance & Society*, 11(1/2), 163–176.

Willson, M. (2018). Raising the ideal child? Algorithms, quantification and prediction. *Media, Culture & Society*, 41(5). https://doi.org/10.1177/0163443718798901

Zuboff, S. (2015). Big other: Surveillance capitalism and the prospects of an information civilization. *Journal of Information Technology*, 30(1), 75–89.

Zuboff, S. (2019). *The age of surveillance capitalism: The fight for a human future at the new frontier of power*. Profile Books.

· 3 ·

DATAFICATION AS A PRACTICE
OF THE SELF

Creating Data Selves: Being, Making and Becoming with Personal Data

Marii and Heleen got their first smartphone for their seventh birthday. It was a gift from their parents who thought it would be a good idea to enable them to practice phoning and SMS-ing a bit, before they started their first year at school. The girls were ecstatic and immediately started exploring the opportunities the phone provided. To the great joy of their grandparents, the girls started to make daily phone calls to granny and grandpa, as well as sending SMS messages to their aunt, all of whom were living in other cities. The phone enabled the girls to exercise their agency, to choose with whom and when to communicate, enabling a daily bond to be established between family members living apart. To the great astonishment of the parents, the girls also started making videos and taking photos with their phone. They made short video clips to introduce their favorite toys and family members, and took countless photos of their everyday surroundings—self-shooting themselves into being.

The girls also enjoyed playing various educational games on their phones. They enthusiastically waited for the fireworks to go off—saluting them for the task solved correctly, and proudly showing off with another star being awarded to them for completing the next level in their assignments. They felt proud of their progress, finding real pleasure not only from their gamified success, but also from the self-governance these apps entailed. In the evenings, however, they put aside their phones and started writing small notes in their diaries, containing reflections and personal thoughts about their day. These notes often included information about how many candies they had eaten during the day, or provided a sneak-peek into the whirlwind of emotions they had experienced (for example, frustrations about one of them not willing to play with the dolls' house or expressing great excitement about the cartoon they had seen together). Sometimes the diary entries contained more images than text—drawings depicting Harry Potter and Hermione Granger (their most recent absolute favorites), or data mementos about a family road trip.

In these ways Marii and Heleen are (un)consciously writing and self-shooting themselves into being, sharing bits and pieces about their daily lives, their likes, and dislikes, sharing data that is seemingly irrelevant to anyone outside their immediate family, sharing the everydayness of their lives and their identities. In addition to all the traditional pen-and-paper methods of self-analysis, young people today are able to make use of various technologies, which means they can create new ways of knowing themselves, their bodies, and their minds. The practice of creating and seeing oneself through various data forms is, in fact, something that many children and young people engage in on a daily basis, becoming thus (un)knowingly engaged in personal informatics (also known as personal analytics) and the "quantified self movement."[1]

Although digital technologies have considerably broadened opportunities for self-expression, self-presentation, and self-quantification, these practices actually date back several centuries. In her book *Seeing ourselves through technology: How we use selfies, blogs and wearable devices to see and shape ourselves*, Jill Walker Rettberg (2014) eloquently reveals the pre-digital history of these artifacts that present-day youth have started to love so dearly. In her book, she explores the ongoing remediation related to form and mediums, suggesting that blogs and social media status updates can be viewed as the descendants of diaries and memoirs, and selfies as descendants of visual artists' self-portraits, while the practice of self-tracking could be associated with former genres of accounting and compiling "to-do" lists. In short, all through the centuries individuals have practiced "technologies of the self" (Foucault, 1988), that is, they have engaged in specific techniques (for instance, self-examination or self-administration) to understand themselves. However, the technologies of the self can only be effective when there is an audience to witness and morally approve one's progress (see also Chapter 6).

Today a wide range of "embodied computing devices" (Pedersen & Iliadis, 2020), that is, technologies that exist in topographical (on the body), visceral (in the body), and ambient (around the body) relationships, with the body are available and assist individuals in collecting, managing, and preserving various kinds of personal information. According to Rettberg (2014), for example, smartphones can be viewed as ultimate real-time diaries, as they capture much data automatically, without requiring any manual input from its user. Our phones track our geographic location, they know where we are going and how fast we are moving; they know which videos we are watching, which music we like to listen to, and which news we consume, as well as which apps we use, how fast we type, and with whom we interact. Thus, sometimes, without any conscious agency from the user, and often without us (fully) acknowledging it, our phones are generating and materializing inherent dimensions of human embodiment and practices, leading to the creation of human data assemblages (Lupton, 2020a).

At other times, however, we may consciously and voluntarily decide to make use of a variety of digital tools and devices that enable us to engage in rational and calculative personal data practices, such as self-tracking, through which individuals are "working to problematize, refine and improve their lives" (Lupton, 2020a, p. 84). In fact, the findings of empirical studies indicate that the decision to make use of a range of topographical technologies like wearables, which can provide insights about one's habits (sleep, food), actions (places visited), internal states (mood, blood pressure), and performance values (the number of steps taken, calories consumed) (Rapp & Cena, 2016), could be viewed as "a profound act of selfhood and embodiment" (Lupton, 2020a, p. 84). In addition to many parents who have enthusiastically welcomed various baby-tech items as well as tracking tools (see Chapter 4), and teachers who are making use of different biometric and behavioral technologies in schools (see Chapter 7), children and young people themselves are also increasingly becoming interested in consciously creating their data selves (see also Chapter 6).

Shaping the Self Through Data: From Self-Tracking to Self-Knowledge

In this present-day "data-driven life" that Gary Wolf (2010) famously wrote about in his article for *The New York Times Magazine*, bodies and minds are turned into measurable machines in the pursuit of personal development, better health and wellbeing, or productivity. When living within this "metric culture" (Ajana, 2018), a wide variety of wearable devices, clip-on cameras, and smart objects (such as smartwatches, pendants, smart rings, or bands that can be worn on the wrist, leg, or around the forehead), not to mention various mobile apps, have been launched inviting people to engage in self-monitoring for health, fitness, sport, and wellbeing purposes. Even clothing is becoming smart. For example, a brightly colored sweat-proof, dirt-proof, and water-proof smart jacket, Wiggly, aimed at 5- to 12-year-olds, is a new fashion-tech item intended to lure children into a healthier lifestyle. The jacket plays music and barks out dancing orders that the child needs to follow, and two gyroscope accelerometers are sown into the jacket to capture if the child is completing the dance moves correctly (Sumra, 2018).

In addition to various wearables and fashion-tech items, more than 380,000 mobile health (mHealth) apps are available through Apple and Android operating systems. All these apps are portrayed as tools enabling users to gain novel self-knowledge about their practices, habits, and behavior. Although these "speculative promissory narratives" (Lupton, 2020b, p. 53) are most visible in the marketing jargon and popular media discourses, they are also strongly present in overall sociotechnical imaginaries, that is, "collectively held, institutionally stabilized, and publicly performed visions of desirable futures, animated by shared understandings of forms of social life and social order attainable through, and supportive of, advances in science and technology" such technologies invite (Jasanoff, 2015, p. 4). In fact, one could argue that the increasing popularity of wearables and fashion-tech is largely built on the dataism discourse (van Dijck, 2014; see Chapter 2), as dominant sociotechnical imaginaries about wearable technologies introduce wearables as a solution enabling complex problems to be solved, such as obesity or concerns with mental health. Such a discourse has also been taken up by various organizations, for instance, the World Health Organization (WHO), that has positioned digital technologies as a cost-effective solution against rising levels of obesity and sedentary behavior (WHO, 2011).

These techno-solutionism discourses are often based on the assumption that self-tracking should not be viewed as merely a simple process of collecting data about oneself, but rather, as a cycle of practices, all of which are aimed at increasing self-knowledge and reaching one's self-improvement goals (Kim et al., 2019). In fact, as argued by Lupton (2016, p. 117), self-tracking practices enable the generation of "digital biocapital," as their inherent value to the user comes from generating "intimate biodigital knowledges," such as information about one's sleep patterns, heart rate, mood, or menstruation cycle, and so on. Empirical studies (Lupton, 2020c) with young self-trackers indicate that young people acknowledge and value the affordances these technologies provide, as, through the human data assemblages that emerge from the tracked data, they are able to gain insights about their physical or mental health, most of which would have otherwise remained hidden and imperceptible. These insights and new knowledge gained, however, could then be used to changing one's behaviors, habits, and practices. In short, it is believed that continuous tracking "leads to the ability to see a deficiency, and that in turn leads to the ability to act" (Neff & Nafus, 2016, p. 24). Thus, there is a strong pedagogical element (Lupton, 2020b) embedded within the design and public discourses about wearables, as by engaging in self-tracking individuals are invited to follow the neoliberal self-optimization discourse by taking greater control of their lives. In short, as proposed by Barassi (2020), the growing popularity of such technologies among both older and younger generations alike is largely built on our deepest and darkest fears—"our fears of not being productive or efficient enough, of being left behind, or of not being in control of our lives" (Barassi, 2020, p. 99).

Due to the "ideology of healthism" that is pervading the lives of adolescence (Depper & Howe, 2017), such self-optimization discourse is probably most visible in the context of various health wearables and mHealth apps that encourage young people to approach health as a personal practice, an individual responsibility (Rich et al., 2020). The findings from a recent survey among 11- to 18-year-old young people from South West England (N = 1019) reveal that young people have indeed become "new digital health consumers"—52% of the survey respondents claimed they used various technological tools for regulating their bodies, including tracking their sleep patterns, measuring their calorie intake, monitoring their mood, tracking their physical exercises, heart rate, or menstruation (Rich et al., 2020). The uptake of mHealth behavior support apps, including apps for fitness, sleep, meditation, and medication reminders, among teens (aged 14–17) and young adults (aged 18–22) in the U.S. is even greater—64% of participants in a survey by Rideout and Fox (2018, p. 10) had used such apps. Such numbers indicate that the use of embodied technologies has become a mundane daily, although sometimes perhaps quite short-lived (Potapov et al., 2019; Schaefer et al., 2016), practice for many young people.

In addition to a wide variety of physical health and fitness technologies, numerous mobile mental health apps are available for download. Some of these offer opportunities for self-diagnosis, monitoring, symptom management or treatment, while others are more focused on providing support and exercises about mindfulness, meditation, or relaxation. Even though the number of mental health apps that have been specifically developed for children and young people is still rather limited (see Grist, Porter, & Stallard, 2017 for a systematic review), many young people, especially those suffering from mental health problems, have been found to make use of such tools. In comparison to 58% of young people without symptoms, 76% of those suffering from moderate or severe depressive symptoms claimed to be using mental health apps prior to the COVID-19 pandemic (Rideout & Fox, 2018).

During the pandemic, it has been noted that the mental health of young people has deteriorated all around the world (for an overview, see Ford, John, & Gunnell, 2021; Lieberoth et al., 2021), leading to a surge in the uptake of various mental health, stress management, mindfulness, and relaxation apps, both among grown-ups as well as children and young people. For example, Smiling Mind, a free mobile phone app offering mental health services and mindfulness exercises for young Australians, saw a 350% increase in its uptake among children younger than 12 (James, 2021), and a ThinkNinja app providing free self-help knowledge and skills for 10- to 18-year-olds across the UK saw a similar spike of 168% during the pandemic (Staines, 2020). In addition to young people's own desire to seek mental health support during the COVID-19 lockdown months, parents also encouraged the uptake of such apps. For instance, 25% of the parents of the 13- to 18-year-olds (N = 977) in the U.S. participating in the National Poll on Children's Health claimed that they had encouraged their child to try a web-based program or mHealth app to improve their mental health; 60% of those believed that their advice had been useful (C.S. Mott Children's Hospital, 2021). In the context of the latter finding, however, it is important to note that a vast majority of the mental health apps that are currently on the market have not undergone any expert vetting or evidence testing (Psihogios, Stiles-Shields, & Neary, 2020). Therefore, even though the promotional materials of many mental health apps claim that their tools provide easy and quick help (Parker et al., 2018), and young users expect such apps to be evidence-based, built on credible, scientific, or clinical evidence (Garrido et al., 2019), the evidence of the effectiveness of such apps targeting pre-adolescence and adolescence is lacking (see Grist et al., 2017).

In addition to the promise of increased self-knowledge, wearable technologies, and mHealth apps, fitness and health wearables are often promoted as being fun, that is, the sociotechnical imaginaries of self-quantification suggest that "self-quantification is a game we play with ourselves" (Hulsey, 2020, p. 154). Although there is nothing new in rewarding desirable behavior (for example, giving grades at school), new digital technologies have led this neoliberal self-governance to an entirely new level, turning surveillance into something pleasurable (Whitson, 2013). With the use of various gamified nudges, wearable technologies are encouraging their users to engage in "ludic labor" (Willmot, Fraser, & Lammes, 2017), indicating that the aspect of playfulness has entered the spaces (for example, school; see Chapter 7) that were not considered playful before, practices (such as losing weight or exercising) that were otherwise considered tedious, time-consuming and hard work. So, on the one hand, gamified self-improvement apps evoke a certain kind of agency—that of an active subject willing to succumb to self-governance while striving for self-realization and self-management. On the other hand, however, as this constant and willing self-surveillance is embedded within a series of gamified techniques that nudge the individual into self-discipline, the self-tracker is turned into a docile body, that is, a body "that can be subjected, used, transferred, and improved" (Foucault, 1977, p. 136). Those wanting to succeed in this "game" and engage in the monitoring of the self for various points and rewards need to adhere to the standards set by the algorithms by which they are judged. This often means that young users of wearables orient their ideas of physical fitness, and what constitutes "health," "fitness," or the "ideal body shape," to the targets and norms set by the wearables and apps they are using (Depper & Howe, 2017; Goodyear, Kerner, & Quennerstedt, 2019). For example, 14- to 17-year-old girls' experiences and reflections from using health and fitness apps indicate that despite criticizing such apps for their preoccupation with the "perfect body" and normative standards of socially acceptable levels of BMI (body mass index), they still wanted to progress towards that "ideal" rather than strive to abandon the performative nature of a health culture (Depper & Howe, 2017).

This example suggests that within the mHealth apps and wearables, gamification works as a manifestation of biopower, that is, "numerous and diverse techniques for achieving the subjugation of bodies and the control of populations" (Foucault, 1998, p. 40). Thus, despite the pleasurable and fun component that the devices hold, they can also be experienced as disciplining devices (Lupton, 2020b) through which young people (un)knowingly not only exercise new forms of governance of themselves, but also turn themselves into new objects of surveillance (Shore & Wright, 2018). Although the human data assemblages that emerge from the practice focus on the individual, according to Neff and Nafus (2016, p. 3), the data also stems from "fundamental beliefs about how societies function." Thus, in the context of health-tracking data, the questions of power and control, as well as issues related to individual agency and identity creation, cannot be avoided while human beings are "increasingly becoming *data subjects* whose responsiveness to data signals is expected, even taken as virtuous" (Couldry & Mejias, 2019, p. 134; original emphasis).

The findings of empirical studies indicate that young people often feel that embodied computing technologies tend to jeopardize their agency. Potapov et al.'s findings (2019) reveal that young self-trackers become disillusioned when realizing that they end up being measured against what adults believe to be good and desirable behavior and activities (Potapov et al., 2019). In short, they are often annoyed by the power dynamic between the device and the user, regardless of the fact that the teens themselves are both the producers as well as interpreters of the data. For example, some of the teens in the Potapov et al. (2019) study viewed Fitbit's nudges as "nagging," a behavior they otherwise associated with authority figures like parents and teachers. Similarly, young users (aged 13–25) of the mental health apps have also emphasized that they did not want to be "*talked down to* or to feel that the app was just for kids" (Garrido et al., 2019, p. 9; original emphasis). Such findings suggest that the young are often disappointed by the fact that they are unable to demonstrate their autonomy, either in the ways they are interacting with the content of the app or by customizing and personalizing its visual aspects (Garrido et al., 2019). Recent analysis by Ito et al. (2020, p. 18) of mental health apps (N = 45) intended for children and young adults tend to confirm the above, suggesting that the majority of mHealth apps only tend to do "surface-level tailoring to make the app seem relevant to youth" while otherwise still mirroring the content and intervention types associated with apps intended for adult users.

Studies reveal that conflicts between young self-trackers' needs and inter-ests, on the one hand, and the promises of the technologies, on the other, are quick to emerge. As is the case with all the other data (boyd & Crawford, 2011), the data produced through self-tracking tools only becomes mean-ingful when it is analyzed in relation to something else, some other data. However, as argued by Pantzar and Ruckenstein (2017), self-trackers often expect mechanical objectivity from their collected data; that is, following the tenets of dataism (van Dijck, 2014) they expect the numbers to provide them with an "authentic," "precise," and "accurate" view of the self, something that Foucault (2012) has referred to as the "clinical gaze." In fact, as argued by Lupton (2020a), even though the information generated and processed through digital technologies is very intimate, labeling it as "data" starts to depersonalize and dehumanize its source. Digitized representations of various bodily processes and attributes are often materialized in metric or graphical forms through graphs, tables, signs, or signals, and many young users tend to struggle with making sense of them (Schaefer et al., 2016). While using wearables and mHealth apps one thus needs to develop a "data sense," which Lupton (2020a, p. 76) considers "the key to how people enact their lively data and the agential capacities that emerge." Furthermore, empirical stud-ies (Pantzar & Ruckenstein, 2017) indicate that reading and interpreting the data in isolation from the social context and situation is not only diffi-cult for the self-trackers, but also undesirable. When looking at the numbers provided by the technologies, how other conditions may have affected the data needs to be interpreted, that is, rather than seeking scientific neutrality and objectivity, one really needs to engage in "data sense-making" (Lupton, 2020a, p. 77), acknowledging the fact that human data assemblages should be "configured within broader networks and environments which again are mutually articulated and co-constitutive." In this respect, the data can only become meaningful when used in combination with one's previous bodily knowledge and the datafied knowledge provided by the technology (Fors & Pink, 2017). Studies with young people (Goodyear et al., 2019; Potapov et al., 2019) reveal that teenagers tend to lose interest and trust in the wearables as soon as they experience that the normative judgments made explicit by the wearables contradicted their own judgments about their health behavior. For example, the findings of Potapov et al. (2019) suggest that young people can drop out of using Fitbit when they feel the device is treating them unfairly— like when their daily target of steps it not acknowledging the fact that they also cycle to school and play football. Similarly, young urban Fitbit users have been found to be frustrated by the constant data losses that resulted from their decisions to clip the device onto their clothes and not wear them on their wrist (Schaefer et al., 2016). This suggests that rather than passively acknowledging and adapting to the digital data, young self-trackers are also making use of the physical sensations and affects while interpreting it, that is, "engaging in creative acts of data sense" (Lupton, 2020a, p. 89).

The chosen reference framework also influences the meaning self-trackers attribute to the collected data (Kneidinger-Müller, 2018). First, the importance of the comparative approach matters at the individual level, that is, the generated time-stamped data (Nafus, 2016) needs to be compared to one's own previous self-knowledge. Rettberg (2014, p. 87) argues that individuals tend to look at their data doubles created in a similar manner as they used to gaze into the reflection of themselves in the mirror, "wondering who we were and who we might be." Second, the comparative approach matters at the social level, while one's peers become an important marker against whom one's data is compared with (Schaefer et al., 2016; see also Chapter 6 of this book). In fact, as proposed by Lomborg and Frandsen (2016), self-tracking should be viewed as a social and cultural practice that is fundamentally communicative. The mere act of wearing a wearable or having an app on one's phone already triggers certain meanings and capacities (Lupton, 2020b). For instance, a teenager wearing a Fitbit can be viewed as a healthy individual, someone who is interested and invested in their health, while another teenager who has downloaded a mobile Mood Diary to their phone may end up being stigmatized because of potential mental health problems (Grist et al., 2017; Kenny, Dooley, & Fitzgerald, 2016). This helps to illustrate the overall performative nature of the culture of self-tracking.

Establishing a relational and affective connection with the generated by human-non-human assemblage is crucially important for young people (Lupton, 2020c). On the one hand, empirical studies (Gowin et al., 2015) suggest that young people tend to personify their apps, describing their experiences of being motivated and coached, but also ashamed and scolded by their devices. On the other hand, however, they want to be able to share their experiences and interact with their peers to establish a sense of belonging and connection (Kenny et al., 2016). For this reason numerous online communities and forums (such as for Fitbit or Strava) have been created both within and outside of the apps. Some self-trackers value sharing the "snapshots" of their personal data assemblages (Lupton, 2016) on ephemeral social media like Snapchat, which are built on "data self-destruct mechanisms"

(Charteris, Gregory, & Masters, 2014), and provide users with an opportunity to determine how long their messages can be viewed before they are automatically deleted. Others make use of archival social media such as Facebook or Twitter that could hold the materializations of their "quantified past" (Elsden, Kirk, & Durrant, 2015) for a longer period. For example, the users of the DataIsBeautiful forum on Reddit are accustomed to sharing graphs, tables, "activity rings," and other types of visualizations of data that they have gathered through self-tracking apps. Through these "data selfies," that is, "representations of one's 'self,' typically presented as a visualization of quantitative data" (Robards, Lyall, & Morgan, 2020, p. 1), they not only tell very personal and emotive stories, but also package these stories in a visually appealing way to be consumed by others. As argued by Robards et al., these data selfies can sometimes be viewed as confessional, as they "attempt to present the author in a kind of unbiased, 'laid bare' transparent way" (2020, p. 2), also inviting new norms about personal information disclosure. Thus, even though individuals do not tend to view self-tracking tools as self-presentations, they "do preserve and present images of us" (Rettberg, 2014, p. 62). Furthermore, in the era of surveillance capitalism, one should not forget that "data traces are speaking for and about individuals in ways that were not possible before" (Barassi, 2020, p. 134).

Becoming a Self-Quantified Commodity

In the era of data-driven surveillance capitalism, "private self-tracking" turns into "exploited self-tracking" (Lupton, 2016), as users' personal data is often repurposed for the financial benefit of others. Considering that many technologies that are providing opportunities for self-tracking are either free or low cost, one cannot but be reminded of a saying, "If you are not paying for it, you are the product."

In comparison to the data generated during the analog times, the self-tracking data is not only considerably greater but also more meticulous. Furthermore, most wearables and apps are connected to cloud computing databases, that is, people's personal data is extended well beyond their own bodies (Lupton, 2020b). As different datasets can be combined to generate data profiles of people, and the collected personal data can be sold to third parties, the users of self-tracking technologies become commodified (Mosco, 2017) and turned into a value for the service providers. In short, through the generation of data, the quantified self becomes not just the "prosuming self," that is, both a producer and consumer of one's own data, but also a "prosumed self," that is, "an active entrepreneurial subject that produces the 'right' kinds of data which satisfy market expectations and requirements" (Charitsis, 2016, p. 38).

Health wearables and mHealth apps mainly valorize on the biometric and behavioral information that the devices enable to collect and harvest about the user base. According to Zuboff (2019, p. 247), such a valorization on users' health data is also an "eloquent testimony to the health care system's failure to serve the needs of second-modernity individuals that we know access health data and advice from our phone while these pocket computers aggressively access us." The greatest value for the companies comes not from a person's explicit personal information and health data, but from the "behavioral surplus data" (Zuboff, 2019) going beyond the service and product use. According to analysis by Cosgrove et al. (2021, p. 612), a mental health app Mindstrong, for example, is mainly interested in "digital phenotyping," that is, collecting data about its users' touchscreen behaviors (such as scrolling, typing, and clicking), to predict their cognition and mood, reducing a user's humanity, not to mention their autonomy and agency, to a mere collection of data points.

It is important to note that such technologies often "operate in an uncertain regulatory space" (Hutton et al., 2018), meaning that mHealth apps and health wearables are not provided with the necessary scrutiny that is given to other medical data. Hence, it is not surprising that various privacy problems emerge. In a study based on a novel heuristic evaluation method, Hutton et al. (2018) evaluated a state of privacy in a wide range of mHealth and self-tracking apps. Their analysis revealed that most apps in their sample (N = 64) did not meet the necessary privacy requirements. Most of the apps (51) in their sample collected personal data from users, but only 29 had included information in their service or privacy policy about how the data would be used and with whom it would be shared (Hutton et al., 2018). In a similar review of mental health apps (N = 36) by Huckvale, Torous, and Larsen (2019), it was found that 81% (29) of the apps in the sample transmitted data to the analytics, marketing, or advertising services of Google and Facebook, while only 59% (17) disclosed this transmission in their policy. The presumption that the greater proportion of children and young people "have an extensive and nuanced comprehension" of issues such as third party sale of data, analytics, and applications, let alone the legalese used in the terms of services, is "overly optimistic," as Berman and Albright (2017), representatives of the UNICEF Office, argue.

At the same time, empirical studies (Lupton, 2020b, c) indicate that most young self-trackers are not concerned about personal privacy issues and do not tend to consider the potential that the data could be exploited by third parties. Rather, they tend to believe that their personal data has little value to anyone else but themselves (Lupton, 2020c), or they do not view the third party use of their personal data as a problem (Selwyn & Pangrazio, 2018). In fact, studies with young people (Pybus, Cotè, & Blanke, 2015; Selwyn & Pangrazio, 2018) suggest that there is a growing sense of apathy among the young in the context of their personal data use and privacy. In short, with regards to digital data, young people lack the so-called "citizen agency" (Kennedy, Poell, & van Dijk, 2015), and tend to accept life as it is within the dataveillance economy. On the one hand, such a stance could be interpreted as an illustration of poor data awareness and literacy skills. On the other hand, however, as posed by Lupton (2020a, p. 120) "the agential capacities that people can mobilize in response to these issues are limited by the affordances of the technologies that collect and distribute personal data." Due to the growing imbalance between the individuals who produce the data and those who monetize this data, various scholars (see, for example, Kennedy et al., 2015; Pybus et al., 2015) have emphasized the need to focus on providing young people with adequate knowledge and skills to enhance their data, code, and algorithmic literacies so as to enable more *"knowing publics* (rather than just *known* publics)" to emerge (Kennedy & Moss, 2015, p. 2; original emphasis).

Bodies Emitting Information from Within: Biohacking the Self

Human upgrading can surely happen through education or through increased self-knowledge that self-tracking devices offer, but not only via these means. Various visceral technologies, that is, embodied computing devices that "resonate internally, interacting with the body's core" (Pedersen & Iliadis, 2020, p. xxii), are able to provide even more advanced options to "upgrade" oneself. In fact, as argued by Pedersen (2020), we are presently witnessing a change through which human bodies are becoming platforms.

News stories (Griffiths, 2015; Messer, 2019) announce that some young people have made use of microchip implants to "upgrade" themselves.

Microchip implants, sometimes also referred to as "human microchip implants" (Rodriguez, 2019: p. 1598), or RFID implants, that is, radio-frequency identification implants (Michael & Michael, 2013), were initially used to identify allied airplanes during the Second World War, and later for tracking livestock and pet animals for their identification (Smith, 2008). More recently, however, microchips have started to be implanted into human bodies for medical and research reasons, but also for personal recreational use.

Microchip implants allow users to automatically open doors, trigger computers and printers, pay for their purchases (Gauttier, 2019), store train tickets (Petersen, 2019), or embed their college ID and contact information (Messer, 2019), and can thereby be used to replace various artifacts such as house and car keys, credit cards, or passwords. The youngest known biohacker in the world, 15-year-old Bryon Wake, for example, is using a microchip implant to unlock his smartphone, play music on Bluetooth speakers, and share his contact details by touching his hand against another person's smartphone (Griffiths, 2015). This shows that in many respects microchip implants are used as items of convenience (Petersen, 2019). This is also why microchip implants have been adopted not just by various technology enthusiasts, hobbyists, and biohackers interested in self-modifications (Heffernan, Vetere, & Chang, 2016), but more recently also by employers (for example, in Belgium, Estonia, Sweden, and the U.S.; see Petersen, 2019). But tech innovations will not stop here. According to a recent survey, *Work 2035* by Citrix, 77% of business leaders (N = 300) currently believe that by 2035, under-the-skin microchips and sensors will boost worker performance and productivity (Citrix, 2021).

Such predictions are largely based on the fact that the members of the millennial generation have been noted to express the most favorable perceptions of insideable technologies (Perakslis & Michael, 2012), that is, technologies that are put under your skin (Gauttier, 2019). In fact, people's willingness to implant their bodies with microchips has been gradually growing. The findings of a Global Shapers survey from 2017, for instance, revealed that 44.3% of young people would not agree with embedding an implant under their skin or in their brain, even when faced with the possibility of increasing their capabilities (World Economic Forum, 2017). In 2021, however, 57% of workers from France, Germany, the Netherlands, the U.S., and the UK (N = 1500) claim to be willing to implant their bodies with microchips if this was a safe way to boost their performance (Citrix, 2021). According to *The age of inclusive intelligence* (Dentsu, 2021), by 2030, two-thirds of people would consider having a microchip put into their brain so as to improve their physical senses, or life expectancy, or to learn some new skills to improve their job prospects (Dentsu, 2021). This suggests that members of the younger generations are open to exploring such a "'creepy or cool' trade off" (Wissinger, 2020, p. 189).

Interviews with Estonian employees with microchip implants (N = 14), carried out by Andra Siibak and Marleen Otsus, also indicate that in comparison to the members of older generations, among whom such technologies trigger the "yuck factor" (Petersen, 2019), young people are tending to embrace the various technological innovations with growing interest and enthusiasm. Most of the interviewees from Estonia who had embedded microchips under their skin were young adults in their 20ies, claiming that they had voluntarily accepted a microchip implant offered by their employer as they believed the technology to be compatible not only with existing organizational values and culture, but also with their own personal needs and values. The interviews revealed that decisions such as whether to adopt or reject the innovation were mainly held among like-minded colleagues and their closest peers, who were believed to share such an interest in technology, and were in favor of adopting the innovation themselves. In fact, like the teenagers Bryan and Evan, whose microchipping stories have been covered by the press (Griffiths, 2015; Messer, 2019), several of the Estonian interviewees stated that they had not told their family members, most often parents and older relatives, about their microchip implant. Such a decision was most often based on the assumption that the subjective evaluations of the microchip implants among the members of older generations would not be compatible with the personal needs, values, and experiences of the young. All the interviewees claimed that the adoption of microchip implants had made their lives more convenient and enabled them to simplify their daily lives. They enjoyed the fact that they did not have the hassle of having to have keys or cards when opening their office doors, and were used to using the microchip when running various work-related errands, for example, printing, sending meeting notes from the smart board directly to email, or when buying coffee and snacks from the vending machines. Some of the interviewees had also used microchip implants for personal identification outside of their work environment, for example, when accessing a gym or renting a bike. Hence, despite the fact that microchip implants have been viewed as "a technology of controls, limits, and rights" (Michael et al., 2020, p. 102), most of the interviewees tended to describe the innovation as a "liberating technology." All the interviewees agreed that if there were more opportunities to use the microchip implants, the perceived relative advantage of the innovation would be even more significant, and the innovation would spread within society to a greater degree. For example, several of the interviewees expressed a hope that one day the microchip implant could be connected to their ID card, while several others looked forward to a chance to use it for personal identification on public transport or while making payments. Furthermore, some expressed a wish to connect their microchip implants with their medical records, and for using the device to measure their blood sugar levels, track their sleep patterns, and so on, that is, they wanted to be able to use the microchip implants for routine self-tracking of their health. At the same time, even though microchip implants have been considered to be "highly intrusive to our overall physical and mental privacy" (Michael et al., 2020, p. 114), none of the interviewees expressed any privacy or ethical concerns in relation to their adoption. Thus, it appears that members of the younger generation have adopted and accepted the idea that the human body is the greatest data platform, bound to generate value in the age of surveillance capitalism.

The emerging cultural practice of self-tracking as a "good" and desirable practice of the self along with the dataism discussed in Chapter 2 provides the reference framework in which the mediatized practices of children, parents, families, and educators are enacted and rendered meaningful.

Note

1 The "quantified self movement" has emerged to promote "self-knowledge through numbers." The label was coined by Gary Wolf and Kevin Kelly, two editors of *Wired* magazine, who used it first informally in 2007 as a name for a local collaboration of users and technology makers interested in the automated collection of data. Resulting from the increasing availability of wearable devices and mobile phone apps, a growing number of people around the world are embracing the practices of self-quantification, measuring and analysing the details of their daily lives, habits, activities, behavior, or health. Hence, the term is now used to describe almost any form of self-tracking.

References

Ajana, B. (2018). Introduction: Metric culture and the over-examined life. In B. Ajana (Ed.), *Metric culture: Ontologies of self-tracking practices* (pp. 1–9). Emerald.

Barassi, V. (2020). *Child | Data | Citizen. How tech-companies are profiling us from before birth.* The MIT Press.

Berman, G., & Albright, K. (2017). *Children and the data cycle: Rights and ethics in a big data world.* Innocenti Working Papers 2017-05. UNICEF Office of Research – Innocenti.

boyd, D., & Crawford, K. (2011). *Six provocations for big data.* SSRN Scholarly Paper ID 1926431. Social Science Research Network. http://papers.ssrn.com/abstract=1926431

Charitsis, V. (2016). Prosuming (the) self. *Ephemera: Theory & Politics in Organization, 16*(3), 37–59.

Charteris, J., Gregory, S., & Masters, Y. (2014). Snapchat "selfies:" The case of disappearing data. In B. Hegarty, J. McDonald, & S.-K. Loke (Eds.), *Rhetoric and reality: Critical perspectives on educational technology* (pp. 389–393). Proceedings Ascilite Dunedin.

Citrix (2021). *Work 2035: How people and technology will pioneer new ways of working.* www.citrix.com/fieldwork/employee-experience/new-ways-of-working-2035.html

Cosgrove, L., Karter, J. M., Morrill, Z., & McGinley, M. (2021). Psychology and surveillance capitalism: The risk of pushing mental health apps during the COVID-19 pandemic. *Journal of Humanistic Psychology, 60*(5), 611–625.

Couldry, N., & Mejias, U. (2019). *The costs of connection: How data is colonizing human life and appropriating it for capitalism.* Stanford University Press.

C.S. Mott Children's Hospital (2021). How the pandemic has impacted teen mental health. National poll on children's health. *Mott Poll Report, 38*(2). https://mottpoll.org/reports/how-pandemic-has-impacted-teen-mental-health

Dentsu (2021). *The age of inclusive intelligence.* https://consumervision.dentsu.com/consumer-vision-2030/start

Depper, A., & Howe, P. D. (2017). Are we fit yet? English adolescent girls' experiences of health and fitness apps. *Health Sociology Review, 26*(1), 98–112.

Elsden, C., Kirk, D. S., & Durrant, A. C. (2015). A quantified past: Toward design for remembering with personal informatics. *Human-Computer Interaction, 31*(6), 518–557.

Ford, T., John, A., & Gunnell, D. (2021). Mental health of children and young people during the pandemic. *BMJ, 372,* 614. https://doi.org/10.1136/bmj.n614

Fors, V., & Pink, S. (2017). Pedagogy as possibility: Health interventions as digital openness. *Social Sciences, 6*(2), 59.

Foucault, M. (1977). *Discipline and punish: The birth of the prison.* Vintage Books.

Foucault, M. (1988). Technologies of the self. In L. H. Martin, H. Gutman, & P. H. Hutton (Eds.), *Technologies of the self. A seminar with Michel Foucault* (pp. 16–49). Tavistock.

Foucault, M. (1998). *The will to knowledge. Vol 1. The history of sexuality.* Penguin.

Foucault, M. (2012). *The birth of the clinic.* Routledge.

Garrido, S., Cheers, D., Boydell, K., et al., (2019). Young people's responses to six smartphone apps for anxiety and depression: Focus group study. *JMIR Mental Health, 6*(10), 1–14.

Gauttier, S. (2019). "I've got you under my skin"—The role of ethical consideration in the (non-) acceptance of insideables in the workplace. *Technology in Society, 56,* 93–108.

Goodyear, V. A., Kerner, C., & Quennerstedt, M. (2019). Young people's uses of wearable healthy lifestyle technologies: Surveillance, self-surveillance and resistance. *Sport, Education and Society, 24*(3), 212–225.

Gowin, M., Cheney, M., Gwin, S., & Franklin Wann, T. (2015). Health and fitness app use in college students: A qualitative study. *American Journal of Health Education, 46*(4), 223–230.

Griffiths, S. (2015). Don't try this at home! Teenager, 15, implants a microchip in his HAND to control his smartphone and play music. *Daily Mail*, June 29. www.dailymail.co.uk/sciencetech/article-3143349/Don-t-try-home-Teenager-15-implants-microchip-HAND-control-smartphone-play-music.html

Grist, R., Porter, J., & Stallard, P. (2017). Mental health mobile apps for preadolescents and adolescents: A systematic review. *Journal of Medical Internet Research*, 19(5), e176.

Heffernan, K. J., Vetere, F., & Chang, S. (2016). You put what, where? Hobbyist use of insertable devices. In *CHI'16: Proceedings of the 2016 CHI Conference on Human Factors in Computing Systems*, 1798–1809.

Huckvale, K., Torous, J., & Larsen, M. E. (2019). Assessment of the data sharing and privacy practices of smartphone apps for depression and smoking cessation. *JAMA Network Open*, 2(4), e192542.

Hulsey, N. (2020). *Games in everyday life: For play*. Emerald.

Hutton, L., Price, B. A., Kelly, R., et al. (2018). Assessing the privacy of mHealth apps for self-tracking: Heuristic evaluation approach. *JMIR mHealth and uHealth*, 6(10), e185.

Ito, M., Odgers, C., Schueller, S., et al. (2020). *Social media and youth wellbeing: What we know and where we could go*. Connected Learning Alliance. https://clalliance.org/publications/social-media-and-youth-wellbeing-what-we-know-and-where-we-could-go/

James, E. (2021). Kids' mental health takes hit in pandemic. *The West Australian*, February 20. https://thewest.com.au/news/health/kids-mental-health-takes-hit-in-pandemic-ng-s-2050414

Jasanoff, S. (2015). Future imperfect: Science, technology and the imaginations of modernity. In S. Jasanoff & S. H. Kim (Eds.), *Dreamscapes of modernity: Sociotechnical imaginaries and the fabrication of power* (pp. 1–33). University of Chicago Press.

Kennedy, H., & Moss, G. (2015). Known or knowing publics? Social media data mining and the question of public agency. *Big Data & Society*, 2(2), 1–11.

Kennedy, H., Poell, T., & van Dijk, J. (2015). Data and agency. *Big Data & Society*, 2(2), 1–7.

Kenny, R., Dooley, B., & Fitzgerald, A. (2016). Developing mental health mobile apps: Exploring adolescents' perspective. *Health Informatics Journal*, 22(2), 265–275.

Kim, S.-I., Jo, E., Ryu, M., et al. (2019). Experiences of adolescents with autism spectrum disorder using custom trackers. In *The 13th International Conference on Pervasive Computing Technologies for Healthcare* (PervasiveHealth'19), May 20–23, Trento, Italy. ACM.

Kneidinger-Müller, B. (2018). Self-tracking data as digital traces of identity: A theoretical analysis of contextual factors of self-observation practices. *International Journal of Communication*, 12, 629–646.

Lieberoth, A., Lin, S.-Y., Stöckli, S., et al. (2021). Stress and worry in the 2020 coronavirus pandemic: Relationships to trust and compliance with preventive measures across 48 countries in the COVID iSTRESS global survey. *Royal Society Open Science*, 8, 200589. https://doi.org/10.1098/rsos.200589

Lomborg, S., & Frandsen, K. (2016). Self-tracking as communication. *Information, Communication & Society*, 19(7), 1015–1027.

Lupton, L. (2016). The diverse domains of quantified selves: Self-tracking modes and dataveillance. *Economy and Society*, 45(1), 101–122.

Lupton, D. (2020a). *Data selves*. Polity Press.

Lupton, D. (2020b). Wearable devices: Sociotechnical imaginaries and agential capacities. In I. Pedersen & A. Iliadis (Eds.), *Embodied computing. Wearables, implantables, embeddables, ingestibles* (pp. 49–69). The MIT Press.

Lupton, D. (2020c). "Better understanding about what's going on: | " Young Australians' use of digital technologies for health and fitness. *Sport, Education and Society, 25*(1), 1–13.

Messer, O. (2019). How a teen 'biohacker' embedded his college ID in his hand. *Daily Beast,* October 22. www.thedailybeast.com/how-a-university-of-south-carolina-biohacker-embedded-his-college-id-in-his-hand

Michael, K., & Michael, M. (2013). The future prospects of embedded microchips in humans as unique identifiers: the risks versus the rewards. *Media, Culture & Society, 35*(1), 78–86.

Michael, K., Michael M. G., Perakslis, C., & Abbas, R. (2020). Überveillance and the rise of last-mile implantables: Past, present, and future. In I. Pedersen & A. Iliadis (Eds.), *Embodied computing. Wearables, implantables, embeddables, ingestibles* (pp. 97–130). The MIT Press.

Mosco, V. (2017). *Becoming digital: Toward a post-internet society.* Emerald.

Nafus, D. (2016). Introduction. In D. Nafus (Ed.), *Quantified: Biosensing technologies in everyday life.* The MIT Press.

Neff, G., & Nafus, D. (2016). *Self-tracking.* The MIT Press.

Pantzar, M., & Ruckenstein, M. (2017). Living the metrics: Self-tracking and situated objectivity. *Digital Health, 3,* 1–10.

Parker, L., Bero, L., Gillies, D., et al. (2018). Mental health messages in prominent mental health apps. *Annals of Family Medicine, 16*(4), 338–342.

Pedersen, I. (2020). Will the body become a platform? Body networks, datafied bodies, and AI futures. In I. Pedersen & A. Iliadis (Eds.), *Embodied computing. Wearables, implantables, embeddables, ingestibles* (pp. 21–47). The MIT Press.

Pedersen, I., & Iliadis, A. (Eds.). (2020). *Embodied computing. Wearables, implantables, embeddables, ingestibles.* The MIT Press.

Perakslis, C., & Michael, K. (2012). Indian millennials: Are microchip implants a more secure technology for identification and access control? In M. Arnold, M. R. Gibbs, G. Adamson, & P. Hall (Eds.), *Proceedings of the 2012 IEEE Conference on Technology and Society in Asia, T and SA* (pp. 1–9). IEEE.

Petersen, M. (2019). *The Swedish microchipping phenomenon.* Emerald.

Potapov, K., Lee, V. R., Vasalou, A., & Marshall, P. (2019). Youth concerns and responses to self-tracking tools and personal informatics systems. In *CHI EA'19: Extended Abstracts of the 2019 Conference on Human Factors in Computing Systems.* https://doi.org/10.1145/3290607.3312886

Psihogios, A. M., Stiles-Shields, C., & Neary, M. (2020). The needle in the haystack: Identifying credible mobile health apps for pediatric populations during a pandemic and beyond. *Journal of Pediatric Psychology, 45*(10), 1106–1113.

Pybus, J., Cotè, M., & Blanke, T. (2015). Hacking the social life of big data. *Big Data & Society, 2*(2), 1–10.

Rapp, A., & Cena, F. (2016). Personal informatics for everyday life: How users without prior self-tracking experience engage with personal data. *International Journal of Human-Computer Studies*, 94, 1–17.

Rettberg, J. W. (2014). *Seeing ourselves through technology: How we use selfies, blogs and wearable devices to see and shape ourselves*. Palgrave Macmillan.

Rich, E., Lewis, S., Lupton, D., Miah, A., & Piwek, L. (2020). *Digital health generation? Young people's use of 'healthy lifestyle' technologies*. University of Bath.

Rideout, V., & Fox, S. (2018). Digital health practices, social media use, and mental well-being among teens and young adults in the U.S. *Articles, Abstracts, and Reports*, 1093. https://digitalcommons.psjhealth.org/publications/1093

Robards, B., Lyall, B., & Moran, C. (2020). Confessional data selfies and intimate digital traces. *New Media & Society*. https://doi.org/10.1177/1461444820934032

Rodriguez, D. A. (2019). Chipping at work: Privacy concerns related to the use of body microchip (RFID) implants in the employer-employee context. *Iowa Law Review*, 104(3), 1581–1611.

Schaefer, S. E., Carter Ching, C., Breen, H., & German, J. B. (2016). Wearing, thinking, and moving: Testing the feasibility of fitness tracking with urban youth. *American Journal of Health Education*, 47(1), 8–16.

Selwyn, N., & Pangrazio, L. (2018). Doing data differently? Developing personal data tactics and strategies amongst young mobile media users. *Big Data & Society*, 5(1), 1–12.

Shore, C., & Wright, S. (2018). Performance management and the audited self. In B. Ajana (Ed.), *Metric culture: Ontologies of self-tracking practices* (pp. 11–35). Emerald.

Smith, C. E. (2008). Human microchip implantation. *Journal of Technology Management & Innovation*, 3(3), 151–160.

Staines, R. (2020). Kids' mental health app sees spike in users in COVID-19 crises. *PharmaPhorum*, April 7. https://pharmaphorum.com/news/kids-mental-health-app-sees-spike-in-users-in-covid-19-crisis/

Sumra, H. (2018). Wiggly is like a wearable Dance Dance Revolution jacket for your kids. *Wearable*, October 17. www.wareable.com/smart-clothing/wiggly-dancing-jacket-kids-6624

van Dijck, J. (2014). Datafication, dataism and dataveillance: Big data between scientific paradigm and ideology. *Surveillance and Society*, 12(2), 197–208. https://doi.org/10.24908/ss.v12i2.4776

Whitson, J. R. (2013). Gaming the quantified self. *Surveillance & Society*, 11(1/2), 163–176.

WHO (World Health Organization) (2011). *mHealth: New horizons for health through technologies*. *Global Observatory Series*, 3. https://apps.who.int/iris/handle/10665/44607

Willmott, C., Fraser, E., & Lammes, S. (2017). "I am he. I am he. Siri rules." Work and play with the Apple Watch. *European Journal of Cultural Studies*, 21(1), 78–95.

Wissinger, E. (2020). Click-click-gimme-gimme: Pleasures and perils of the "opt in" world of fashion tech. In I. Pedersen & A. Iliadis (Eds.), *Embodied computing. Wearables, implantables, embeddables, ingestibles* (pp. 187–209). The MIT Press.

Wolf, G. (2010). The data-driven life. *The New York Magazine*, April 28. www.nytimes.com/2010/05/02/magazine/02self-measurement-t.html?pagewanted=all&_r=0

World Economic Forum (2017). *Global Shapers Survey*. www.es.amnesty.org/fileadmin/noticias/
    ShapersSurvey2017_Full_Report_24Aug__002__01.pdf
Zuboff, S. (2019). *The age of surveillance capitalism: The fight for a human future at the new frontier
    of power*. Profile Books.

MEDIATIZED PARENTING AS DATAFIED PARENTING

Hypervigilance of Transcendent Parenting

Lim (2020) has recently argued that in the context of Western urban middle-class societies, always on and always-on-hand mobile media means parents are able to transcend the physical distance between themselves and their children, enabling "transcendent parenting," that is, a practice indicating "the apparent ceaselessness of parenting duties" (Lim, 2020, p. 5). Parents living in a technology-saturated society have thus needed to become accustomed to parenting 24/7, as various parenting duties may interrupt their other social roles, obligations, and duties at any time or any place. In fact, this parental state of "hypervigilance" (Katz, 2001) has been gradually growing since 2000, both as a response to common fears and insecurities about children's wellbeing, but also as a response to the guilt and anxiety many parents experience while being away from their children due to work obligations. In our present-day media-saturated society, where various digital technologies lure parents in by a promise of constant connection, this has helped pave the way to intensive mediatized parenting (Clark, 2013; Nelson, 2010). In fact, as argued by Veronica Barassi (2020, p. 29), such hyperconnectivity "has become *a way of life*," or rather, "everything has become *onlife*" (p. 30; original emphasis), indicating that many parents have become dependent on technologies and smart devices to enable them to fulfill their parental roles. Such dependency, as claimed by Barassi (2020), is the exact reason why children are becoming datafied before birth.

While parents have always worried and watched over their children, since 2010 various labels such as "helicopters," "hovercrafts," "hummingbirds," "stealth fighters," or "black hawks" (Clark, 2013; LeMoyne & Buchanan, 2011) have been coined both by the popular press and by academics to refer to overprotective parents who tend to micro-manage their children's lives, and much of this parental gaze has "become technologized" (Howell, 2010, p. 1). More than a decade ago, scholars were already reporting "a new stance of anxiety" (Nelson, 2010, p. 516) emerging, particularly among middle-class parents who tend to constantly worry about the safety and development of their children. Due to this growing parental anxiety, which is believed to be deeply rooted in our present-day risk society (Ericson & Haggerty, 2006), many parents have thus started to take additional steps to monitor their children more closely than ever before. In fact, as argued by Lupton, Pedersen, and Thomas (2016), parents in general, and mothers in particular, are constantly pressured to take part in dataveillance, for example, taking responsibility for finding, generating, and using digitized information about childcare. While such dataveillance is often understood in negative terms as a restriction of autonomy and privacy of those who are being watched (Lupton et al., 2016), as claimed by Lupton (2020b), in family settings, dataveillance can also entail an expression of love and attentiveness. Thus, in the realm of caring dataveillance, digital devices become part of the "materialities of care" (Lupton, 2020b, p. 399), where parental control is justified for assuring children's health and wellbeing.

Various technology companies and service providers are supplying a myriad of technological solutions for easing those parental anxieties. Hundreds of digital devices and thousands of mobile apps have been brought onto the market in recent years with the aim of enabling parents to be able to create "virtual togetherness with their children over distance" (Gabriels, 2016, p. 176). Furthermore, such devices and various digital platforms (for example, social media) trigger various forms of "intimate surveillance" (Leaver, 2017; Lupton, 2020a), that is, "a mode of watching that takes place when people observe other people who are close to them" (Lupton, 2020a, p. 102), which has become a popular practice associated with normal parental care (Lupton & Williamson, 2017). At the same time, some scholars (Bonafide, Jamison, & Foglia, 2017; Nelson, 2010) have become increasingly concerned that this (over)reliance on various digital technologies and parenting apps has not actually helped to ease parental concerns, but has instead intensified them, turning the present-day childhood into "a critical site of datafication and dataveillance" (Mascheroni, 2020, p. 798).

Creating Digital Data Shadows for the Unborn Child

Digital platforms have become inseparable from the precarious lives of present-day parents(-to-be). The role of parental discussion forums, social media, and "mommy blogs" in everyday routines has become so ubiquitous that the platforms have become "the digital mundane" (Wilson & Chivers Yochim, 2017, p. 16), helping parents navigate the complexities that becoming and being a parent entails.

Since the early days of the internet, pregnant women have turned to online discussion forums and websites (Lupton et al., 2016) or "mommy blogs" (Morrison, 2011; Orton-Johnson, 2017) for emotional support and information about pregnancy and childrearing. Although mothers usually assume primary responsibility for the wellbeing of the child, fathers-to-be have also been found to use the internet, and social media in particular, both for practicing "caring fatherhood," that is, communicating with other fathers for encouragement, confirmation, and advice (Eriksson & Salzmann-Erikson, 2012), as well as to "learn how to be a good father" (Ammari & Schoenebeck, 2015, p. 8). Sharing personal information online has become "a communal data practice" (Lupton, 2020a, p. 101), where personal stories, experiences, and feelings become part of the "crowdsourced body of knowledge" (Lupton, 2020a, p. 101) that is deeply enwoven into the fabric of social life in the era of the "sharing economy." So in a sense these platforms not only help to build parents' social capital and shape their identities as future parents, but also help to coin their imaginaries of a "good parenting" practice. Hence, as argued by Neiterman (2012), the contemporary notions of pregnancy entail the performance of pregnancy, something that women first need to master by (1) seeking information and advice to learn how to be pregnant; (2) adapting new routines of self-care; and (3) performing normalized pregnancy routines.

As claimed by Gillies (2010, p. 4), in the contemporary neoliberal world, good parenting has become "a technical exercise—something that you can either get right or wrong." Furthermore, it is often assumed that parental competencies cannot only be taught and learned, but also purchased and con-sumed (cf. Tiidenberg & Baym, 2017). The latter aspect has, of course, not gone unnoticed by the data-hungry gaze of the marketers who are eagerly sinking their algorithmic claws into every corner of the internet. Thus, while the future mothers are actively Googling for health advice, looking for some ideas from BabyCentre for how to decorate a nursery, or posting their bump selfies on Instagram, "the datafication of the unborn has become unavoidable" (Barassi, 2020, p. 39). In fact, as suggested by Barassi (2020), it has become impossible to keep one's pregnancy a secret from all the trackers, bots, cookies, and other data sniffers that feed the data brokers for targeted advertising and predictive analytics.

Although some parents have tried their best to consciously hide the fact that they are expecting or planning to conceive, these attempts have often ended with the realization that it has become impossible not to be tracked. For example, Vertesi (2014), a sociologist of technology at Princeton University, who wrote in *Time Magazine* about her own personal experiment of trying to hide her pregnancy, concluded her article with a bitter acknowledgment that "avoiding the big-data dragnet meant that I not only looked like a rude family member or an inconsiderate friend, but I also looked like a bad citizen." During the big data era of marketed advertising, the data from prospective mothers has come to mean lucrative business for big corporations, data com-panies, and retail stores (Target, for example, is notorious for its "pregnancy prediction score;" cf. Duhigg, 2012).

In recent years, however, the mediation of the unborn child in a technology-saturated society has reached another new dimension (Thomas & Lupton, 2016). Fertility or menstrual cycle tracking apps, that is, repro-ductive health trackers, aimed at women who either want to conceive or to avoid conceiving (Gambier-Ross, McLernon, & Morgan, 2018), and preg-nancy apps that enable pregnant women to track their pregnancies and to access pregnancy-related information have become immensely popular (Lee & Moon, 2016). In fact, this niche of the "quantified self" movement has become so popular all around the world that, according to Hughson et al. (2018, p. 1), "most pregnant women in high-income countries [are] now using them." During 2021–28, the compound annual growth rate of the pregnancy tracker apps market is expected to hit a massive +11% revenue (KSU/*The Sentinel Newspaper*, 2021). At the same time, it should be acknowledged that it is mostly middle-class urban families who use such devices, whereas already marginalized groups—for example, women with a lower income, ethnic or racial minorities, other hard-to-reach populations, as well as groups that have lower English language proficiency and digital or health literacy—are caught up in the "vicious cycle of digital exclusion" (Baum, Newman, & Biedrzycki, 2014, p. 12).

These digital inequalities were magnified even further due to the COVID-19 pandemic, during which many pregnant women experienced difficulties in accessing healthcare (Karavadra et al., 2020). Since many prenatal appointments during the pandemic were carried out either through various telemedicine or video-conferencing platforms (such as Zoom), prenatal healthcare also relied on the "*systematic coercion of digital participation*" (Barassi, 2020, p. 46; original emphasis), indicating that future mothers were forced to give up their personal data simply because the services they depended on had become increasingly automated and datafied. Declining these services, however, could result in these mothers not only harming their physical and mental wellbeing, but also the life of their child. Furthermore, according to NordVPN researchers, the average number of installed pregnancy apps during the COVID-19 lockdown in spring 2020 grew globally by 13% compared to 2019 (*Welp Magazine*, 2020). Although NordVPN researchers associate this increased interest in pregnancy apps with a "compulsory intimacy" (*Welp Magazine*, 2020), it could be hypothesized that many of these downloads were actually a direct result of the problems pregnant women experienced with accessing healthcare. So, as a result of not being able to have regular doctors' appointments in person, many of the women were simply coerced into creating human data assemblages of themselves and of their unborn children.

The greatest lure of pregnancy apps is associated with the fact that they provide women with an opportunity to track their pregnancies by inserting intimate health data and personal identifying information both about the mother and the unborn child, such as diet before conception, conception date, parents' thoughts, medical history, number of kicks in the womb, and potential due date (Barassi, 2020). Studies have also indicated that the users of these pregnancy apps often value the "highly agential capacity of digital technologies" (Lupton, 2020a, p. 115), which provide them with an opportunity to become better aware of their own bodies by providing new insights and sensory responses they otherwise might not be able to sense. On the one hand, such self-surveillance enables not only valuable self-knowledge and assurance to be produced, but on the other, as is evident from Lupton's studies (2020a), also helps women to develop a relationship with their fetuses. Therefore, as argued by Barassi (2020), the emotional dimension of the data cannot be overlooked.

At the same time, however, research reveals that pregnant women often fail to acknowledge the amount of personal data they leave behind that "extends well beyond any original intention that they may have had gathering them" (Lupton, 2020a, p. 109). Furthermore, they fail to recognize the affordances their personal data could provide to other actors, for example, marketers, employers, insurance offices, etc. In fact, the findings of empirical studies (cf. Lupton, 2020a) indicate that some users of pregnancy apps are simply unaware of the continuous dataveillance that they are under, while others reveal a total lack of interest and concern in privacy issues—the users simply cannot imagine that their mundane everyday practices and the data these evoke could be of any use to anyone. It is thus crucial to acknowledge that the practice of self-monitoring reproductive health tracking apps cannot be separated from discussions about the political economy of big data and capitalist data relations that pose a considerable risk to privacy.

The findings of a recent study by Consumer Report's Digital Lab reveal that all five popular period tracking apps included in the study—BabyCenter, Clue, Flo, My Calendar, and Ovia—were sharing user data with advertisers; and in the case of the Ovia app, both employers and insurance companies were able to access a vast range of aggregated data about its users (Rosato, 2020). According to an article published in *The Washington Post*, the Ovia user data shared with employers most probably included information about the average age, number of children, and current trimester; the average time it took the women to get pregnant; the percentage who had high-risk pregnancies and who conceived after a stretch of infertility, who had C-sections, or who gave birth prematurely; and how soon the new mothers had returned to work (see Harwell, 2019). This suggests that the data traces collected through pregnancy apps can be used for making various assumptions and conclusions about the users, both in the employment context and beyond. Considering that the data policies drafted by the service providers do not generally address the issue of privacy as clearly as they should, and tend to direct all responsibilities related to privacy to the users (Barassi, 2020; Bert et al., 2015), many users are unaware of the potential risks. However, in addition to sharing medical and private health data with the service providers and their potential third parties, the parents are also creating and commodifying a data footprint for their unborn child. Thus, as argued by Barassi (2017, p. 2), we are witnessing not only the "commodification of the lived experience of expectant parents, but also the politics of exploitation of the data flows of the unborn," contributing to the emergence of the datafied child. Even though many parents are making use of these reproductive health trackers on a voluntary basis, the commodified form of data relations that these devices evoke bind its users tightly into surveillance capitalism.

Babies Under the Data Gaze

Parents of newborns are often anxious, as the situation they find themselves in is new, uncertain, and seemingly out of control. Babytech (also known as famtech), with its countless apps, gadgets, and services, is mostly targeted at millennial parents with the aim of making parenting experiences easier and in the hope of keeping babies healthy. Although the market of this "new mom economy" is still relatively new, in 2019 *Forbes* estimated its market size to be US$46 billion, and sure to grow in the coming years (Klich, 2019). The growing popularity of the babytech industry thus serves as an illustration of the continuous technological and data fetishism among parents who are anxiously trying to live up to the societal imaginaries of a "good parent." In fact, as suggested by Johnson (2014, p. 346), products of the babytech industry are meant to sell the promise of becoming a better and more relaxed parent, and are thus constructed as "empowering technologies" through which women can take control of their babies' health and wellbeing. Downloading apps that can alert you when your baby has rolled over, woken up, or peed in their diaper can be really helpful for first-time parents. Devices and gadgets that notify parents when their baby is hungry, cold, or simply tired also make parents' childrearing experiences easier. However, all the personal data traces that these apps and gadgets provoke feed into the growing surveillance capitalism.

Much of the success of the babytech industry has been built on aggressive marketing jargon the service providers use that is believed to "stimulate unnecessary fear, uncertainty, and self-doubt in parents about their abilities to keep their infants safe" (Bonafide et al., 2017, p. 1). A variety of intimate surveillance apps and devices are thus closely intertwined with parental caring practices aiming to assure the parent that their children's wellbeing, health, and development depend on making the right consumer choices. The findings of a content analysis of more than 1000 consumer reviews of baby monitors in Epinions.com, for instance, suggest that parents themselves also "participate in the 'selling' of anxiety and of attitudes toward the appropriateness of careful monitoring—or surveillance—of children" (Nelson, 2008, p. 519). In fact, Nelson's analysis suggests that parents using baby monitors seem to believe that "they have both a 'right' and a moral obligation to know what is going on with their own child" (2008, p. 533). In short, anxious parents do not view parental anxieties or the spread of surveillance as a problem, but rather embrace these as widespread and normalized parts of the digitalized society and present- day parenting practice.

Baby tracking apps have also been criticized for silencing the everyday mundane and personal experiences that mothers have, for not considering what Helen Thornham (2019, p. 179) refers to as "maternal subjectivity." The findings of Thornham's ethnographic study indicate that the "datalogical construction" produced by the baby tracking apps offers "a clean and simple, 'scientific' and atomized metric" (Thornham, 2019) of motherhood, where the subjective experiences of mothers, full of different kinds of emotions and anxieties and everyday frustrations, but also joy or pain, simply do not fit. In fact, as suggested by Holloway, Mascheroni, and Inglis (2020), baby wearables are a perfect example of the neoliberal gendered responsibilization discourse. Through push notifications and nudges that are dependent on the datafication of the baby's body, these wearables aim to provide mothers with true knowledge, not just subjective, embodied judgments that can easily be deceptive or unreliable. As argued by Johnson (2014, p. 346), these gadgets aim to turn mothers into experts though disciplinary "push responsibilization;" however, such "device-ification of mothering" (Johnson, 2014, p. 346) does not consider the fact that these technologies instrumentalize and quantify the baby's and mother's body according to a very particular set of measurements. For example, although baby wearables enable parents to track the duration and frequency of sleep and to count intentional attempts to breastfeed, they do not enable parents to measure the quality of sleep or count for all the unsuccessful attempts to breastfeed.

Another big concern, especially for first-time parents, is the baby's health and development. Although there are no "medical indications for monitoring healthy infants at home" (Bonafide et al., 2017, p. 2), many parents have started to make use of baby monitors or smartphone apps that can be integrated with sensors built into leg bands, diaper clips, socks, or onesies to monitor the baby's health (for example, checking heart rate, skin temperature, and oxygen concentration, and generating alarms for apnea, tachycardia, bradycardia, and/or oxygen desaturation). Even though most of the consumer infant physiologic monitor websites avoid direct statements that their products treat, diagnose, or prevent disease, their advertised role is to alert parents when something is wrong with their infant's cardiorespiratory health (Bonafide et al., 2017). Furthermore, as baby monitors are sold as consumer rather than medical devices, none of the service providers are required to carry out observational studies or randomized trials to find scientific evidence for backing up their claims (King, 2014), leaving parents with information that is not medically sound. In fact, recent research reveals that such devices have serious problems with accuracy (Bonafide et al., 2018), thus, rather than reassuring parents and easing their anxieties, it is argued that the use of such devices "may generate anxiety and a false assumption that their infant is at risk of dying" (Bonafide et al., 2017, p. 3).

In addition to various digital devices and apps that enable parents to monitor their children, numerous parents continue to rely on the help of babysitters. As finding a reliable babysitter is hard work, California-based start-up Predictim provided its services for parents in their search for a "perfect babysitter" (Harwell, 2018). Predictim made use of AI to vet babysitters' behavior, offering a risk rating of each applicant based on a scan through the babysitter's various social media profiles, online criminal history databases, and other online sources (Klazema, 2019). The start-up advertised that its system was not only able to evaluate babysitters on various personality traits (for example, politeness, ability to work with others, and positivity), but was also able to detect potential problems with drug abuse or possible bullying behavior. The service charged US$25 for each scan, which could potentially end up with a score decision: "this person is very likely to display the undesired behavior (high likelihood of being a bad hire)" (Lee, 2018). Predictim's service, however, was soon met with harsh public criticism, and after Facebook, Instagram, and Twitter blocked the company from accessing their data, for violating rules on user surveillance and data privacy (Klazema, 2019), the company had to suspend its operations for good.

Caring Dataveillance: Use of Parental Controls and Other Tracking Devices

Present-day parents have adopted a "philosophy of protectiveness" (Simpson, 2014, p. 275) that is so deep-rooted in their parenting practices that these concerns and anxieties do not ease up even when their children are older. On the contrary, various technological devices, mobile applications, and parental controls (such as content filtering software, internet blockers, and add-on monitoring software) have been taken into use so as to monitor children's whereabouts, both in the online and offline worlds.

Although recent EU Kids Online findings (Smahel et al., 2020) suggest that the number of children claiming their parents make use of such techno-logical aids is relatively insignificant (an EU average of 22% or less), a study by the Pew Research Center indicates that a considerable number (52%) of parents of teens (13- to 17-year-olds) report the use of parental controls (Anderson, 2019). Such a noticeable difference in the adoption of parental controls between parents in the EU and the U.S. could be explained not only by the differences in dominant parental styles (cf. Ghosh et al., 2018) and childrearing values (cf. Mascheroni, 2014), but also by the cultural differences in understanding and contextualizing children's privacy (Cino, Mascheroni, & Wartella, 2020). Findings of a recent quantitative and qualitative content analysis study of users' reviews (N = 154) of Circle Home Plus—a small box that regulates through parental controls all the domestic connected devices and, through an app, all the mobile devices—posted on Amazon and Searchman, for example—reveal that parents who incorporate Circle into a repertoire of enabling mediation strategies express more critical views about the ways in which the device constrains children's agency and voice (Cino et al., 2020). Parents who are more enthusiastic about the tool, however, belong to the group of "anxiety-reducing restrictive caregivers" who combine restrictive mediation with "an ethic of respectful connectedness that emphasizes paren-tal authority when using the media within and outside the domestic walls" (Cino et al., 2020, p. 213). Studies also indicate that the socioeconomic status of families (cf. Clark, 2013), as well as the educational attainment of the par-ents and their digital literacy skills (cf. Nikken & Schols, 2015), might play a role in their adoption of parental controls. For example, according to Nelson (2010), upper- and middle-class parents tend to view various parental controls and filters as "constraining technologies," and therefore avoid using them.

A wide variety of parental controls have been brought to the market either to help parents to ensure their children's online safety or to limit their children's screen time. Despite their questionable effectiveness (Zaman & Nouwen, 2016), parents mainly start using these apps in the hope that they will enable them to set place, time, and content restrictions for their children's device use. For example, they can give parents control over where, how long, and what kind of content the child can access online, or with whom they can interact. Some other parental controls may also help to set limits on various online activities, such as entertainment, social media, and online games (for example, disabling features for sharing content). Facebook's messaging app for families with children, Messenger Kids, also recently introduced new features that provide parents with more oversight and control over their children's chats (Perez, 2020). These new features enable parents to see who their child is chatting with and how often, to view recent photos and videos sent through chat, to access the child's reported and block list, or to download the child's chats, images, and videos, both sent and received. Both Apple (Family Setup) and Microsoft (Family Safety) have also launched new features that function both as a parental control app and a location-tracking app, raising concerns about potential "interpersonal privacy" (Stoilova, Nandagiri & Livingstone, 2019) breaches by the parents.

The use of parental controls is, however, also associated with various commercial privacy concerns (Livingstone, Stoilova, & Nandagiri, 2019). Findings from Feal et al.'s (2020) in-depth study of Android parental control apps available in Google Play Store (N = 46) reveal that 72% of the apps included in their analysis share data with third parties, and in 67% of the cases this sharing happens without explicit and verifiable parental consent. The privacy policies of many of these apps tend to under-report the amount of data they share with other parties. Research by Ali and colleagues (2020, p. 11) introduced similar cautionary results, claiming that many parental control apps on the market have pervasive security and privacy issues, that rather than ensuring safety, could actually "undermine children's online and real-world safety."

Today's children are rarely able to enjoy walking alone to school, biking around the neighborhood, or playing outside with their friends while completely out of reach of their parents. The "world's longest umbilical cord" (Shellenbarger, 2005), the mobile phone, is often there, enabling parents to "exercise control from a distance, without interaction" (Gabriels, 2016, p. 176). Since the beginning of the 20th century, additional technological advancements, other tracking devices, and apps have been brought to the market in support of transcendent parenting practices (Lim, 2020). Although EU Kids Online 2020 findings suggests that the use of these intimate surveillance technologies is still relatively less common within the EU (an EU average of 15% of children report such an experience) (Smahel et al., 2020, p. 75), the sheer variety of apps and devices on the market provides a reason to believe that the use of such technologies will keep growing in their popularity.

Many of the other tracking devices offer real-life tracking opportunities that enable parents to pinpoint the exact location and whereabouts of the child; some even provide the child's transit speed (cf. Siibak, 2019). Many devices also come with an SOS or panic button, so that when the child is in trouble, they can immediately contact their parents either through two-way voice communication or a video option. Others provide a geo-fencing option, which enables parents to mark concrete locations on the map and to turn them into so-called safety zones (specific locations where the child is allowed to be), and in case the child has wandered outside of the safety zone, the parents will be immediately notified. Some apps also alert parents when the child is visiting a new place or when they arrive home too late. More expensive ones, such as the Amber Alert GPS Locator, even tap into the U.S. National Sex Offender Database and alert parents when the child is within 500 feet of a registered sex offender.

There is also a variety of school bus tracking apps (for example, Here Comes the Bus) available for parents concerned about their younger children's bus rides, while some others either have a driver tracking feature (for example, Life360), or specialize on driver tracking (for example, RoadReady, SafeDrive, Hum), and are thus eagerly used by parents who are concerned about their teenage drivers (Jargon, 2020). In addition to offering some peace of mind to anxious parents, some of these apps also provide data in the context of teen driver premiums—those teen drivers who have downloaded the app and, according to apps imaginaries, are considered safe drivers, can save money from their car insurance. This is a vivid illustration of how the commercialization of an individual's behavioral data works in the age of surveillance capitalism.

Some more recent technological advancements have become so discreet that their usage might go totally unnoticed by the child. For example, 2019 Edison Award winner in "personal protection system," B'zT, comes in the form of a washable tracker patch and chipset that can be embedded in clothing, such as a t-shirt, with an alarm that goes off every time the child wanders away to notify the parents (Siibak, 2019). This means that parents are able to use tracking devices without the consent and knowledge of their child, eloquently illustrating the claim that "spying has become an enhanced parenting tool," as argued by Marx and Steeves (2010, p. 205). EU Kids Online survey findings from Estonia also suggest that children (aged 9–17) are often unaware of the intimate dataveillance practices their parents are undertaking—although 22% of Estonian parents reported making use of some tracking technologies to monitor their child, only 13% of the children from the same families were aware of such surveillance (Sukk & Soo, 2018).

The marketing discourse encourages parental use of such technology by assuring them that by making the right kind of consumer choices, parents can actually "make the world a better—and in this case, safer—place" for their children (Hasinoff, 2017, p. 497). Such a protective and connected stance, however, can lead to a no-risk culture, altering and limiting children's experiences (Bundy et al., 2009). In fact, some authors argue that limited exposure to risks not only obstructs the development of resilience (Abbas et al., 2011, p. 26), but also puts children in a vulnerable and dependent position (Meyer, 2007). Furthermore, as claimed by Livingstone and Byrne (2018, p. 27), the use of parenting apps and the wish to protect children clashes with the wish to allow children the freedom to discover, learn, and grow on their own.

A recent Q methodology study combined with semi-structured individual interviews with middle-class parents in Estonia (N = 20; 18 mothers and 2 fathers) who used child-tracking technologies revealed three subjective parental viewpoints on the topic (see Table 4.1) (Sukk & Siibak, 2021).

Table 4.1. Subjective parental viewpoints extracted from a Q methodology study (Sukk & Siibak, 2021: 13-14)

Tech-trusting parent
• Has complete trust in tracking apps; views them as keeping the family safe.
• Believes that tracking helps to ease parental concerns.
• Believes that parents have the right to control their children.
• Believes that tracking does not limit children's privacy and personal freedom.
• Is not concerned about data privacy risks or trade-offs.

Cautious parent
• Has doubts about tracking apps: tracking can backfire and offer a false sense of security.
• Believes that tracking exploits parents' fears.
• Believes in children's autonomy: parents do not have the right to control their children.
• Believes that tracking devices are somewhat of a risk to children's privacy.
• Believes that location information can lead to privacy risks.

Careful authoritarian parent
• Has doubts about the sense of security tracking apps offer.
• Believes that apps are marketers' response to parental fears, and that they pose significant privacy risks.
• Believes that parents have the right to extensive control over children.
• Believes it is not necessary to ask for children's permission for tracking.
• Has problems with trusting children.

The most commonly held imagined affordance associated with the use of other tracking technologies by both the "tech-trusting" and "cautious" parents in Sukk and Siibak's (2021) study, was the idea that these apps help to make sure their families are safe. On the one hand, these parents believed that tracking apps helped to assure the children that their parents could keep them safe. On the other hand, the parents believed that these technologies provided them with agential capacities, meaning an easing of their own unnecessary worries. These parents also tended to view the use of tracking technologies as a parental right, as they believed it was their responsibility and parental duty to keep their children safe, and other tracking devices enabled them to cast a protective eye over their children. Practices of caring dataveillance (Lupton, 2020b) were thus deeply rooted in the reasoning of the parents as they agreed that sometimes they needed to protect their children from themselves, even if the children did not want that protection. At the same time, these parents also associated the use of tracking technologies with greater freedom for the child. They believed that the use of other tracking devices meant they could provide their children with a form of "monitored mobility" (Rutherford, 2011, p. 81) that they might otherwise not be willing to grant. Similar experiences were also revealed by Kelli Aia (2020), in the interviews with the parents of teens (aged 14–16) in Estonia who used tracking technologies to monitor them. For example, a mother of a 14-year-old girl explained that she was willing to allow her daughter to travel alone to a larger city to stay the night with a friend because she trusted that the tracking data would provide her with the necessary reassurance about her daughter's whereabouts. Although some parents tended to have full trust in the location data provided by the apps, and considered such technologies uncritically to be almost "truth-making machines" (Gregg, 2013, p. 307), several of them had also experienced that the data produced by these devices was not always accurate. The unreliability of the data received resulted in growing parental anxieties and concerns about the wellbeing of the child. A mother of a 10-year-old boy, for instance, described an instance when her son had taken a bus alone to participate in an event on the other side of town, but due to data breakage (Pink et al., 2018), the tracking app showed as though the boy had not reached his destination. Similar experiences indicating the unreliability of the apps were also shared by pre-teens (aged 7–13) in Estonia who were aware of being tracked by their parents (Sukk & Siibak, 2021). Even though the majority of the pre-teens in the Sukk and Siibak's (2021) sample (N = 20) were ready to place trust both in their parents and in the tracking technology, some of them had still experienced instances where the location data sent through the apps had been incorrect, for example, the app showed that the child was still at home although they were, in fact, in school. Similar data unreliability issues (inoperable geo-fencing functions, faulty SOS buttons) have been uncovered by the Norwegian Consumer Council's report (2017) on children's smartwatches.

Interviews with mothers of teens (aged 14–16) in Estonia reveal that the activities of the children themselves could also result in the data being broken down (Aia, 2020). Several interviewed mothers described how their children tried to escape from the technologized parental gaze either by deinstalling the tracking app from their phones, manipulating their location data, or leaving their phones behind or turning them off.

Such attempts to break the data flow were usually a direct result of some prior negative incident between the parent and the child (a row, a misunderstanding, etc.). In some cases, for example, parents also agreed that their use of tracking technologies had resulted in creating embarrassing moments for the child (Aia, 2020). For example, a mother of a 15-year-old boy confessed that on one occasion, after several unanswered phone calls to her son, she looked up his location from the app and drove to him to invite him home for dinner. Such an incident was obviously not looked on too keenly by the son who was spending time with his friends and was embarrassed by the sudden intrusion, indicating that he saw such tracking by his mother as an intrusion of his privacy. Although all the parents in the study saw trust as the cornerstone of parent–child relationships, they also considered privacy as something that needed to be earned—that is, they believed that there should be a direct link between the amount of responsibility that the children showed, and the amount of privacy they were allowed to have (Sukk & Siibak, 2021). Parents who had experienced problems with their children were thus more likely to use other tracking technologies.

Still, the analysis of the Q methodology study and interview data of preteens (aged 7–13) suggest that younger children do not really mind being tracked or see any harm in parental surveillance, that is, they did not consider their parents exercising caring dataveillance as an intrusion of their privacy (Sukk & Siibak, 2021). Only the pre-teens associated with the "privacy-sensitive child" expressed more reservations about tracking and had a salient need for privacy (see Table 4.2).

These children also strongly agreed with the statement that they would sometimes like to be alone without their parents knowing where they were, for example, when they felt like skipping their sports training. Children loaded on

Table 4.2. Children's subjective viewpoints extracted from a Q methodology study (Sukk & Siibak, 2021: 14)

Compliant child
- At ease with tracking.
- Believes that parents have the right to complete control over their children.
- Believes that children must do as their parents say.
- Believes that tracking does not invade their privacy.
- Believes that tracking needs to be discussed in families.
- Believes that one cannot solely rely on apps; children themselves are responsible for their safety.

Autonomous child
- Finds tracking apps useful.
- Is self-aware and autonomous.
- Believes that parents should not track children without their knowledge.
- Believes that parents do not have the right to control their children.
- Believes that they can do well without their parents constantly tracking them.
- Thinks that children are responsible for their own safety.

Privacy-sensitive child
- Is not against tracking, but has some reservations about it.
- Thinks parents should not track their children in secret.
- Wishes to be alone sometimes without parents knowing where they are.
- Believes that children can avoid tracking successfully.
- Does not take responsibility for their own safety and wellbeing.

---

the "privacy-sensitive child" thus expressed a stronger need to negotiate the degree and kind of privacy co-ownership (Petronio, 2002) with their parents, whereas the "compliant children" and "autonomous children" (see Table 4.2) were rather at ease with their parents' intimate surveillance, and considered it to be even useful, at times (Sukk & Siibak, 2021).

At the same time, all the children in the sample emphasized the need to be involved in the decisions related to the adoption of tracking technologies (Sukk & Siibak, 2021). Even though the parents interviewed by Sukk and Siibak (2021) claimed to have involved their children in the adoption decision, interviews with the children indicated that on many occasions the children had either found out about the tracking themselves or felt excluded from these discussions. This indicates that authoritarian and child obedience-oriented childrearing values might have played a significant role in the family processes and dynamics of the study participants. Hence, rather than protecting "the innocence of childhood" (Malone, 2007, p. 515), ignoring and disregarding children's views on the matter might lead to the breach of confidentiality and privacy boundary turbulence in the parent–child relationship (Petronio, 2002).

Interviews and a Q methodology study with Estonian pre-teens (Sukk & Siibak, 2021) who are accustomed to intimate surveillance by their parents thus indicates that pre-teens in the sample tended to view their parents as confidants, that is, people worthy of accessing and co-owning their private information, and they did not therefore perceive tracking as a practice through which they were giving up control of their private information (Petronio, 2002). In short, in the children's minds, the practices of caring dataveillance did not seem to harm family members' understandings of privacy boundaries and trust in a family relationship (cf. Ervasti, Laitakari, & Hillukkala, 2016). Such a positive attitude to caring dataveillance could potentially be explained by their relatively young age (cf. Ervasti et al., 2016); however, a desire to have more control over one's privacy is more likely to change when the child is growing up.

The findings of the Q methodology study also reveal that parental tracking may promote a certain degree of irresponsibility in children (Sukk & Siibak, 2021). Pre-teens belonging to the "autonomous" and "privacy-sensitive" child factors, for instance, believed that it was purely their parents' duty to be responsible for the wellbeing and safety of their children. Such findings coincide with the claims of Fahlquist (2013), who has argued that parental use of geo-location tracking might be interpreted as a sign of someone else being in control and taking responsibility. Similar claims have also been voiced by Rooney (2010), who has argued that when tracking practices are in place, children are denied the opportunity to show they are capable of being responsible. Such tendencies have unfortunately become characteristic of the neoliberal parenting regimes where parenting can be exercised "on demand" (Furedi, 2002). Furthermore, due to the perpetual mobile connections, a transcendent parent is kept on "permanent standby for emergency calls or routine communication" (Lim, 2020, p. 5) and dependent on the data traces that their children leave behind.

It is highly likely that such data traces will be used and exploited by third parties. Various tests (see, for example, Norwegian Consumer Council, 2017) have uncovered critical security flaws in children's smartwatches. For example, a test by the Norwegian Consumer Council (2017) revealed that some smartwatches enabled strangers to eavesdrop on a child, talk to them behind their parent's back, use the watch's camera to take their picture, or even stalk them. Furthermore, the analysis indicated that the user terms of service for these gadgets were often not only inadequate and unclear, but could also "deny consumers their basic consumer and privacy rights" (2017, p. 4), and hence, the user's private data could be tracked and used for commercial purposes. Regardless of all these concerning findings, the parents using other tracking devices similar to those using pregnancy trackers (Lupton, 2020b) or babytech gadgets are not really worried about potential privacy breaches. Most of the Estonian parents participating in the interviews and the Q methodology study (Sukk & Siibak, 2021), for instance, claimed that they had "nothing to hide" (Solove, 2007). On the one hand, they found it hard to believe that there could be any real value in the data these tracking technologies collected. On the other hand, they also claimed they were powerless to stop the data collection, and believed that the value these technologies brought to their everyday lives outweighed the potential privacy risks (Sukk & Siibak, 2021). Thus, many of the parents seemed to have bought the marketing myth that other tracking technologies would enable them to "reduce or even eradicate all risks for their children" (Lim, 2020, p. 98), and simply blindly accepted the terms of service. It is becoming increasingly important to remind today's parents that "parenting issues will not be solved just because 'there is an app for that'" (Zaman & Nouwen, 2016, p. 6). Rather, it is important to acknowledge that various digital parenting tools—from pregnancy apps and baby monitors to parental controls and tracking devices—tend to one-sidedly focus on the protective and preventive features (Zaman & Nouwen, 2016), while almost entirely discarding the issues related to the digital rights of the child.

Sharenting: Creating Digital Footprints for the Child

As noted, sharing the joys and challenges of parenthood and documenting children's lives publicly has become a norm in the social media era (Blum-Ross & Livingstone, 2017; Clark et al., 2015; Lipu & Siibak, 2019), and parents are encouraged to share images and stories related to their experiences (Blum-Ross & Livingstone, 2017). However, either by performing "intensive pregnancy" on Instagram (Tiidenberg & Baym, 2017), sharing the first ultrasound image of the fetus on social media (Leaver & Highfield, 2018), or posting photos of the successes of potty-training parents create "digital shadows" (Leaver, 2015, p. 150) for their children, sometimes even before they are born.

Parents sharing photos of their children in social media, posting in parental forums, or keeping blogs do not necessarily associate these practices with jeopardizing their children's privacy (Lipu & Siibak, 2019). Rather, on many occasions parents argue that through sharenting they aim to collect and restore precious memories of their children growing up (Blum-Ross & Livingstone, 2017). Sharenting can thus also be viewed as an opportunity for parents to exercise their agential capacity to create valuable data mementos (Lupton, 2020a) that can be recorded and preserved for posterity. Sharenting can also be performed as a remedy against the increasing privatization and individualization of parenthood, and especially motherhood; in fact, survey data collected among a representative sample of 1000 Italian parents of children aged 0–8 showed that new mothers incorporated sharenting in their repertoire of communicative practices aimed at both finding emotional support online and receiving approval for their acceptable enactment of the "intensive" "good mothering" model (Mascheroni et al., 2021). However, by doing this, they also contributed to creating the human data assemblages (Mascheroni et al., 2021) of their children growing up as members of "the generation tagged" (Oswald, James, & Nottingham, 2016).

This is especially the case with micro-microcelebrities (Abidin, 2015), that is, the children of influencer parents, who are often born into social media (Maheshwari, 2019). What for many parents started off as a creative escapade and an opportunity to build social capital has now turned into a global business with the potential for considerable monetary gain. Within the U.S. alone there are 4.5 million "mom influencers" (Krueger, 2019) who are used to monetizing, marketizing, and creating value from their living rooms. Many companies have thus turned their attention to the parental outsourcing industry where they can also advertise their products and services through paid sponsorships and endorsements with "mom influencers" who are creating value by sharing private details of their family's and children's everyday lives.

The case of the Fisher family (#FishFam), one of the forerunners of family vlogging, serves as a vivid example where a highly commercial form of sharenting has brought the family both international recognition and economic capital. All four siblings of the Fisher family have become recognized micro-microcelebrities, whose YouTube channels and personal Instagram accounts are managed by their parents Madison and Kyler Fisher who "curate [their] identities into being" (Leaver, 2015). The success of the "family influencer" is based on the tremendous success of identical twin sisters Taytum and Oakley Fisher (@taytumandoakley) who, by the age of four, have become some of the best-known "kid influencers" in the world, with more than 3 million followers on Instagram, enabling the family to earn more than US$200,000 a month from brand deals and advertising revenue. The two younger siblings of the Fisher family—Halston and Ollie—became internet celebrities way before they were born. Months before baby Halston (@halston.blake) was born, she had more than 62,000 followers on her Instagram account (at the age of one she had 626,000 followers) (Martin, 2019); Oliver's live birth video from August 2020 has, however, already gained more than 2 million views on YouTube, and everyone can receive daily updates of his development on his Instagram account (@oliver.rhettfisher). These four siblings of the Fisher family, similar to the millions of other micro-microcelebrities, will one day "inherit digital publics, personae, and careers" (Abidin, 2015) as an outcome of their parents' sharenting practices. In short, while creating and curating their children's data selves, parents end up crafting not just data footprints for their child, but also a "digital tattoo which is difficult to erase" (Donovan, 2020, p. 49).

Interviews with 9- to 13-year-old pre-teens (N = 14) and their mothers (N = 14) in Estonia indicate, however, that not only do the children feel annoyed and frustrated by their parents' sharenting choices, but they would also like their parents to involve them in the decisions as to what content can be shared (Lipu & Siibak, 2019). Several of the pre-teens in the study claimed that their parents were not used to asking their children's permission before sharing their images on social media. Furthermore, even if the pre-teens had voiced their concerns about the choice of photos, in cases where parents had uploaded images the pre-teens considered to be embarrassing or unflattering, these requests were often not responded to (Lipu & Siibak, 2019). In short, most of the pre-teens in the sample engaged in active boundary coordination efforts (Petronio, 2002) in the hopes of co-managing their online identities. Despite the fact that some mothers in the sample expressed the need to consult with their child before uploading an image or tagging them on social media, most rarely considered their child's opinion. Even when the parents knew that their children resented sharenting, the analysis of both pre-teens' and mothers' interviews revealed that there were still mothers who continued the practice despite their children's wishes. These mothers tended to justify their stance by claiming that parents have a right to decide and to control which information they share about their children, especially if the children are still quite young. Similarly, Italian parents—including those who engage in sharenting on a regular basis—are not used to asking their children for permission before sharing photos or videos portraying them (Mascheroni et al., 2021: forthcoming). Such a stance also illustrates that failing to take children's privacy expectations seriously may lead to privacy boundary turbulence (Petronio, 2002).

Privacy boundary turbulence is also more likely to occur when parents and children have very different attitudes about how often parents should ask for permission to post about their child on social media (Moser, Chen, & Schoenebeck, 2017). For example, the findings from Hiniker et al. (2016, p. 1385) suggest that, "children were twice as likely to report that parents should not 'overshare' by posting information about their children online without permission." Although various policy documents (for example, Recommendation CM/REC(2018)x of the Committee of Ministers to Member States) emphasize the role of parents and caregivers in protecting children's privacy, personal data, and online reputation, and the need to respect the confidentiality of their correspondence, Blum-Ross and Livingstone (2017, p. 122) rightfully claim that parents are "yet to find an approach to representing relational identities in ways that deal fairly with both parents and their children."

Finding the right balance between the perceived societal expectation of portraying oneself as a loving mother while also respecting a child's right to privacy is indeed difficult, as semi-structured interviews with Estonian mothers of 0- to 3-year-olds (N = 20) (Siibak & Traks, 2019) and the survey of Italian parents of young children reveal (Mascheroni et al., 2021). Analysis of the interviews with mothers, millennial mothers in particular, revealed that many of them have started to feel uneasy when posting photos of their children on social media (Siibak & Traks, 2019). In fact, similar to other findings (see, for example, Autenrieth, 2018), the majority of young mothers in the sample claimed to have consciously decided either not to share any images of their children on social media, or to limit both the number and audience of such posts. Furthermore, some of the young mothers had also started to engage in a practice Autenrieth (2018, p. 226) referred to as "anti-sharenting," that is, engaging in "specific practices of (un)-showing" that place the focus on the photographic and spatial contexts of the image rather than the child. On such occasions post-production (for example, digital stickers of emojis) is most often used to "replace" the facial expressions of their child in order to preserve their privacy (Siibak & Traks, 2019). This indicates that the mothers are determined to steward their children's privacy and identities online, by deciding themselves what is appropriate to share about their children online as well as trying to ensure that their family and friends also respect and maintain the integrity of those rules.

The question of what kind of content is appropriate to sharent online also usually evokes mixed feelings in children. For example, interviews with Estonian pre-teens indicate that, on the one hand, they are happy and proud when they notice their parents sharing posts about their achievements on social media (for example, doing well in sports/in school/in hobbies) or had posted photos reflecting their happy family life (Lipu & Siibak, 2019). On the other hand, they resented their parents sharing unflattering visuals (for example, "ugly photos" or "when my hair is messed up") or their use of endearments (for example, "my sweetheart," "my little princess," and "my sunshine") in public social media posts. Thus, they wanted to be able to voice their opinion so as not to allow their parents to upload embarrassing, visually unflattering, or otherwise negative posts that would reflect negatively on their self-image. Due to the searchability, scalability, replicability, and persistency of social media data, as well as the lack of control the young people feel about the sharenting process, teenagers are increasingly concerned about the potential future consequences of sharenting (Ouvrein & Verswijvel, 2019). Studies report that teenagers feel frustrated, annoyed, and humiliated by photos in which a child "behaves weird or looks weird" or in which the child is naked (Ouvrein & Verswijvel, 2019, p. 16). Such content could thus be viewed as "dirty data" (Lupton, 2020a) that can be used for making assessments, judgments, and predictions about the child, leading to future data harms.

Parents' sharenting practices on social media can, for example, make the child vulnerable to (cyber)bullying (Siibak & Tamme, 2013), child pornography, identity theft, or digital kidnapping (Abidin, 2015). The latter refers to instances when a stranger steals a photo of a child from social media and uses it in a different context, often inventing new narratives around the persona of the child or claiming the child as their own. Sometimes a set of hashtags, such as #babyrp or #adoptionrp, are used together with the stolen photo to indicate that the owner of the account is role-playing; on other occasions, however, digital kidnapping may also lead to a real cybercrime (for example, identity theft of the child), or an online grooming incident. Although digital kidnapping is a rather rare threat, interviews with Estonian mothers of 0- to 3-year-olds (N = 20) revealed that some of the mothers had both noticed as well as experienced it themselves (Siibak & Traks, 2019). For example, one mother described how a stranger had stolen photos of her children from her personal blog and uploaded them on a dating website, claiming that the children could be bought as sex slaves. Other interviewed mothers had noticed instances when strangers had posted photos of digitally kidnapped children on different mommy groups on Facebook, accompanied with a narrative claiming that the child depicted in the photo was seriously ill and in need of expensive medical care that the parent, that is, the digital kidnapper, was unable to cover. On these occasions, the kidnappers were hoping to find sympathizers from the community with the hope of raising money to "cure" the child (Siibak & Traks, 2019). Although these examples reveal the gloomiest potential scenarios sharenting could lead to, raising parents' awareness of the topic is crucial.

References

Abbas, R., Michael, K., Michael, M., & Aloudat, A. (2011). Emerging forms of covert surveillance using GPS-enabled devices. *Journal of Cases on Information Technology*, *13*(2), 19–33.

Abidin, C. (2015). Micromicrocelebrity: Branding babies on the internet. *M/C Journal*, *18*(5) https://doi.org/10.5204/mcj.1022.

Aia, K. (2020). Jälgimisrakendused kui digitaalse lapsevanema abivahendid: kasutajate arvamused ja kogemused. [Tracking apps as digital parenting tools: user's opinions and experiences]. Bachelor Thesis. Institute of Social Studies. University of Tartu.

Ali, S., Elgharabawy, M., Duchaussoy, Q., Mannan, M., & Youssef, A. (2020). Betrayed by the guardian: Security and privacy risks of parental control solutions. In *Annual Computer Security Applications Conference (ACSAC 2020)*, December 7–11, Austin, USA. ACM Press.

Ammari, T., & Schoenebeck, S. (2015). Understanding and supporting fathers and fatherhood on social media sites. In *Proceedings of the 33rd Annual ACM Conference on Human Factors in Computing Systems* (pp. 1905–1914). ACM Press.

Anderson, M. (2019). How parents feel about—and manage—their teens' online behavior and screen time. Pew Research Center, March 22. www.pewresearch.org/fact-tank/2019/03/22/how-parents-feel-about-and-manage-their-teens-online-behavior-and-screen-time

Autenrieth, U. (2018). Family photography in a networked age. Anti-sharenting as a reaction to risk assessment and behaviour adaption. In G. Mascheroni, C. Ponte, & A. Jorge (Eds.), *Digital parenting: The challenges for families in the digital age* (pp. 219–231). Nordicom.

Barassi, V. (2017). BabyVeillance? Expecting parents, online surveillance and the cultural specificity of pregnancy apps. *Social Media + Society*, *3*(2). doi: https://doi.org/10.1177/205630511770718

Barassi, V. (2020). *Child | Data | Citizen. How tech-companies are profiling us from before birth.* The MIT Press.

Baum, F., Newman, L., & Biedrzycki, K. (2014). Vicious cycles: Digital technologies and determinants of health in Australia. *Health Promotion International*, *29*(2), 349–360.

Bert, F., Passi, S., Scaioli, G., Gualano, M. R., & Siliquini, R. (2015). There comes a baby! What should I do? Smartphones' pregnancy-related applications: A web-based overview. *Health Informatics Journal, 22*(3), 608–617.

Blum-Ross, A., & Livingstone, S. (2017). "Sharenting," parent blogging and the boundaries of the digital self. *Popular Communication, 15*(2), 110–125.

Bonafide, C. P., Jamison, D., & Foglia, E. (2017). The emerging market of smartphone-integrated infant physiologic monitors. *JAMA Network, 317*(4), 353–354.

Bonafide, C. P., Localio, A. R., Ferro, D. F., et al. (2018). Accuracy of pulse oxiometry-based home baby monitors. *JAMA Network, 320*(7), 717–719.

Bundy, A. C., Luckett, T., Tranter, P. J., et al. (2009). The risk is that there is "no risk": A simple innovative intervention to increase children's activity levels. *International Journal of Food Science and Technology, 17*, 33–45.

Cino, D., Mascheroni, G., & Wartella, E. (2020). "The kids hate it, but we love it!" Parents' reviews of Circle. *Media and Communication, 8*(4), 208–217. http://dx.doi.org/10.17645/mac.v8i4.3247

Clark, L. S. (2013). *The parent app: Understanding families in the digital age.* Oxford University Press.

Clark, S. J., et al. (2015). *Parents on social media: Likes and dislikes of sharenting.* C.S. Mott Children's Hospital, University of Michigan Department of Pediatrics and Communicable Diseases, & University of Michigan Child Health Evaluation and Research Unit. https://mottpoll.org/sites/default/files/documents/031615_sharenting_0.pdf

Donovan, S. (2020). ' "Sharenting": The forgotten children of the GDPR. *Peace Human Rights Governance, 4*(1), 35–59.

Duhigg, C. (2012). How companies learn your secrets. *The New York Times Magazine.* February 19. www.nytimes.com/2012/02/19/magazine/shopping-habits.html?pagewanted=all&_r=0

Ericson, R., & Haggerty, K. (2006). *The new politics of surveillance and visibility.* University of Toronto Press.

Eriksson, H., & Salzmann-Erikson, M. (2012). Supporting a caring fatherhood in cyberspace— An analysis of communication about caring within an online forum for fathers. *Scandinavian Journal of Caring Sciences, 27*(1), 63–69.

Ervasti, M., Laitakari, J., & Hillukkala, M. (2016). "I want to know where my child is at all times"—Field study of a location-aware safety service for schoolchildren. *Behaviour & Information Technology, 35*(10), 833–852.

Feal, Á., Calciati, P., Vallina-Rodriguez, N., Troncoso, C., & Gorla, A. (2020). Angel or devil? A privacy study of mobile parental control apps. *Proceedings on Privacy Enhancing Technologies, 2020*(2), 314–335. https://doi.org/10.2478/popets-2020-0029

Furedi, F. (2002). *Culture of fear: Risk-taking and the morality of low expectation.* Continuum.

Gabriels, K. (2016). "I keep a close watch on this child of mine": A moral critique of other-tracking apps. *Ethics and Information Technology, 18*(3), 175–184.

Gambier-Ross, K., McLernon, D., & Morgan, H. (2018). A mixed methods exploratory study of women's relationships with and uses of fertility tracking apps. *Digital Health, 4*.

Ghosh, A. K., Badillo-Urquiola, K., Rosson, M. B., HengXu, J. Carroll, M., & Wisniewski, P. J. (2018). A matter of control or safety? Examining parental use of technical monitoring apps on teens' mobile devices. In *Proceedings of the 2018 CHI Conference on Human Factors in Computing Systems (CHI'18)* (pp. 1–14). ACM Press.

Gillies, V. (2010). Is poor parenting a class issue? Contextualising anti-social behaviour and family life. In M. Klett-Davies (Ed.), *Is parenting a class issue?* (pp. 44–61). Family and Parenting Institute.

Gregg, M. (2013). Spousebusting: Intimacy, adultery, and surveillance technology. *Surveillance & Society, 11*(3), 301–310.

Harwell, D. (2018). Wanted: The "perfect babysitter." Must pass AI scan for respect and attitude. *The Washington Post*, November 23. www.washingtonpost.com/technology/2018/11/16/wanted-perfect-babysitter-must-pass-ai-scan-respect-attitude/

Harwell, D. (2019). Tracking your pregnancy on an app may be more public than you think. *The Washington Post*, April 10. www.bostonglobe.com/news/nation/2019/04/10/tracking-your-pregnancy-app-may-more-public-than-you-think/pclaUa5SDzDgdYj99lPTbO/story.html

Hasinoff, A. (2017). Where are you? Location tracking and the promise of child safety. *Television & New Media, 18*(6), 496–512.

Hiniker, A., Schoenebeck, S., & Kientz, J. (2016). *Not at the dinner table: Parents' and children's perspectives on family technology rules.* ACM Press. http://dx.doi.org/10.1145/2818048.2819940

Holloway, D., Mascheroni, G., & Inglis, S. (2020). The quantified baby: Discourses of consumption. In L. Tsaliki & D. Chronaki (Eds.), *Discourses of anxiety over childhood and youth across cultures* (pp. 99–118). Palgrave Macmillan. https://doi.org/10.1007/978-3-030-46436-3_5

Howell, J. P. (2010). Parents, watching: Introducing surveillance into modern American parenting. PhD (Doctor of Philosophy) thesis, University of Iowa. https://doi.org/10.17077/etd.a4wpg2r2

Hughson, J. P., Daly, O. J., Woodward-Kron, R., Hajek, J., & Story, D. (2018). The rise of pregnancy apps and the implications for culturally and linguistically diverse women: Narrative review. *JMIR mHealth and uHealth, 6*(11), e189.

Jargon, J. (2020). The terror of teen drivers: Parents track their kids without being in the car. *The Washington Post*, March 3. www.wsj.com/articles/the-terror-of-teen-drivers-parents-track-their-kids-without-being-in-the-car-11583231401

Johnson, S. A. (2014). "Maternal devices," social media and the self-management of pregnancy, mothering and child health. *Societies, 4*(2), 330–350.

Karavadra, B., Stockl, A., Prosser-Snelling, E., Simpson, P., & Morris, E. (2020). Women's perceptions of COVID-19 and their healthcare experiences: A qualitative thematic analysis of a national survey of pregnant women in the United Kingdom. *BMC Pregnancy Childbirth, 20*(600), 1–8.

Katz, C. (2001). The state goes home: Local hypervigilance and the global retreat from social reproduction. *Social Justice, 28*(3), 47–56.

King, D. (2014). Marketing wearable home baby monitors: Real peace of mind? *BMJ (Clinical Research Edition), 349*, g6639.

Klazema, M. (2019). Predictim's new babysitter background check faces racial bias and FCRA controvers. *Backgroundchecks*, January 4. www.backgroundchecks.com/blog/predictim-s-new-babysitter-background-check-faces-racial-bias-and-fcra-controvers

Klich, T. (2019). The new mom economy: Meet the startups disrupting the $46 billion millennial parenting market. *Forbes*, May 10. www.forbes.com/sites/tanyaklich/2019/05/10/the-new-mom-economy-meet-the-startups-disrupting-the-46-billion-millennial-parenting-market/?sh=36804efa5130

Krueger, A. (2019). When mom slams a brand on Instagram. *The New York Times*, November 26. www.nytimes.com/2019/11/26/business/mommy-influencers.html?smtyp=cur&smid=fb-nytimes

KSU/The Sentinel Newspaper (2021). Pregnancy tracker apps market shooting at CAGR+11% by 2028 with Everyday Health, The Knot, Ovuline, Fehners Software, Nighp Software, WebMD, Blogsoft, HelloBaby, BabyCenter, Baby Bump. February 21. https://ksusentinel.com/2021/02/18/pregnancy-tracker-apps-market-shooting-at-cagr-11-by-2028-with-everyday-health-the-knot-ovuline-fehners-software-nighp-software-webmd-blogsoft-hellobaby-babycenter-baby-bump/

Leaver, T. (2015). Born digital? Presence, privacy, and intimate surveillance. In J. Hartley & W. Qu (Eds.), *Re-orientation: Translingual transcultural transmedia. Studies in narrative, language, identity, and knowledge* (pp. 149–160). Fudan University Press.

Leaver, T. (2017). Intimate surveillance: Normalizing parental monitoring and mediation of infants online. *Social Media + Society*, 3(2), 1–10.

Leaver, T., & Highfield, T. (2018). Visualising the ends of identity: Pre-birth and post-death on Instagram. *Information, Communication & Society*, 21(1), 30–45.

Lee, D. (2018). Predictim babysitter app: Facebook and Twitter take action. BBC News, November 27. www.bbc.com/news/technology-46354276

Lee, Y., & Moon, M. (2016). Utilization and content evaluation of mobile applications for pregnancy, birth, and child care. *Healthcare Informatics Research*, 22(2), 73–80.

LeMoyne, T., & Buchanan, T. (2011). Does "hovering" matter? Helicopter parenting and its effects on well-being. *Sociological Spectrum*, 31(4), 399–418.

Lim, S. S. (2020) *Transcendent parenting: Raising children in the digital age.* Oxford University Press.

Lipu, M., & Siibak, A. (2019). "Take it down!" Estonian parents' and pre-teens' opinions and experiences with sharenting. *Media International Australia*, 170(1), 57–67.

Livingstone, S., & Byrne, J. (2018). Parenting in the digital age. In G. Mascheroni, C. Ponte, & A. Jorge (Eds.), *Digital parenting: The challenges for families in the digital age* (pp. 19–30). Nordicom.

Livingstone, S., Stoilova, M., & Nandagiri, R. (2019). *Children's data and privacy online: Growing up in a digital age. An evidence review.* London School of Economics and Political Science.

Lupton, D. (2020a). *Data selves: More-than-human perspectives.* Polity.

Lupton, D. (2020b). Caring dataveillance: Women's use of apps to monitor pregnancy and children. In L. Green, D. Holloway, K. Stevenson, L. Haddon, & T. Leaver (Eds.), *The Routledge companion to digital media and children* (pp. 393–402). Routledge.

Lupton, D., Pedersen, S., & Thomas, G. M. (2016). Parenting and digital media: From the early web to contemporary digital society. *Sociology Compass*, 10(8), 730–743.

Lupton, D., & Williamson, B. (2017). The datafied child: The dataveillance of children and implications for their rights. *New Media & Society, 19*(5), 780–794.

Maheshwari, S. (2019). Online and making thousands, at age 4: Meet the Kidfluencers. *The New York Times*, March 1. www.nytimes.com/2019/03/01/business/media/social-media-influencers-kids.html

Malone, K. (2007). The bubble-wrap generation: Children growing up in walled gardens. *Environmental Education Research, 13*(4), 513–527.

Martin, B. (2019). Halston Fisher has 62,000 Instagram followers—She just hasn't been born yet. *Los Angeles Magazine*, January 10. www.lamag.com/lalifeandstyle/fisher-family-taytum-oakley-halston/

Marx, G., & Steeves, V. (2010). From the beginning: Children as subjects and agents of surveillance. *Surveillance & Society, 7*(3/4), 192–230.

Mascheroni, G. (2014). Parenting the mobile internet in Italian households: Parents' and children's discourses. *Journal of Children and Media, 8*(4), 440–456.

Mascheroni, G. (2020). Datafied childhoods: Contextualising datafication in everyday life. *Current Sociology, 68*(6), 798–813.

Mascheroni, G., Cino, D., Zaffaroni, L. G., & Amadori, G. (2021). (Non-)sharenting as a form of maternal care? The dilemmas of mothers of 0- to 8-year-old children. In *71st Annual ICA Conference Engaging the Essential Work of Care: Communication, Connectedness and Social Justice*. May 27–31.

Meyer, A. (2007). The moral rhetoric of childhood. *Childhood, 14*(1), 85–104.

Morrison, A. (2011). "Suffused by feeling and affect": The intimate public of personal mommy blogging. *Biography, 34*(1), 37–55.

Moser, C., Chen, T., & Schoenebeck, S. (2017). *Parents' and children's preferences about parents sharing about children on social media*. ACM Press. https://dl.acm.org/doi/10.1145/3025453.3025587

Neiterman, E. (2012). Doing pregnancy: Pregnant embodiment as performance. *Women's Studies International Forum, 35*, 372–383.

Nelson, M. (2008). Watching children: Describing the use of baby monitors on Epinions.com. *Journal of Family Issues, 29*(4), 516–538.

Nelson, M. (2010). *Parenting out of control: Anxious parents in uncertain times*. New York University Press.

Nikken, P., & Schols, M. (2015). How and why parents guide the media use of young children. *Journal of Child and Family Studies, 24*, 3423–3435.

Norwegian Consumer Council (2017). *#WatchOut. Analysis of smartwatches for children*. https://www.forbrukerradet.no/side/significant-security-flaws-in-smartwatches-for-children/

Orton-Johnson, K. (2017). Mummy blogs and representations of motherhood: "Bad mummies" and their readers. *Social Media + Society, 3*(2), 1–10.

Oswald, M., James, H., & Nottingham, E. (2016). The not-so-secret life of five-year-olds: Legal and ethical issues relating to disclosure of information and the depiction of children on broadcast and social media. *Journal of Media Law, 8*(2), 198–228.

Ouvrein, G., & Verswijvel, K. (2019). Sharenting: Parental adoration or public humiliation? A focus group study on adolescents' experiences with sharenting against the background of their own impression management. *Children and Youth Services Review*, 99, 319–327.

Perez, S. (2020). Messenger Kids adds expanded parental controls, details how much kids' data Facebook collects. *TechCrunch*, February 4. https://techcrunch.com/2020/02/04/messenger-kids-adds-expanded-parental-controls-details-how-much-kids-data-facebook-collects/

Petronio, S. (2002). *Boundaries of privacy: Dialectics of disclosure*. State University of New York Press.

Pink, S., Ruckenstein, M., Willim, R., & Duque, M. (2018). Broken data: Conceptualising data in the emerging world. *Big Data & Society*, 5(1), 1–13.

Rooney, T. (2010). Trusting children: How do surveillance technologies alter a child's experience of trust, risk, and responsibility? *Surveillance & Society*, 7(3/4), 344–355.

Rosato, D. (2020). What your period tracker app knows about you. Consumer Reports, January 28. www.consumerreports.org/health-privacy/what-your-period-tracker-app-knows-about-you/

Rutherford, M. B. (2011). *Adult supervision required: Private freedom and public constraints for parents and children*. Rutgers University Press.

Shellenbarger, S. (2005). Tucking the kids in—In the dorm: Colleges ward off overinvolved parents. *The Wall Street Journal*, July 28. www.wsj.com/articles/SB112250452603298007

Siibak, A. (2019). Digital parenting and the datafied child. In T. Burns & F. Gottschalk (Eds.), *Educating 21st century children. Emotional well-being in the digital age* (pp. 103-118). OECD Publishing.

Siibak, A., & Tamme, V. (2013). "Who introduced Granny to Facebook?" An exploration of everyday family interactions in web-based communication environments. *Northern Lights Film and Media Studies Yearbook*, 11(1), 71-89.

Siibak, A., & Traks, K. (2019). The dark sides of sharenting. *Catalan Journal of Communication & Cultural Studies*, 11(1), 115–121. doi: https://doi.org/10.1386/cjcs.11.1.115_1

Simpson, B. (2014). Tracking children, constructing fear: GPS and the manufacture of family safety. *Information & Communications Technology Law*, 23(3), 273–285.

Smahel, D., Machackova, H., Mascheroni, G., et al. (2020). *EU Kids Online 2020: Survey results from 19 countries*. London School of Economics and Political Science. http://eprints.lse.ac.uk/103294/

Solove, D. (2007). 'I've got nothing to hide' and other misunderstanding of privacy. *San Diego Law Review*, 44, 745–772.

Stoilova, M., Nandagiri, R., & Livingstone, S. (2019). Children's understanding of personal data and privacy online—A systematic evidence mapping. *Information, Communication & Society*, 24(4). www.tandfonline.com/doi/abs/10.1080/1369118X.2019.1657164?journalCode=rics20

Sukk, M., & Siibak, A. (2021). Caring dataveillance and the construction of "good parenting": Estonian parents' and pre-teens' reflections on the usage of tracking technologies. *Communications: The European Journal of Communication Research*, 46(3), 1–22.

Sukk, M., & Soo, K. (2018). *EU kids onlineĭ eesti 2018. Aasta uuringu esialgsed tulemused.* Ühiskonnateaduste instituut, Tartu. www.yti.ut.ee

Thomas, G. M., & Lupton, D. (2016). Threats and thrills: Pregnancy apps, risk and consumption. *Health, Risk & Society, 17*(7–8), 495–509.

Thornham, H. (2019). Algorithmic vulnerabilities and the datalogical: Early motherhood and tracking-as-care regimes. *Convergence, 25*(2), 171–185.

Tiidenberg, K., & Baym, N. K. (2017). Learn it, buy it, work it: Intensive pregnancy on Instagram. *Social Media + Society, 3*(1), 1–13.

Vertesi, J. (2014). My experiment opting out of big data made me look like a criminal. *Time Magazine*, May 1. https://time.com/83200/privacy-internet-big-data-opt-out/

Welp Magazine (2020). The spring lockdown has led to record downloads of pregnancy tracking apps globally. https://welpmagazine.com/the-spring-lockdown-has-led-to-record-downloads-of-pregnancy-tracking-apps-globally/

Wilson, J. A., & Chivers Yochim, E. (2017). *Mothering through precarity: Women's work and digital media.* Duke University Press.

Zaman, B., & Nouwen, M. (2016). *Parental controls: Advice for parents, researchers and industry.* EU Kids Online. www.eukidsonline.net

· 5 ·

MEDIATIZED HOMES
AS DATAFIED HOMES

The Modern Home as a Mediatized Home

Children today are growing up in media-saturated homes, and this increasing mediatization of family life is complicating care and parenting practices (see Chapter 4), refashioning our homes into datafied environments. However, as Livingstone and Blum-Ross (2020) point out, assuming digital media as the major agent of change obscures the complex factors that are profoundly reshaping family—and the very meaning of home—from within and from without. Insomuch as positioning digital media as the problem (or the solution) of contemporary family life is flawed, blaming the latest technological objects for corrupting the privacy of the home is equally problematic.

On its surface, the "smart"[1] home, equipped with various digital media and internet-connected objects, is constructed as marking a profound historical shift, which breaks with the modern idea of "home"[2] as a familiar, private, intimate, secure space, apart from the world beyond its walls. However, we should acknowledge how the concept of the home as an autonomous entity is itself a paradox. Looking at the historical and sociocultural developments of the idea of home reveals its contingent and relational nature.

In fact, the modern imaginary of the home is a socially situated construction, which can be traced to the new ideals of privacy and domesticity that first emerged in the lives of bourgeois families in Europe in the 18th century. The home as the center of private and family life is "literally, [one of the] principal achievements of the Bourgeois Age" (Rybczynski, 1986, p. 75; see also Mallett, 2004). Conversely, "the family in preindustrial society was characterized by *sociability* rather than *privacy*" (Hareven, 1991, p. 256; original emphasis), and the boundaries between the domestic space and the public world were rather flexible and even negligible. As such, the notion of domesticity centered on privacy, intimacy, familiarity, and comfort is a specifically modern phenomenon. Therefore, as Roger Silverstone wrote, the modern notion of "home" is constitutively relational, for it is a product of the distinction between the private and the public:

> A place with boundaries to define and defend . . . Private. Personal. Inside. Familiar. Mine. All these terms have their opposite. And home is the product of their distinction. It is always relative. Always set against the public, the impersonal, the outside, unfamiliar, yours. (Silverstone, 1999, p. 89)

The concept of home is inextricably bound up with the major societal and technological transformations that marked the transition from pre-modern to modern societies. It is with the processes of industrialization and urbanization in the late 19th century that the idea of the home as the private haven for the nuclear family became the dominant household pattern. Indeed, industrialization led to the removal of the workplace from the home and the transfer of former households' functions, such as education, to outside institutions. These changes "resulted in the emergence of the home as a specialized site for the family's consumption, childrearing, and private life" (Hareven, 1991, p. 259). Through the provision of the necessary transportation and communication technologies, industrialization also enabled the (material and symbolic) construction of the modern home in response to urbanization—namely, as a retreat from the hustle and bustle of urban life. From its origins, therefore, the home depended on the outside, on the provision of urban services, public spaces, and, more importantly for our focus here, on the media.

Rather than external elements that impinge on the notion, and the experience, of home, the media, hence, is a constitutive component of family and domestic life. Not only is the media an integral part of the "general texture of experience" (Silverstone, 1999, p. 2), thus also shaping our experience of home(ness); more importantly, the modern meaning of home is the product of a specific set of historical and sociocultural conditions in which the media has assumed an increasingly central role. Such transformations have been defined by Raymond Williams (2003 [1974]) as "mobile privatization." In fact, Williams recognizes broadcast media as the product of the modern urban lifestyle, centered on the separation of the private from the public, the home from the workplace. Simultaneously, however, he emphasizes how the media supported and expanded the idea of the home as the center of family time— the new family time restricted to the home being increasingly mediated and centered round consumption. Mobile privatization combined "a technological utopia and a housing utopia in which domestic technologies, especially electrical communications technologies in the form of home entertainment machines such as radio and, later, television, were the very source and substance of the comfortable life of the modern era" (quoted in Allon, 2003, p. 258). What the concept of mobile privatization illustrates is precisely a form of mediatization (see Chapter 2, this book), that is, the co-determination and interdependence between social processes and the infrastructures and practices of communication. Talking about Williams' view on broadcasting, Silverstone emphasized how the modern home has been co-constituted by social and technological transformations that had the media at their core:

> For Raymond Williams (1974) the media responded to a second wave of bourgeois confidence as families moved from city to suburb. Once again privatization was the theme, as broadcasting systems emerged to enable the dispersal of populations: to link the private home to a public one; indeed to redefine home as a space in which broadcasting was essential, and to define a particular version of home as appropriate to the conduct of everyday life. (Silverstone, 1999, p. 93)

Yet, the process of mobile privatization is not without its own contradictions and tensions—the same contradictions that are inscribed in, and constitutive of, the concept of home itself. On the one side, the integration of broadcast media into the domestic environment constituted the infrastructure around which families organized their spatial geography and timetable (Morley, 2000), thus sustaining the move towards home-centeredness, and the concentration of family life within the household. On the opposite side, in some respects at least, the media have also seemed to undermine the ideal of the nuclear family around which the concept of home has been based (Morley, 2000; Silverstone, 1999). The domestication of an ever-expanding range of media and technological objects exacerbates the tension between the home's constitutive reliance on media, and the media threatening to breach the "sacred" boundaries of the home. It has been argued "the modern home can be said to be a phantasmagoric place, to the extent that electronic media of various kinds allow the radical intrusion of distant events into the space of domesticity" (Morley, 2000, p. 6).

Such a tension, however, is inscribed at the heart of the modern idea of home, as explained earlier. Ultimately, it is the very modern tension between private and public, autonomy and relationality. The media's role in disrupting, transgressing, rearticulating, and, in a word, mediating the boundaries between the private and the public in novel ways is what domestication scholars have labeled their "double articulation:" "information and communication technologies, uniquely, are the means (the media) whereby public and private meanings are mutually negotiated; as well as being the products themselves (through consumption) of such negotiations of meaning" (Silverstone, Hirsch, & Morley, 1992, p. 25).

The media are doubly articulated in the domestic context as both media and objects (goods sold on the market and embedded in public discourses); as both material objects and symbolic content; for their ability to be embedded in the infrastructure of everyday family life, and to disembed family relations beyond the walls of the home; for their potential to connect and disconnect; to articulate together which is separate—providing individual homes with a coherent social experience, such as feeling part of a community—while at the same time transgressing the boundaries and exposing the vulnerability of the home to the outside world (Haddon & Silverstone, 2000). The place and the significance of the home is, thus, mediated and constrained, as well as enhanced by the variety of (digital) media that populates the domestic environment (Silverstone & Hirsch, 1992). And, yet, the media participates in the construction, redefinition and transgression of our domesticity almost unnoticed, for it is absorbed into the contexts of family life up to the point that it becomes a taken-for-granted, normalized, and negligible presence.

It is this dialectic relationship between the media and the modern idea of home, their mutual shaping, which generates the experience "of home as a mediated space, and of media as a domesticated space" (Silverstone, 1999, p. 93). Far from a transformative external force, mediatization, then, is better understood as one of the conditions that shapes our sense and practice of home: the "place called home was never an unmediated experience" (Massey, 1994, p. 164).

The "Smart" Home

Having outlined the profound implication of the media in the social construction of the modern home as simultaneously autonomous and relational, we are tempted to conclude that the "smart" house is nothing but "the culmination or 'end point' of this story, where the home itself becomes a fully technologized/wired place and comes to be defined by the technologies that constitute it" (Morley, 2003, p. 350) Digital media and internet-connected things represent the latest development in the home as a node connected to multiple networks, which started with the introduction of electricity in the first quarter of the 20th century.

However, we cannot simply dismiss the specificity of internet-connected devices—usually grouped under the Internet of Things (IoTs) umbrella—and how they complicate the mutual shaping and social consequences of the mediatized domesticity. Indeed, the datafication of the domestic context relies substantially on the data collected by the IoTs, which complement the data traces family members leave as part of their daily engagements with media of various kinds (see Chapters 4 and 6, this book).

The IoTs, where physical objects are embedded with sensors, software, and connectivity that support the exchange of data, represent, for many, an everyday interface to the internet (Natale & Cook, 2020)—to which we shall return later. The IoTs presently entering our homes are varied, including smart home appliances (such as smart fridges, smart washing machines, robot vacuum cleaners, and the like); security sensors and surveillance cameras (for example, Amazon Ring Doorbell and Google Nest cameras and sensors); energy, lighting, and temperature-sensing technologies (such as smart thermostats and switches); entertainment technologies (smart TVs, smart sound systems, Internet of Toys, etc.); and voice assistants embedded in so-called "home hubs" (Amazon Echo, Google Home,[3] Apple HomePod).

Internet-connected, AI-based technologies are reconfiguring the domestic environment: no longer simply a media-saturated home, but a data-saturated home that "turns its users into a resource that creates data, and extends the surveillance business model that has become entrenched through social media into new domains—domestic, biological, environmental" (Bunz & Meikle, 2018, p. 31). These sensing networks of connected things collect, create, and distribute an increasing variety of "home life data"—a concept through which Barassi (2020) indicates the complexity of information layers that are aggregated, related to one another, and analyzed as a whole, including: "household data" relative to the family's practices and routines of consumption and families' interactions with media and the IoTs; "family data," ranging from sociodemographics to political orientation, religion, health data, etc.; "biometric data," mostly voice, but also images and vital parameters (think of wearables that monitor a baby's oxygen level and heart rate during sleep—see Mascheroni & Holloway, 2019b); and "situational data," consisting both of environmental (number of rooms, social and individual uses of each room) and relational data (any changes in family composition, potential conflicts between family members, etc.). The notion of "home life data" also resonates with Couldry and Mejias' (2019) theorization of the new social order of data capitalism, which extracts and annexes every single piece of human experience—including the intimacy and privacy of the home and family life—as raw, profitable materials for industry (see also Chapter 2, this book). Indeed, the "data relations" (Couldry & Mejias, 2019) between the IoTs and their users—here understood as relations that are both supported by data and generating data—makes us appreciate even more the ground-breaking nature of the domestication of technology approach, which, already three decades ago, observed how we consume technologies while being also, fundamentally, consumed by technologies ourselves (Silverstone et al., 1992). Similarly, the more recent notion of "tool reversibility" (Couldry & Hepp, 2017, p. 132) captures the complex power dynamics at play when we use data-based artifacts that actually use us: certainly, the data are generated as part of our usage practices, but they are sent, interpreted, and reacted on elsewhere. Therefore, these technologies operate on the basis of an invisible data transmission, over which our control is limited, or non-existent. The IoTs, then, seemingly question established notions of (human and machine) agency.

Many scholars have discussed how objects' new acquired ability to gather, generate, and distribute information on their users and the surrounding environment—they can track, address, see, and speak (Bunz & Meikle, 2018)—changes their status and their agency. From the viewpoint of media and communication studies, things have become media that "mediate what has not been mediated before" (Bunz & Meikle, 2018, p. 18). Traditional understandings of media and communication processes are also challenged by internet-connected and AI-powered things. Let's focus on smart speakers and the conversational agents they embed as an example. These technologies "are not simply media in the sense that they serve as interaction nodes between people" (Hepp, 2020, p. 79). We do not simply communicate *through* such media; we now communicate *with* such media. Hepp includes voice assistants embedded in smart speakers and other "artificial companions" among the category of communicative robots, that

> ... are (partially) automated communication media which operate—often but not always on the basis of artificial intelligence—autonomously with the purpose of quasi-communication with human beings in order to enable further algorithmic based functionalities. (Hepp, 2020, p. 78)

The notion of quasi-communication adopted by Hepp emphasizes how these tools are designed to simulate interpersonal interactions and enter into a communicative relationship with its users. Technically speaking, voice assistants, such as Alexa, Google's Assistant and Siri, are a new model of human–computer interaction (Humphry & Chesher, 2020). More precisely, the interaction between conversational agents and human actors follows a command–response pattern: human inputs, in the form of spoken commands, are transmitted to, and processed in, the cloud; the machine's outputs—based on scripts that anticipate a possible range of interactions, invisibly performed by discrete algorithms, software, and platforms—are either a spoken response (such as the weather forecast) or a completed task (switching off the lights, turning on the music, etc.). However, despite the fact that their ability to perform tasks or speech acts is scripted,[4] communicative robots create the impression of responding and adapting to users' queries in a personalized manner (Natale & Cook, 2020). The user's agency is also redefined and constrained: "The agency of the users of voice assistants can be best described as the ability to choose among a pre-defined range of interactions that the companies already anticipated for their systems" (Natale & Cook, 2020, p. 8). However, communicative robots are generally perceived and addressed as communicative partners (Guzman, 2018, 2019). It is by virtue of their anthropomorphization—through the attribution of a name, a naturalistic female voice, and the simulation of an individual (helpful and/or witty) personality—that voice assistants create the illusion of a dialog and inspire feelings of empathy:

> Siri and similar agents are programmed with human-like traits of gender and overt personality, and, equally important, also are designed to enact a specific social role— that of an assistant—in the functions they perform and in the messages they send to the user. (Guzman, 2019, p. 344)

The simulation of a conversation helps conceal the collection, transmission, and algorithmic calculation of users' and environmental data on which basis communicative robots operate.

The interaction between voice assistants and users, however, is not limited to a conversation-like, human-initiated stimulus–response. In fact, in their function of home hubs, smart speakers can record and track household data (for example, when family members wake up, when they take a shower, how often they use the dishwasher, when and for how long the home is empty, etc.), compare it with previously collected data, and adjust lighting, heating, and the activities of connected appliances accordingly. The value of such data is two-fold, serving to improve both users' classification into ever-more accurate profiles, and the system itself, by providing resources for machine learning (Goulden, 2019)—namely, users' conversations are used to train voice recognition software, while household and situational data serve to fine-tune the control of connected appliances, energy, and the like. In this sense, the activity of home hubs is not limited to a command–response interaction: their monitorial operations produce information that is distributed and interpreted to inform further activities. "With this, the internet of things becomes not just a means of collecting or recording data, but enables systems of interpretation and judgement through programmed algorithms that interpret data" (Bunz & Meikle, 2018, p. 14). In producing regular answers—or regular anticipations—to regular behavioral patterns, they create a personalized environment designed around its inhabitants. Moreover, both their spoken responses and their ability to perform tasks of various kinds improve over time, thanks to machine learning-based algorithms as well as users becoming more skilled at adapting their commands to the machine—for example, adjusting the rhythm of speech, raising their voices, or repeating the query are common communication repair strategies adopted by both adults and children when the machine fails to understand their command (Beneteau et al., 2019). This recursive loop contributes to reinforcing the impression of a one-to-one personalization and, in the case of conversational agents, the credibility of their anthropomorphic features. Therefore, the presence of the IoTs in the home—their repeated responses to human inputs—slowly become naturalized, while generating new practices, new routines, and temporalities, which feed into the general processes of meaning-making that hold families together as a cultural system. To borrow Couldry and Hepp's understanding of the family as a communicative figuration (2017, pp. 66–67), the IoTs become a significant component of the family's distinctive "media ensemble" and communication repertoire. Media ensembles and repertoires of practices shape while being shaped by the family as a "constellation of actors" who share common "relevance frames." In this sense, we propose to frame the IoTs, and voice assistants more specifically, as non-intentionally involved in the creation of meaning. However, we recognize how deeply the IoTs are involved in setting the coordinates through which a distinctive constellation of human actors makes sense of such mediated engagements, incorporating sensing technologies in their media ensemble, and normalizing them into their reference frames. "Technology has an effect, but no intention," we can conclude with Bunz and Meikle (2018, p. 21).

Like any other media, the IoTs are not transformative *per se*: it is the way they are domesticated and integrated into the media repertoire of each family, and the way they are made meaningful within the family's culture, that grounds their transformative potential. While both human and machine agency are redefined, and the home as a communicative figuration is transformed in its repertoire of practices and its meanings system by the advent of the IoTs, such transformations are not linear cause–effect relationships (Hepp, 2020). Rather, any transformation in the home as a cultural and relational unit (the practices and the relations it shapes) is the outcome of the complex interplay of media and social processes (Hepp, 2020; Livingstone & Blum-Ross, 2020). As explained earlier, however, acknowledging that agency of the IoTs is not intentional does not mean rejecting or downplaying its effect in the home, or ignoring the questions of (human and machine) agency that the IoTs pose. The family and the home—and the social construction of both—cannot be isolated from the infrastructures and practices of communication that form the background of domestic everyday life, or from its meanings. Rather, we agree that:

> Because their functionality is based on datafication, that is, the collection and processing of large amounts of data, they are part of an automated, data-based construction of reality. (Hepp, 2020, p. 79)

Goulden's (2019) analysis of the family accounts offered by Google and Amazon's home hubs—called, respectively, Google Family and Amazon Household—helps us illustrate this point further. Goulden's starting point is that these "smart home ecosystems" are each designed with a distinctive representation of its users as a family that is inscribed in the interface, which, in turn, shapes its domestication by inhibiting certain practices while encouraging others. More specifically, as much as social media platforms engineer and technologize sociality, turning previously informal, spontaneous acts such as conversation into formalized, quantifiable, and monetizable data (van Dijck, 2013), so does the "platformed family" represent "an engineered simulacra of domesticity, formatted to run on the respective smart home operating system" (Goulden, 2019, p. 3). Both Google Family and Amazon Household provide an infrastructure for the coordination and organization of domestic life, and for the shared consumption of digital content. In so doing, the platformed family requires that the informal, contingent, situated practices of the family are rendered "both encodable within digital systems, and commensurate with the platform's commercial logics" (Goulden, 2019, p. 14). Moreover, family members are required to conform to the structures, roles, and power positions inscribed in the platform, with the Manager and Parent (Google Family) or Adult (Amazon) roles exercising control over the content and apps children have access to, as well as their purchases. Hierarchical roles are also entitled with the ability to remove or add children, and, in the case of Google Family, remove the Parent who is not positioned as Manager of the family account.

Goulden's work on the "platformed family," then, emphasizes how home hubs' agency is exercised both on the level of the production and communication of data and the data-based interaction with users, and on the cultural level—that is, the creation of meanings in response to the meanings and representations encoded in the design of the technological artifact. Goulden argues that normative family models, which are embedded in such platforms, are being imposed on their users. Our approach, which is grounded in phenomenological epistemologies of the everyday and the domestication framework, does not deny platforms' encoding with social norms, yet acknowledges how such normative patterns must be incorporated among the users' meanings and values in order to succeed.

This brings us back to the renegotiation of private/public boundaries that digital media mobilize (Silverstone et al., 1992). Technologized domesticity is the product of a mutual shaping, whereby families consume ICTs while being simultaneously consumed by them. In fact, home hubs introduce services that are simultaneously "a vehicle for domestic consumption, and a vehicle for consuming domestic life" (Goulden, 2019, p. 3). By using such technologies we feed data into the surveillance capitalism system, and in so doing, expand the colonization of private life by extractive rationalities, which further envelops our domesticity into data relations (Couldry & Mejias, 2019). Such colonization, however, is only effective to the extent that it is appropriated, rendered meaningful, and legitimated within the family culture. The platformed family constitutes an attempt to script the structure and practices of a family in a prescriptive manner, to the point it forms "an invisible *built moral environment*" (Goulden, 2019, p. 6; original emphasis) through which the market and public discourses penetrate the domestic at the same time as they construct its autonomy. Yet, their incorporation depends on complex, not fully predictable, hermeneutic agencies.

The Domestication of Smart Speakers

Research on the domestication of smart speakers and voice assistants, then, is of the utmost importance if we want to understand the complex ways in which such technologies mediate between the privacy of the home and the public sphere dominated by the logic of surveillance capitalism, and account for the processes through which families consume, make sense of, negotiate, resist, and eventually naturalize data-based artifacts. However, and despite the fact that Amazon Echo had already been launched in the U.S. at the end of 2014, the study of the social representations and "ideal users" embedded in these technological artifacts has only partially been matched by research on the socially situated practices and contexts in which the meanings encoded in the digital–material interface are enacted, negotiated, or resisted.

One of the first studies observing the use of smart speakers in the domestic context is Lopatovska et al.'s study (2019), based on data collected through an online survey and online structured diary administered to a sample of 19 Alexa users from nine different households, including children (aged 4–10), younger adults (aged 20–39), and older adults (aged 40–60). The findings shed light on two interrelated dimensions of the domestication of Amazon Echo: namely, its objectivation and its incorporation (Silverstone et al., 1992). Most of the participating families positioned the smart speaker in the living room or in the kitchen, thus encouraging shared, rather than privatized, uses. In this way, Alexa is domesticated as a family device, despite its incorporation, that is, its embeddedness, in the media ensemble and the repertoire of family practices varies across age groups. The authors identified two main clusters of activities performed by family members through Alexa: namely, information (including weather forecasts, fact checking, and news) and entertainment (playing music, telling jokes). The most widely reported use of Alexa was checking the weather conditions, except by children, whose main request to Alexa was playing music. The use of Alexa to control networked devices and appliances ranked third. More interestingly, based on the duration of ownership and the participants' perceived satisfaction of their interactions with Alexa, the study suggests that usage declines and varies over time, with some functionalities (such as looking for news) being reduced or dismissed. This reminds us that the domestication of technological artifacts is not a linear or definitive process determined by the functionalities and public representations of the device. Instead, it depends on the social context in which it is received, and how well the artifact fits with the routines, temporalities, and values of a family (Haddon, 2004).

Similarly, a comparative study into the lived experiences and expectations of users in the U.S. and the Netherlands (Pridmore et al., 2019) identifies information, entertainment, and control of other devices (such as switching the lights on or off) as the main uses of smart speakers, but also highlights the more limited experience of Dutch users. In fact, with the exception of the UK (where it was already available by 2016) and France, Ireland, Italy, and Spain (where its launch was delayed until 2018), Amazon Echo was released on the European market in 2017. Similarly, Google Home's release across Europe took place between 2017 and 2018. It is no surprise, then, if research on the domestication of smart speakers in Europe has been slower.

A recent survey of a national representative sample of 1000 Italian parents of children aged 8 and younger, collected as part of the DataChildFutures[5] project by one of the authors, shows that, as of September 2020, 46% of the households with at least one child in this age group owned a smart speaker—more precisely, 17% of the respondents reported having two or more home hubs (Mascheroni & Zaffaroni, 2020). This finding is consistent with prior research showing that households with children are more likely to have access to digital media (Jennings & Wartella, 2013; Lemish, 2015; Livingstone, 2009)—in fact, a survey conducted in February 2020 by the Osservatorio Internet of Things of the Polytechnic School of Milan observed the diffusion of smart speakers in 18% of Italian households. Entertainment and information top the list of activities regularly asked of smart speakers in families with young children: 75% of the respondents reported using Alexa or Google Home to listen to music, 63% for quick factual information, and 51% to listen to the news. Smart speakers have also been incorporated into another range of habitual domestic practices, including looking for cooking recipes (51%), communicating with family and friends (43%), and telling bedtime stories to children (43%). The use of smart speakers as a calendar is also quite popular, to remind people of deadlines and appointments (57%). Half of the respondents have also appropriated "smarter" functionalities such as the control of connected appliances and energy-saving technologies (51%), while only 35% of the respondents reported using their smart speaker to buy things online (Mascheroni & Zaffaroni, 2020).

The domestication of smart speakers is not without tensions and acts of resistance, especially since the news broke of private domestic conversations being transcribed with the purpose of training speech recognition software. In April 2019 Amazon was found to be employing human reviewers who transcribed and annotated conversations in order to minimize errors in Alexa's understanding of human speech (Day, Turner, & Drozdiak, 2019; O'Flaherty, 2019). Following this revelation, and other incidents that occurred in 2018—when Alexa was triggered by a TV ad and ordered cat food by mistake (Sweney, 2018), or when it sent a private conversation between a husband and wife to one of the husband's employees (Warren, 2018)—it became clear that Alexa was "an always on eavesdropping device" that "unintentionally" records sounds unprompted (Clauser, 2019). Users have little control over what is recorded and stored. Journalist Geoffrey Fowler (2019) recounts how he "listened to four years of my Alexa archive and found thousands of fragments of my life: spaghetti-timer requests, joking houseguests and random snippets of 'Downton Abbey.' There were even sensitive conversations that somehow triggered Alexa's 'wake word' to start recording, including my family discussing medication and a friend conducting a business deal." In summer 2019, when the Flemish VRT NWS broadcaster revealed having listened to over a thousand excerpts of leaked recorded conversations in Dutch—153 of which were recorded even if the wake word "Okay Google" was clearly unspoken (Verheyden et al., 2019) and most of which included sensitive information—Google admitted its practice of allowing language analysts to listen to audio recordings from Google Home smart speakers in order to improve voice recognition software (Cuthbertson, 2019).

We would expect that privacy concerns around the uncontrolled recording and centralized storing of data, and the "chilling effects" of corporate algorithmic profiling (Büchi et al., 2020), shape the domestication of smart speakers at home. However, research that examines the influence of privacy and security risks over technologies' adoption found that privacy only partially accounted for non-use of voice assistants: lower perceived utility and a high effort expectancy represented more common barriers to adoption (Liao et al., 2019). Similarly, the qualitative comparative study conducted in the U.S. and the Netherlands, cited above, found a certain degree of resignation among users of voice assistants, who consider dataveillance and profiling an inevitable consequence of using smart speakers (Pridmore et al., 2019). This was particularly prominent among users in the U.S., for whom the belief of having "nothing to hide" coupled with the convenience and utility of home hubs (Pridmore et al., 2019) results in what has been defined as "surveillance realism"—namely, "the nature of acceptance and resignation to the increasing mass collection of data across the social life despite widespread unease and concerns with these infrastructures and systems" (Hintz, Dencik, & Wahl-Jorgensen, 2018, p. 92).

Likewise, a study of the predictors and outcomes of distinctive privacy concerns around social robots points to a "robot privacy paradox," whereby the perceived benefits of social robots, strengthened by social influence—that is, the perceived social pressure to adopt and use a technology—outnumbered the privacy concerns that could hinder the use of social robots (Lutz & Tamó-Larrieux, 2020).

A similar combination of concerns and apathy about the data generated as part of users' interactions with smart speakers is expressed by Italian parents of young children, who would be willing to disclose more personal data if their smart speaker performed better at taking their interests and preferences into account—61% would rather have more personal data collected in exchange for a more personalized response (Mascheroni & Zaffaroni, 2020). This is a striking contrast to the answer provided by a sample of 4272 American owners of smart speakers surveyed by the Pew Research Center, only 33% of whom would trade their privacy for higher personalization (Auxier, 2019). As with Pridmore et al.'s 2019 study, then, we can observe cultural differences in surveillance imaginaries (Lyon, 2018) that inform the adoption, use, and non-use of smart speakers. However, we have to be cautious in comparing these data as such: although it is the same question, it has been asked of two different populations (American adults vs. Italian parents of young children); the two countries were at two different stages of the domestication process (remember that while Amazon Echo was launched in 2014 in the U.S., it was only launched in 2018 in Italy), and this may account for a persisting novelty effect in the latter country; finally, the data collection in the U.S. took place just after the news of Amazon staff listening to and transcribing users' conversations, which may have influenced respondents' views. We may also speculate that less satisfactory experiences with voice assistants in non-English-speaking countries—due to lower speech recognition software's accuracy in languages other than English—motivates users' desire for greater personalization. To conclude, research so far has pointed to a disjuncture between consumers' desires and concerns. More studies adopting a domestication of technology framework could shed light on the diverse, contradictory meanings that are made and remade as technologies enter our homes and are given a place in our lives.

Children and Smart Speakers

The most popular smart speakers are not designed for children, yet their grow-ing diffusion means that children are increasingly more likely to interact with a voice assistant at home. The latest "Common Sense census: Media use by kids age zero to eight" (Rideout & Robb, 2020) observes a substantial increase in the diffusion of smart speakers and children's interaction with them. While in 2017 only 9% of homes in the U.S. with young children had a smart speaker, the number of children's homes with at least one internet-connected, voice-activated device grew to 41% in 2020. It is no surprise, then, that the number of children interacting with voice assistants increased from 14% in 2017 to 25% in 2020, including 23% of 2- to 4-year-olds and 36% of 5- to 8-year-olds. According to the same report, and consistent with the findings of Lopatovska et al.'s study (2019), children mainly use smart speakers to play music (19% of 2- to 4-year-olds and 5- to 8-year-olds), followed by fooling around with the voice assistant (12% of 2- to 4-year-olds and 25% of 5- to 8-year-olds) and getting information (7% of 2- to 4-year-olds and 25% of 5- to 8-year-olds). Across both age groups, the use of smart speakers as storytellers is reported by a minority of the interviewed children (4%). In the Italian study presented earlier, 30% of the interviewed parents reported that their children use smart speakers autonomously, while 38% use them under parental super-vision (Mascheroni & Zaffaroni, 2020).

The use of smart speakers by children raises concerns for the recording and storing of their personal data. In fact, Amazon was sued in June 2019 for illegally recording and storing children's conversations without parental consent (Thorne, 2019). The lawsuits followed the complaint filed to the Federal Trade Commission (FTC) by the Campaign for a Commercial-Free Childhood and (CCFC) and the Center for Digital Democracy (CDD), lead-ing to a coalition of 19 groups that accused Amazon of violating the Children's Online Privacy Protection Act (COPPA) with its Echo Dot Kids Edition (Singer, 2019). The company allegedly retained the children's data even after the parents tried to delete the recordings. The child-friendly version of the smart speaker targeted by the advocacy groups, and launched on the market in 2018, included access to children's content, an optimized voice recognition software that would detect children's voices and common mispronunciations, and additional features to appease worried parents—namely, parental control to limit the time and duration of use, a Parent Dashboard to monitor content and usage, and positive reinforcement of politeness when children use the "magic word" "please" to Alexa. Indeed, Amazon's head of FreeTime declared that, "parents have been asking the company to add features that help children learn manners" (Seifert, 2018). Yet, despite being designed for children, Echo Dot Kids was not private-by-design.

A new Echo Dot Kids, containing new privacy features, was launched in June 2019. However, privacy risks persist, as children are likely to encounter and engage—either directly or indirectly—with other smart speakers present at home. Children's data, then, are being continuously collected through aggregated profiles, even when using Amazon Household or Google Family platforms. Veronica Barassi (2020) warns against the risks of often-inaccurate data that are used to profile children, as well as, again, the systematic discrimination of algorithmic bias. Her ethnographic work with families in the U.S. and the UK also points to how parents differently domesticated home hubs, or not, according to their concerns over datafication and privacy: some parents resisted smart speakers altogether, choosing not to buy them; others reported consciously limiting their voice interactions with Alexa in order to limit data collection and to protect their children; while others were less concerned, arguing that the data collected by voice assistants were not sensitive and could not be coupled with other sensitive information such as social security or credit card numbers (Barassi, 2020). A combination of unawareness of the surveillance business model of home hubs and "surveillance realism" (Hintz et al., 2018) makes parents inure to the home as a reservoir of data for surveillance capitalism.

Beyond raising issues of datafication of family life, the entrance of home hubs into the domestic environment shapes, while being shaped by, family practices and relations. A study conducted in the U.S. with 10 families with children aged 0–16—based on pre- and post-deployment interviews, and recordings of the families' interactions with Alexa for four weeks—shows how the domestication of Alexa involved negotiations and conflicts among the parents and their children (Beneteau et al., 2020). On the positive side, the parents and children engaged in practices of co-use, where the parents scaffolded their children's interaction with the voice assistant—for example, suggesting how to rephrase a question or other repair communication strategies. In this way, younger children's communicative skills were expanded through their parents' scaffolding of mediated interaction with the smart speakers. Moreover, smart speakers democratized younger children's access to technology by providing a more natural interaction compared to screens and keyboards. However, the researchers recount numerous examples of the children trying to take control of the voice assistant through what they call "instrumental or subversive interruptions" (Beneteau et al., 2020, p. 5), where the children hijacked the device to impose their desired outputs (such as music) or to annoy their parents. Finally, Alexa was incorporated by the parents into practices of "augmented parenting" (Beneteau et al., 2020, p. 5), namely, in a more innocuous way, as a neutral third party mediator to help make decisions (such as to when to plan a visit to the park), but also in a more deceitful way, to obtain children's obedience, such as when a mother set the timer on the mobile app to persuade her son that it came from Alexa and it was time to go to sleep.

Garg and Sengupta's study (2020) with 18 families, based on interviews and Google Home Activity logs, examined the domestication of smart speakers over a longer period of time—participating families had owned a home hub from six months to two years before the study. The findings confirm that parents and children use smart speakers differently. Adults used Google Home mainly for automation—to control smart lighting, thermostats, and cameras—or to play music—which was integrated into different daily routines. Conversely, children's voice logs indicated that playing games, listening to music, searching for information, and engaging in small talk were the most common uses. Parents scaffolded children's interactions with the voice assistant over the first two or three months, until the child learned to adapt the communication style using shorter sentences and raising their speaking volume, etc. Moreover, observing usage patterns over time, the authors were able to conclude that the personification of the device by children is not limited to the initial domestication, but continues over time, and results in the development of an emotional attachment. The interviews also explored reasons for intermittent non-use, including family holidays, loss of interest and utility, and, in some families, privacy issues. Six of the 18 families expressed concern over Google Home recording sensitive information, even in the absence of its "wake" word. The children too found it "creepy" (Garg & Sengupta, 2020, p. 15).

Children's interactions with smart speakers also open up questions concerning their cognitive and psychological development. Research in this area draws on experimental studies in developmental psychology, focused on the cognitive, emotional, and moral consequences of interactions with social robots, which provide insights into how children make sense of machines that attempt to act like humans. In fact, such studies show how children's interaction with social robots is not only shaped by the appearance of the robot (humanoid versus non-humanoid), but also by the diverse representations of robots that children hold; that is, either human-like, pet-like or machine-like. More specifically, scholars emphasized how children's understandings of animacy, liveliness, and intelligence (Turkle, 2006) varied according to age and development (Cameron et al., 2017), but also based on their prior experiences with robots (Bernstein & Crowley, 2008). In a more recent study, which applied to social robots' insights from prior research on children's learning of prosocial behavior, Peter, Kühne, and Barco (2021) found that more prosocial robots elicited a more intense prosocial response in children. Yet, prosocial robots' influence over knowledge and perception of social norms is less linear: while children who interacted with a prosocial robot were more inclined to believe that their peers also typically engaged in prosocial behavior (descriptive norms of sharing), they did not consider sharing as more socially legitimate (injunctive norms). The explanation that Peter and his co-authors suggest is that social robots are not perceived as competent and authoritative others like parents, but rather, as peers. The question, then, is to what extent existing categories of living and non-living map onto the categories applied to robots. According to the new ontological category (NOC) hypothesis (Kahn, Gary & Shen, 2013), social robots are assigned to an emerging category at the intersection of natural and artifactual entities. The moral consequences are potentially disruptive, involving a partial objectification of social robots that could extend to humans and could be detrimental to children's development (Kahn et al., 2013). An echo of such concerns is reflected in the debate around the opportunity, or not, of teaching children good manners with voice assistants. As explained earlier, American parents' worry that children who learn to give harsh orders to smart speakers would command humans in the same way is behind Amazon's choice to equip their Dot Kids Edition with positive reinforcement of politeness. This is, however, a simplistic techno-solution to a complex problem, which could actually have the opposite effect in reinforcing children in their belief that AI is human-like (Elgan, 2018).

Lovato and Piper (2019) argue that, while smart speakers remove some of the obstacles that prevent young children from being autonomous in online searches (namely, spelling and typing), we should not underplay other developmental factors. More specifically—and similarly to Peter et al.'s study (2021)—they question voice assistants' ability to act as "more knowledgeable others" (Vygotsky, 1978) who scaffold the child in learning how to ask the right questions, and trying to figure out the answer, thus supporting their development of language and reasoning skills. The authors also ask how the specific language required to effectively interact with smart speakers will shape how children learn to use language to ask for information.

A further challenge that voice assistants pose to children lies in their role as web interfaces. Indeed, "voice assistants give the impression of access to vast, nearly unlimited information that users customarily attributed to the Web, but dramatically reduce control over Web access to users, affecting their capacity to browse, explore and retrieve the plurality of information available through the Web" (Natale & Cook, 2020, p. 4). By making information retrieval opaque and narrowing down the number of results for each query, voice assistants not only limit access to the variety of online sources, but also undermine children's acquisition of critical navigation skills, such as the ability to check the reliability of information sources and, therefore, to cope with misinformation and disinformation. The human-like characterization of voice assistants will also likely impact on the perceived credibility and authority of the information provided (Natale & Cook, 2020), in ways that are yet to be examined. Growing up while getting used to accessing online content through the mediation of human-like voice-activated AI can lead to the naturalization of algorithmic, data-driven selection (van Dijck, Poell, & de Waal, 2018). Beyond the impression of a vast, almost infinite repertoire of digital sources, smart speakers narrow down access to a predetermined, selected range of content based on children's and parents' datafied practices—and the practices of other families assigned to the same "measurable types" (Cheney-Lippold, 2017; see also Chapters 2 and 8, this book).

Children and the Internet of Toys

Smart speakers are by far the most pervasive, yet not the only, internet-connected device that children today have access to at home: in 2017, the Family Online Safety Institute (FOSI, 2017) found that 35% of children aged 0–12 own or have access to a connected toy, while 31% have access to a wearable device such as a smart watch. Similarly, the DataChildFutures study of Italian parents of children aged 0–8 shows that 40% of the households studied had at least one internet-connected toy and 57% owned at least one smart wearable device. While the majority of children (60%) were allowed to engage autonomously with a connected toy, only 11.5% could use a wearable device without parental supervision (Mascheroni & Zaffaroni, 2020).

The Internet of Toys (IoToys) includes a range of toys that are internet-connected, often controlled via a smartphone or tablet app, and programmable and/or often simulating human interaction through voice recognition and speech.[6] In the public discourse, internet-connected toys have been mostly associated with their security and privacy issues. The growing public concern for children's privacy has been sparked by a successful campaign launched by the Norwegian Consumer Council in November 2016, which was later embarked on by the BEUC (The European Consumer Organisation), and resulted in a report filed with the European Data Protection Supervisor and the International Consumer Protection and Enforcement Network (ICPEN). Similar complaints have been filed with the U.S. FTC by U.S. advocacy groups for children, consumers, and privacy, including the CCFC (Mascheroni & Holloway, 2017). The campaign exposed the security and safety failures of two toys—the talking doll My Friend Cayla and the i-Que Intelligent Robot by Genesis Toys—including lack of control, by parents, over the storage and sharing of children's data with third parties and deceitful Terms and Conditions; unauthorized Bluetooth access from any smartphone or tablet within 50 meters; and hidden advertising, in the form of sponsored brands and products included in the scripted interactions. The campaign culminated with the ban of Cayla from the German market, and the invitation, by the German Federal Network Agency, to destroy the doll (Oltermann, 2017).

Major toys manufacturers have also been under the spotlight. In 2015, the vulnerability of Mattel's Hello Barbie was exposed by white-hat hackers[7] (Gibbs, 2015). Two years later, the company canceled the launch of its digital nanny, Aristotle, a smart speaker and baby monitor designed to entertain children with bedtime stories, teach them literacy and reading, and to soothe and comfort a crying child—after advocacy groups, pediatricians, psychologists, and parents raised concerns about the consequences for children's privacy, development, and wellbeing (Rabkin Peachman, 2017).

While most media coverage and academic literature has focused on the privacy implications of internet-connected toys, a further risk is evident when examining the datafication and algorithmic processing mobilized in the child–IoToys interaction as a Customer Relationship Management (CRM) data practice (Steeves, 2020)—that is, the scripted flow of conversation as a means of controlling a child's responses to Hello Barbie fits within a predetermined narrative and stimulates a highly emotional response in the child. "Mattel uses the algorithm to ensure that the corporation has a privileged place in the dialogue as a one-sided conversationalist who controls the flow of the conversation" (Steeves, 2020, p. 6). The child's agency is constrained by the scripted conversation, in that they are given the possibility of having a meaningful conversation with their doll only on condition that they follow the script. It is the high degree of control over the child–toy dialog, as informed by data extraction and abstraction, which offers a glimpse into the deceitful marketing strategies that datafication enables. In other words, beyond concerns over the control and use of children's intimate data, IoToys raise concerns for the forms of hidden, highly emotional, and hyper-personalized advertising that AI enables, disguised beneath the doll's or the toy's suggestion in their "spontaneous" conversations with a child. Datafication intensifies and exacerbates the commodification of childhood.

Research on the appropriation of IoToys in the domestic context shows complex and varied "connected play" practices (Marsh, 2019), which suggests negotiations around the preferred meanings encoded in such toys, transcending the boundaries between digital and non-digital play, online and offline, material and immaterial, public and private, global and local. For example, Marsh's observations of young children's interaction with Furby Connect show how the anthropomorphic features of social robotic toys can equally be embraced in children's play practices or resisted as alienating and "creepy" (2019). Children's and parents' domestication of IoToys cover a broad spectrum of positions between the two poles of "anthropomorphic" and "uncanny" playful encounters (Marsh, 2019), depending on their prior experiences with robotic toys and digital media, the role of digital technologies within the family media culture, their play cultures, and so on. Similarly, Berriman and Mascheroni's analysis of the digital materialities of connected toys found that their more media-like, hybrid nature involves a renegotiation of the meanings and practice of play: while connected toys "demand," rather than simply encourage, specific play practices—for example, care and nurturing— nonetheless children enact such affordances and enliven the toys in diverse and complex ways (Berriman & Mascheroni, 2019).

Analyzing in-depth qualitative, mixed-method data collected as part of a four-country project funded by the Australian Research Council, Mascheroni, Zaman, and Holloway (2020) examined the domestication of an interactive robotic toy called Cozmo, which is controlled and programmable by means of an app. The analysis show how its domestication is shaped by a combination of factors: the toy's materiality and technological features—namely, the toy needs to be plugged in and the app requires specific hardware and software in order to function; children's busy everyday lives, their favorite play and media practices—YouTubers and PlayStation games topping the list of their favorite online activities; parents' concern with limiting screen time; and the family's orientation towards technologies and mediated family time. All these factors meant a partial incorporation of the toy into the children's domestic routines: the time spent playing with Cozmo© gradually diminished and became less rewarding if the child stopped exploring new functionalities or abstained from programming the robot. Partial incorporation translates into a partial conversion: even though the children and their parents personified Cozmo©, the emotional attachment was only temporary. Moreover, the toy failed to become part of the child's social identity because its conversion into a symbolic token for social interaction with their peers was limited due to its little diffusion among the child's friends. However, this led to intermittent moments of redomestication during friends' visits at home.

Growing Up in Mediatized Homes

In this chapter, we have argued how children's homes are increasingly media- and data-saturated. However, recognizing that children are growing up amidst a variety of media and technologies that give shape to a datafied environment does not mean to argue against the diversity of children's and families' situated experiences, or to ignore how the adoption and use of digital media is fundamentally uneven. Rather, the domestication of technology approach has highlighted how similar media ensembles and repertoires of media practices can actually have different meanings for different families, based on their situated practical and emotional adaptation to technological artifacts. Ultimately, the main teaching of the domestication of technology approach is that "how one experiences ICTs is not completely determined by technological functionality or public representations; it is also structured by the social context in which it is received" (Haddon, 2003: 47).

Social inequalities shape the ways in which datafication is experienced, understood, and dealt with (Barassi, 2020) (We shall return to this in Chapter 8.). However, while different layers of digital divide reproduce and exacerbate existing inequalities, socioeconomic inequalities do not simply map onto digital inequalities. Already back in 2007 Sonia Livingstone had distinguished among media-rich, media-poor, and traditional homes, to emphasize how parents' imaginaries around technologies shape the cultural and cognitive framework of media use. Livingstone and Blum-Ross's latest research with families across London equally questions the validity of crosscut divisions among upper-, middle-, and lower-class families to explain the mediatization of contemporary homes, pointing to "the rise of a common parenting culture—arguably middle-class in its ethos of individualized achievement and itself a response to the individualization of risk in reflexive modernity—that encompasses poorer families too" (2020, p. 83). Yet, their vivid journey into the lived experiences of diverse families shows how, despite a pervasive parenting culture centered round technology-based expressive empowerment, and similar levels of mediatization of family lives, inequalities persist: in the number and quality of the devices available at home; the formal and informal learning opportunities available to children; and, more importantly, the outcomes of digital engagement for children's future.

The uneven experiences of mediatization and datafication among children have been amplified in the current situation, characterized by the global coronavirus pandemic (COVID-19). With school closures and lockdown implemented in many countries, digital media and online platforms have become essential resources for learning, social interaction, play, and entertainment. Data collected in July 2020 through an online survey of children aged 10–18 and their parents as part of a cross-country study coordinated by the JRC (Vuorikari et al., 2020) show that in most European countries schools moved classes online, through a combination of video conferencing tools (such as Zoom, Microsoft Teams, Hangouts, and Skype), digital learning platforms (Google Classroom, ClassDojo, etc.), messaging apps, emails, social media, and traditional paper books and exercise sheets. Therefore, in many countries, such as Italy, the lockdown represented an opportunity for tech giants to expand the datafication of the home and education at the same time (see Chapter 7, this book). Moreover, the pandemic also brought to the fore inequalities among homes that would, under different conditions, be considered as media-rich. For example, data collected in Italy as part of the above-mentioned European study found that 27% of parents lamented that the devices available at home were not sufficient for everyone to engage in remote learning or working when needed. Larger families were particularly disadvantaged: the number of available devices per child tends to decrease with household size, dropping from 1.7 computers and 1.1 tablets per child in single-child families down to 0.6 computers and 0.7 tablets per child in households with five children (Mascheroni et al., 2021).

Therefore, the forced reliance on digital media and platforms during the lockdown resulted not only in a further normalization of data relations (Couldry & Mejias, 2019) in children's lives; it also exposed the diverse, unequal experiences of children growing up in mediatized homes.

Notes

1 Strictly speaking, "smart" homes are defined as those that are equipped with internet-connected appliances, which are integrated and able to anticipate the needs of the inhabitants (see Harper, 2003). In what follows, however, we adopt the notion of "smart" homes in a broader sense, to suggest how deeply IoTs objects (not necessarily appliances) have been incorporated into the domestic context.

2 We do not mean to dismiss the complexity of the concept of "home," or to conflate it, unproblematically, with the family—its content—and the house or apartment—its physical container. However, a thorough discussion of the home as a multidimensional concept exceeds the scope of this chapter. For more, see Hareven (1991) and Mallett (2004). On the concept of "home" from a media and communications perspective, see Silverstone (1999) and Morley (2000).

3 Now re-branded Google Nest after Nest Labs merged with the Google Home team in 2018, after their initial acquisition by Google in 2014.

4 An example of how even AI-powered voice assistants are informed by scripted conversation is offered by Amazon's explanation to several users complaining that Alexa burst out laughing without reason: "In rare circumstances, Alexa can mistakenly hear the phrase 'Alexa, laugh'" when other words are spoken, Amazon said in an emailed statement. "We are changing that phrase to be 'Alexa, can you laugh?' which is less likely to have false positives, and we are disabling the short utterance 'Alexa, laugh'" (Chokshi, 2018).

5 DataChildFutures (https://datachildfutures.it/en/home-english/) is funded by the Fondazione Cariplo to investigate the data practices of Italian families with children aged 0–8. Using a combination of qualitative (longitudinal research) and quantitative (survey, computational) methods, it will shed light on the social and cultural consequences of the normalization of dataveillance in everyday life: namely, transforming not only parenting and growing up, but ultimately social imaginaries. Ipsos administered the survey online on a nationally representative sample of parents. Parents were asked to respond to each survey question having in mind the focal child in their family. The focal child was selected at random using a computer algorithm from a prior question that asked parents to report the age and gender of all their 0- to 8-year-old children.

6 For a more detailed review of IoToys, see Mascheroni and Holloway (2017, 2019a).

7 White-hat hackers are also called "ethical hackers," as they usually perform a vulnerability assessment to increase the security of systems.

References

Allon, F. (2003). An ontology of everyday control. Space, media flows and "smart" living in the absolute present. In N. Couldry & A. McCarthy (Eds.), *Media/space: Place, scale and culture in a media age* (pp. 253–274). Routledge.

Auxier, B. (2019). 5 things to know about Americans and their smart speakers. Pew Research Center Fact Tank, November 21. www.pewresearch.org/fact-tank/2019/11/21/5-things-to-know-about-americans-and-their-smart-speakers/

Barassi, V. (2020). *Child | Data | Citizen. How tech-companies are profiling us from before Birth.* The MIT Press.

Beneteau, E., Boone, A., Wu, Y., Kientz, J., Yip, J., & Hiniker, A. (2020). Parenting with Alexa: Exploring the introduction of smart speakers on family dynamics. *CHI'20: Proceedings of the 2020 CHI Conference on Human Factors in Computing Systems,* April 21, 1–13. https://doi.org/10.1145/3313831.3376344

Beneteau, E., Richards, O., Zhang, M., Kientz, J., Yip, J., & Hiniker, A. (2019). Communication breakdowns between families and Alexa. *CHI'19: Proceedings of the 2019 CHI Conference on Human Factors in Computing Systems,* May, Paper No. 243, 1–13. https://doi.org/10.1145/3290605.3300473

Bernstein, D., & Crowley, K. (2008). Searching for signs of intelligent life: An investigation of young children's beliefs about robot intelligence. *Journal of the Learning Sciences, 17*(2), 225–247.

Berriman, L., & Mascheroni, G. (2019). Exploring the affordances of smart toys and connected play in practice. *New Media & Society, 21*(4), 797–814. https://doi.org/10.1177/1461444818807119

Büchi, M., Fosch-Villaronga, E., Lutz, C., Tamò-Larrieux, A., Velidi, S., & Viljoen, S. (2020). The chilling effects of algorithmic profiling: Mapping the issues. *The Computer Law and Security Report, 36,* 105367. https://doi.org/10.1016/j.clsr.2019.105367

Bunz, M., & Meikle, G. (2018). *The Internet of Things.* Polity.

Cameron, D., Fernando, S., Collins, E. C., et al. (2017). You made him be alive: Children's perceptions of animacy in a humanoid robot. In *Lecture Notes in Computer Science. The 6th International Conference on Biomimetic and Biohybrid Systems* (Living Machines 2017), July 25–28, Stanford University. https://doi.org/10.1007/978-3-319-63537-8_7

Cheney-Lippold, J. (2017). *We are data: Algorithms and the making of our digital selves.* New York University Press.

Chokshi, N. (2018). Amazon knows why Alexa was laughing at its customers. *The New York Times,* March 8. www.nytimes.com/2018/03/08/business/alexa-laugh-amazon-echo.html

Clauser, G. (2019). Amazon's Alexa never stops listening to you. Should you worry? *The New York Times,* August 8. www.nytimes.com/wirecutter/blog/amazons-alexa-never-stops-listening-to-you/

Couldry, N., & Hepp, A. (2017). *The mediated construction of reality.* Polity.

Couldry, N., & Mejias, U. A. (2019). *The costs of connection: How data is colonizing human life and appropriating it for capitalism.* Stanford University Press.

Cuthbertson, A. (2019). Google defends listening to private conversations on Google Home—but what intimate moments are recorded? *The Independent,* July 12. www.independent.co.uk/life-style/gadgets-and-tech/news/google-home-recordings-listen-privacy-amazon-alexa-hack-a9002096.html

Day, M., Turner, G., & Drozdiak, N. (2019). Thousands of Amazon workers listen to Alexa users' conversations. *Time,* April 11. https://time.com/5568815/amazon-workers-listen-to-alexa/

Elgan, M. (2018). The case against teaching kids to be polite to Alexa. *Fast Company,* June 24. www.fastcompany.com/40588020/the-case-against-teaching-kids-to-be-polite-to-alexa

FOSI (Family Online Safety Institute) (2017). *Connected families: How parents think and feel about wearables, toys, and the Internet of Things.* www.fosi.org/policy-research/connected-families

Fowler, G. A. (2019). Alexa has been eavesdropping on you this whole time. *The Washington Post,* May 6. www.washingtonpost.com/technology/2019/05/06/alexa-has-been-eavesdropping-you-this-whole-time/

Garg, R., & Sengupta, S. (2020). He is just like me: A study of the long-term use of smart speakers by parents and children. *Proceedings of the ACM on Interactive, Mobile, Wearable and Ubiquitous Technologies, 4*(1), 1–24. https://doi.org/10.1145/3381002

Gibbs, S. (2015). Hackers can hijack Wi-Fi Hello Barbie to spy on your children. *The Guardian,* November 26. www.theguardian.com/technology/2015/nov/26/hackers-can-hijack-wi-fi-hello-barbie-to-spy-on-your-children

Goulden, M. (2019). "*Delete the family*": Platform families and the colonisation of the smart home. *Information, Communication & Society.* https://doi.org/10.1080/1369118X.2019.1668454

Guzman, A. L. (2018). What is human–machine communication, anyway? In L. Guzman (Ed.), *Human–machine communication: Rethinking communication, technology, and ourselves* (pp. 1–28). Peter Lang.

Guzman, A. L. (2019). Voices in and of the machine: Source orientation toward mobile virtual assistants. *Computers in Human Behavior, 90,* 343–350.

Haddon, L. (2003). Domestication and mobile telephony. In J. E. Katz (Ed.), *Machines that become us: The social context of personal communication technology* (pp. 43–56). Transaction Publishers.

Haddon, L. (2004). *Information and communication technologies in everyday life: A concise introduction and research guide.* Berg.

Haddon, L., & Silverstone, R. (2000). Information and communication technologies and everyday life: Individual and social dimensions. In K. Ducatel, J. Webster, & W. Herrman (Eds.), *The Information Society in Europe: Work and life in an age of globalization* (pp. 233–258). Rowman & Littlefield.

Hareven, T. K. (1991). The home and the family in historical perspective. *Social Research, 58*(1), 253–285.

Harper, R. (Ed.). (2003). *Inside the smart home.* Springer.

Hepp, A. (2020). *Deep mediatization.* Routledge.

Hintz, A., Dencik, L., & Wahl-Jorgensen, K. (2018). *Digital citizenship in a datafied society.* Polity.

Humphry, J., & Chesher, C. (2020). Preparing for smart voice assistants: Cultural histories and media innovations. *New Media & Society.* https://doi.org/10.1177/1461444820923679

Jennings, N., & Wartella, E. (2013). Technology and the family. In A. L. Vangelisti (Ed.), *The Routledge handbook of family communication* (2nd ed.) (pp. 448–462). Routledge.

Kahn, P. H., Gary, H. E., & Shen, S. (2013). Children's social relationships with current and near-future robots. *Child Development Perspectives, 7*(1), 32–37.

Lemish, D. (2015). *Children and media: A global perspective.* Wiley Blackwell.

Liao, Y., Vitak, J., Kumar, P., Zimmer, M., & Kritikos, K. (2019). Understanding the role of privacy and trust in intelligent personal assistant adoption. In *International Conference on Information* (pp. 102–113). Springer.

Livingstone, S. (2007). Strategies of parental regulation in the media-rich home. *Computers in Human Behavior, 23*(2), 920–941. https://doi.org/10.1016/j.chb.2005.08.002

Livingstone, S. (2009). *Children and the internet.* Polity.

Livingstone, S., & Blum-Ross, A. (2020). *Parenting for a digital future: How hopes and fears about technology shape children's lives.* Oxford University Press.

Lopatovska, I., Rink, K., Knight, I., et al. (2019). Talk to me: Exploring user interactions with the Amazon Alexa. *Journal of Librarianship and Information Science, 51*(4), 984–997. https://doi.org/10.1177/0961000618759414

Lovato, S. B., & Piper, A. M. (2019). Young children and voice search: What we know from human–computer interaction research. *Frontiers in Psychology, 10,* 8. https://doi.org/10.3389/fpsyg.2019.00008

Lutz, C., & Tamó-Larrieux, A. (2020). The robot privacy paradox: Understanding how privacy concerns shape intentions to use social robots. *Human-Machine Communication, 1,* 87–111. https://doi.org/10.30658/hmc.1.6

Lyon, D. (2018) *The culture of surveillance: Watching as a way of life.* Polity.

Mallett, S. (2004). Understanding home: A critical review of the literature. *The Sociological Review, 52*(1), 62–89. https://doi.org/10.1111/j.1467-954X.2004.00442.x

Marsh, J. (2019). The uncanny valley revisited: Play with the internet of toys. In G. Mascheroni & D. Holloway (Eds.), *The Internet of Toys: Practices, affordances and the political economy of children's smart play* (pp. 47–65). Palgrave.

Mascheroni, G., & Holloway, D. (Eds.). (2017). *The Internet of Toys: A report on media and social discourses around young children and IoToys.* DigiLitEY. http://digilitey.eu/wp-content/uploads/2017/01/IoToys-June-2017-reduced.pdf

Mascheroni, G., & Holloway, D. (Eds.). (2019a). *The Internet of Toys: Practices, affordances and the political economy of children's smart play.* Palgrave.

Mascheroni, G., & Holloway, D. (2019b). The quantified child: Discourses and practices of dataveillance in different life stages. In O. Erstad, R. Flewitt, B. Kümmerling-meibauer, & I. Pereira (Eds.), *The Routledge handbook of digital literacies in early childhood* (pp. 354–365). Routledge.

Mascheroni, G., Saeed, M., Valenza, M., et al. (2021). *Learning at a distance: Children's remote learning experiences in Italy during the COVID-19 pandemic.* Innocenti Research Report, UNICEF Office of Research – Innocenti. www.unicef-irc.org/publications/1182-learning-at-a-distance-childrens-remote-learning-experiences-in-italy-during-the-covid-19-pandemic.html

Mascheroni, G., & Zaffaroni, L. G. (2020). The datafication of childhood at home: The data practices, meanings and affects of parents of young children. *Association of Internet Researchers (AoIR) Selected Papers of Internet Research 2020 Life.* https://doi.org/10.5210/spir.v2020i0.11136

Mascheroni, G., Zaman, B., & Holloway, D. (2020). Child–robotic toy interactions as a form of communication: Processes of (de- and re-)domestication. *ICA 70th Annual Conference* [virtual].

Massey, D. (1994). *Space, place and gender.* Polity.

Morley, D. (2000). *Home territories: Media, mobility and identity*. Routledge.

Morley, D. (2003) What's "home" got to do with it? Contradictory dynamics in the domestication of technology and the dislocation of domesticity. *European Journal of Cultural Studies*, 6 (4), 435–458. https://doi.org/10.1177/13675494030064001

Natale, S., & Cook, H. (2020). Browsing with Alexa: Interrogating the impact of voice assistants as web interfaces. *Media, Culture & Society*. https://doi.org/10.1177/0163443720983295

O'Flaherty, K. (2019). Amazon staff are listening to Alexa conversations—Here's what to do. *Forbes*, April 12. www.forbes.com/sites/kateoflahertyuk/2019/04/12/amazon-staff-are-listening-to-alexa-conversations-heres-what-to-do/

Oltermann, P. (2017). German parents told to destroy doll that can spy on children. *The Guardian*, February 17. www.theguardian.com/world/2017/feb/17/german-parents-told-to-destroy-my-friend-cayla-doll-spy-on-children

Osservatorio Internet of Things (2020). *Smart home: Dove c'è IoT, c'è casa [Smart home: Home is where the IoT is]*. www.osservatori.net/it/ricerche/comunicati-stampa/smart-home-mercato-italiano-da-530-milioni-di-euro

Peter, J., Kühne, R., & Barco, A. (2021). Can social robots affect children's prosocial behavior? An experimental study on prosocial robot models. *Computers in Human Behavior*. https://doi.org/10.1016/j.chb.2021.106712

Pridmore, J., Vitak, J., Trottier, D., et al. (2019). Intelligent personal assistants and the intercultural negotiations of dataveillance in platformed households. *Surveillance & Society*, 17(1/2), 125–131.

Rabkin Peachman, R. (2017). Mattel pulls Aristotle children's device after privacy concerns. *The New York Times*, October 5. www.nytimes.com/2017/10/05/well/family/mattel-aristotle-privacy.html

Rideout, V., & Robb, M. B. (2020). The Common Sense census: Media use by kids age zero to eight, 2020. Common Sense Media. www.commonsensemedia.org/research/the-common-sense-census-media-use-by-kids-age-zero-to-eight-2020

Rybczynski, W. (1986). *Home: A short history of an idea*. Penguin Books.

Seifert, D. (2018). Amazon's new Echo Dot Kids Edition comes with a colorful case and parental controls. *The Verge*, April 25. www.theverge.com/2018/4/25/17276164/amazon-echo-dot-kids-edition-freetime-price-announcement-features-specs

Silverstone, R. (1999). *Why study the media?* SAGE Publications Ltd.

Silverstone, R., & Hirsch, E. (1992). Introduction. In R. Silverstone & E. Hirsch (Eds.), *Consuming technologies: Media and information in domestic space* (pp. 1–11). Routledge.

Silverstone, R., Hirsch, E. & Morley, D. (1992). Information and communication technologies and the moral economy of the household. In R. Silverstone & E. Hirsch (Eds.), *Consuming technologies: Media and information in domestic space* (pp. 13–28). Routledge.

Singer, N. (2019). Amazon flunks children's privacy, advocacy groups charge. *The New York Times*, May 9. www.nytimes.com/2019/05/09/technology/amazon-childrens-privacy-echo-dot-kids.html

Steeves, V. (2020). A dialogic analysis of Hello Barbie's conversations with children. *Big Data & Society*, 7(1). https://doi.org/10.1177/2053951720919151

Sweney, M. (2018). Hey Alexa, is it true a TV advert made Amazon Echo order cat food? *The Guardian*, February 14. www.theguardian.com/technology/2018/feb/14/amazon-alexa-ad-avoids-ban-after-viewer-complaint-ordered-cat-food?CMP=share_btn_tw

Thorne, J. (2019). Does Alexa illegally record children? Amazon sued for allegedly storing conversations without consent. *GeekWire*, June 12. www.geekwire.com/2019/alexa-illegally-record-children-amazon-sued-allegedly-storing-conversations-without-consent

Turkle, S. (2006). Tamagotchi diary. *London Review of Books*, 28(8), 36–37.

van Dijck, J. (2013). *The culture of connectivity: A critical history of social media*. Oxford University Press.

van Dijck, J., Poell, T., & de Waal, M. (2018). *The platform society: Public values in a connective world*. Oxford University Press.

Verheyden, T., Baert, D., van Hee, L., & van den Heuvel, R. (2019). Google employees are eavesdropping, even in your living room, VRT NWS has discovered. *VRT News Flanders*, July 10. www.vrt.be/vrtnws/en/2019/07/10/google-employees-are-eaves dropping-even-in-flemish-living-rooms/

Vuorikari, R., Velicu, A., Chaudron, S., Cachia, R., & Di Gioia, R. (2020). *How families handled emergency remote schooling during the Covid-19 lockdown in spring 2020—Summary of key findings from families with children in 11 European countries*. Publications Office of the European Union. https://doi.org/10.2760/31977

Vygotsky, L. S. (1978). *Mind in society: The development of higher mental process*. Harvard University Press.

Warren, T. (2018). Amazon explains how Alexa recorded a private conversation and sent it to another user. *The Verge*, May 24. www.theverge.com/2018/5/24/17391898/amazon-alexa-private-conversation-recording-explanation

Williams, R. (2003 [1974]). *Television: Technology and cultural form*. Routledge.

· 6 ·

THE MEDIATIZED PEER NETWORK

Children's Peer (Digital) Cultures

For children growing up today—at least for those living in media-saturated homes—digital media form an invisible, yet material, infrastructure for their everyday interactions with peers: creating and sustaining friendship ties, hanging around with peers, and expressing and performing their own identity are increasingly dependent on platforms and technologies that profit from harvesting and manipulating users' data.

Both identity and friendship, and their co-constitution, have been central themes in research on children, the internet, and mobile communication since its beginnings. The question has been to what extent and how mobile communication, social network sites (SNSs), and other online platforms have transformed both the practice of keeping in touch with friends and, relatedly, the identity spaces where children creatively engage in their self-presentation. In fact, sociologists maintain that, even under the pressure of the increasing complexity and uncertainties of life in a globalized, individualized, and consumerist society—or perhaps precisely because of such challenges—identity has never been an individual accomplishment. Rather, it is always a relational and situated process, embedded in the practices, contexts, communication repertoires, and norms of peer cultures. In a word, identities are constituted and performed through social interactions—through both identification with, and differentiation from, the peer group (Buckingham, 2008; Corsaro & Eder, 1990). Under the conditions of deep mediatization (Couldry & Hepp, 2017), children's identities and interpersonal relations are increasingly mediatized (Bond, 2014; boyd, 2014; Livingstone, 2009; Livingstone & Sefton-Green, 2016)—that is, shaped by the role that digital media play in children's lives.

Clark (2013) distinguishes three interrelated roles that media play in the habitual, experiential, and symbolic dimensions of children's everyday life, thus shaping how children experience themselves as individuals and as members of a peer group. First, digital media function "*mythically*" as they provide cultural resources in the form of "stories that resonate with us" (Clark, 2013, p. 79; original emphasis): narratives, role models, and behavioral patterns that children employ in the social construction of their own identities. Second, Clark identifies a pragmatic function of digital media, as they provide the communicative contexts in which identities and/in interaction are played out—that is, digital media reconfigure the peer group communication repertoires by enabling practices of nearly "perpetual contact" (Katz & Aakhus, 2002). Finally, digital media provide resources for self-expression and identity performance not just because of the stories they tell—their content—or for the relations they mediate, but for their "double articulation" as both material and symbolic objects (Haddon & Silverstone, 2000; see also Chapter 5, this book). Thus, technological artifacts "also function *symbolically*, as young people own commercially produced products such as mobile phones, televisions, and MP3 players or iPods that say something to others about who we are" (Clark, 2013, p. 79; original emphasis).

Similarly, in her ethnographic investigation of the practices and meanings of consumption among a diverse range of families in the U.S., Pugh (2009) showed how children incorporate media content and technological artifacts in their constant efforts to belong to their peer group. The media—encompassing both their material and symbolic dimension—are converted into behavioral scripts and symbolic tokens in order to signal children's "dignity" to take part in the everyday interaction rituals that mark the boundaries of the peer group. In fact, through their everyday interactions, together children shape and reproduce what Pugh calls the "economy of dignity:" "children collect or confer dignity among themselves, according to their (shifting) consensus about what sort of objects or experiences are supposed to count for it" (Pugh, 2009, p. 7). Therefore, drawing on the work of both Clark (2013) and

Pugh (2009), we can conclude that the definition of the peer culture—and accordingly, both the sense of belonging to the peer group and the sense of self—is sustained, at least partly, through digital media: their content, their symbolic value, and their functional support to co-present interaction.

Children are generally recognized as forerunners in the adoption of new devices, platforms, and communicative practices. Moreover, digital media and peer cultures are perceived as so inextricably linked that the mobile phone first, and specific social media platforms later, have even been assumed as defining features of the younger generations and their cultures. The notion of a "mobile youth culture" (Vanden Abeele, 2016)—followed by other successful classifications at the interplay of marketing and public discourse such as "generation Facebook" (Hamel, 2009) or "generation TikTok" (Tett, 2020)—is emblematic of how digital media, and their distinctive modes of communication, are seen as both enabling the expression of children's cultures and reinforcing their distinctiveness and distance from the adults' world. Research has shown how mobile communication rituals—such as the use of "texting argot" (Ling, 2008) before the widespread adoption of automated predictive text software such as T9—have been used to mark the distinction between the in-group and the out-group. In fact, "a central assumption of the mobile youth culture concept is that, today, youths assert generational distinctiveness through their mobile media practices and meanings" (Vanden Abeele, 2016, p. 87). Similarly, we can talk about "children's internet culture" (Livingstone, 2013) to refer not only to the distinctive ways in which they act and interact online as compared to adults, but, more fundamentally, to how greater parts of "their lives (identity, pleasure, pain, relationships) are altered by the fact of their digital, networked, online mediation" (Livingstone, 2013, p. 115). While these labels contribute to emphasize the mutual shaping between changing childhood and changing media, they are problematic for many reasons. First, to speak of children's internet culture or mobile youth culture runs the risk of overlooking the diversity of children (Stoilova et al., 2020), and the heterogeneity of their mobile and online practices (Stoilova et al., 2020; Vanden Abeele, 2016). The social consequences of the mediatization of childhood, including the implications for children's agency (Livingstone, 2013; Mascheroni, 2020), are equally plural and diverse.

The online spaces for sociability, self-expression, youthful experimentation, play, and learning are, for the most part, commercially owned and driven by the business logic of data capitalism. Now, more than ever, children's identities, interactions, and cultures are implicated with and defined by "data relations" (Couldry & Mejias, 2019; see also Chapters 2 and 8, this book): they are increasingly dependent on the same technologies that enable the extraction of data from the flow of everyday life practices and identities, and their conversion into profitable resources for data capitalism. While providing material support for relational maintenance and identity creation, commercial platforms extend the logic of datafication into the "once-private processes of identity, personal relationships" and peer cultures (Livingstone & Sefton-Green, 2016, p. 7). However, children are not merely "objects of data (about whom data is produced)" (Ruppert, Isin, & Bigo, 2017, p. 3). Narrowing the focus on the commodification of childhood and the political economy of children's data runs the risk of underplaying the contribution of the everyday practices of children themselves (see also Chapter 3):

> Indeed, a closer examination of children's internet culture reveals counter processes that qualify grand claims about childhood engulfed by increasing commercialization and globalization—the embedded nature of local meanings, the agency and creativity of children's activities and meaning-making online and offline ... (Livingstone, 2013, p. 117)

Therefore, and as already outlined in Chapter 2, while this book aims to provide a critique of the normalization of data relations in children's lives, we adopt a non-media-centric yet child-centered approach that, in line with the developments in the sociology of childhood, recognizes children as active agents and interpreters of their own social worlds. Children's interpretive agency is at the core of the notion of "interpretive reproduction," a notion developed by William Corsaro (2017) to emphasize the double articulation of socialization as both a top-down and bottom-up practice, in which children participate not only by imitating adults and internalizing culture, but also by making sense of, reproducing, and reinventing it from below (James, 2013). More specifically, interpretive reproduction is "made up of three types of collective action: (1) children's creative appropriation of information and knowledge from the adults' world; (2) children's production and participation in a series of peer cultures; and (3) children's contribution to the reproduction and extension of the adult culture" (Corsaro, 2017, p. 44). Children simultaneously participate in two cultures—the adults' and their own—that emerge from their socially shared and creative interiorization of the world of adults.

Children's own contribution to the socialization process is made more prominent in the context of the current deep mediatization (Couldry & Hepp, 2017), when the traditional socialization agencies (the family, the school,

religion, etc.) seem to be complemented, if not displaced, by informal socialization within peer networks and online communicative contexts. In fact, not
only have digital media permeated all contexts of socialization—including
the home, the school, and the peer network—but they are also themselves a
context of socialization (Paus-Hasebrink, 2019). Looking at children's engagement with digital and mobile media through the lens of peer cultures—and
the agentic capacities of children in the process of socialization—helps us to
avoid media panics, stereotypes, and one-sided accounts of the experiences
and meanings of datafication in their everyday lives.

The "Always On" Peer Network, Algorithmic Friendship, and Automated Peer Pressures

The most evident change in children's lives associated with the widespread
adoption of smartphones and social media has been identified in the enhanced
connectedness with peers facilitated by such devices, platforms, and apps.
Mobile communication in particular is known to provide a sense of "full-time
intimate sphere" (Ling, 2008) by creating an "anywhere, anytime" communicative bubble: namely, mobile phones and later, smartphones, have been
used to fill in the gaps between one face-to-face encounter and the next, and
to "extend the interaction beyond the period of co-presence" (Ling, 2008,
p. 128). Such an unprecedented opportunity for children to keep in touch
with their peers has raised concerns for the potential withdrawal from co-
present interaction and social isolation, addiction to screens, etc. However,
contrary to media panics around mobile communication and SNSs as potentially disrupting and replacing co-present interactions, the expanded and privatized communication repertoire that these tools facilitate compensate for
children's limited mobility (in the evenings, for example; see Livingstone &
Sefton-Green, 2016). Another recurrent concern is that children's engagement in online communication would move them away from face-to-face or
mediated interactions with strong ties towards superficial ties with "strangers"—the "displacement-reduction hypotheses" (Mesch, 2013; Valkenburg &
Peter, 2009). However, empirical research has confirmed that children's pre-
existing social ties are mirrored in their online contacts (Livingstone, 2008;
Livingstone & Sefton-Green, 2016): children mainly use their smartphones
and social media to keep in touch with their offline social relations. When
children expand their social circles and form new friendships online, they

mainly do so either to compensate for emotional difficulties and a lack of social interactions offline,[1] or to diversify their social circles beyond the constraints of their local contexts (Mesch, 2013). The extended social access to peers enabled by online and mobile communication represents an opportunity to strengthen friendship ties and is especially valued when face-to-face contacts with peers are reduced, such as during the recent lockdowns implemented to contain the COVID-19 pandemic. For scholars studying a peer group's sociability online and offline, it comes as no surprise that children's experiences during the pandemic have revealed a renewed appreciation for face-to-face interactions, which cannot be fully replaced by mediated proximity. A teenage girl interviewed by *The Guardian* about her own experience of a year at home as a result of the pandemic commented:

> I was barely ever home before. I'd go out with my friends and get back late. The age that I'm at, you just want to be with your friends. We'd hang out down the beach, or in the park or something. It's changed a lot. It's a bit like going back to being a child. I haven't seen anyone for ages . . . We do talk a lot though over social media— Instagram, Snapchat. It's brought us together in that way, but honestly, I just miss actually going out and seeing everyone. (quoted in Godwin, 2021)

In fact, social media platforms and other messaging apps provide the opportunity to hang out with friends (boyd, 2014) and to keep in touch when meeting face-to-face is neither possible nor safe. In terms of its beneficial outcomes for children, this "always on" mode of interaction with peers has been viewed through the lens of the "emancipation approach" (Ling, 2004), which argues that private, unsupervised, and potentially full-time access to a peer group by means of smartphones accelerates children's emancipation from the family sphere (Ling, 2004; Vanden Abeele, 2016). However, scholars have also highlighted the negative consequences of the 24/7 communicative bubble on children's wellbeing, observing how expectations of reciprocal accessibility turn into a source of tension and anxiety for fear of missing out (FOMO) and failing obligations to reciprocate in nearly real time (Bond, 2014; Ling, 2012; Mascheroni & Vincent, 2016).

Indeed, the almost perpetual contact (Katz & Aakhus, 2002) with a peer group is not without costs; rather, it pushes the naturalization of data relations in the context of peer networks even further. In fact, the enhanced connectedness supported by social media platforms and smartphone apps is perfectly aligned with the ideology of connection (Couldry & Mejias, 2019; see also Chapter 2, this book) that sustains data capitalism and presents mediated connections as the natural form of social ties. Only if we contextualize the mediatized peer network against the backdrop of the commercially driven "*requirement* to connect here and now—connect to *this particular* deeply unequal infrastructure" (Couldry & Mejias, 2019, p.16, original emphasis), and in relation to the social legitimation of "social mediation technologies" (Ling, 2012), can we move beyond individual frameworks of pathological use in explaining children's online communication practices—in particular, of their problematic aspects such as stress and fear of being "out of the loop," excessive screen time, pressures to gain popularity by conforming to sexualized stereotypes, and so on. In fact, the social media logic (van Dijck & Poell, 2013) has at its core the technologization of sociality: spontaneous, informal interactions such as conversations among peers are coded and formalized in order for algorithms to read and manipulate them. That is, social connectedness is turned into datafied connectivity and becomes measurable, programmable, and eventually, monetizable.

The engineering of sociality (van Dijck, 2013) through automated scripts and codes—aimed at maximizing users' social interactions by turning them into profitable resources of data—introduces a discrepancy between people's experience and notion of friendship versus platforms' "computable friendships" (Bucher, 2018). Friendship ceases to be merely a relation between two or more individuals, becoming a relation between individuals and a set of algorithms and technological infrastructures. The algorithms and interfaces of social media platforms design particular templates of friendship, and trigger and steer users' social interactions by recommending, expanding, or encouraging certain practices. Facebook friends are the outcome of a process of algorithmic classification: they are "made-up people" (Bucher, 2018), that is, social contacts classified as "friends" on the basis of standard quantifiable measures such as reputation, social impact, latest interaction, frequency of interaction, mode of interaction (whether in private messages or on the wall), and so on. As Bucher explains, "computable friendships hinge on measuring and evaluating users in order to be able to determine their friendship status" (2018, p. 11). The new algorithmic classification of friendship ties responds to a business goal, that is, to stick users on the platform and provide them with a pleasant experience they would be more likely to repeat over time: "Facebook 'wants' friendships to happen in order to increase engagement with the social network, ultimately serving revenue purposes" (Bucher, 2018, p. 11).

Children's desire for being connected with their peer group irrespective of adults' regulations and limited mobility converges and is soldered with the business logic of social media and its technological infrastructures. In this way, the algorithms and interfaces that engineer online sociality strengthen and enhance the social norms that base the maintenance of a peer group on the reciprocal full-time accessibility of its members. The incorporation of smartphones and social media into the peer group's communication repertoire facilitated the social legitimation of the norms governing reciprocal social availability: "data relations" (Couldry & Hepp, 2019) became normalized, taken for granted, and even normative, regulating behavior and reciprocal expectations (Ling, 2012). Analyzing how the normative mobile maintenance expectations (Hall & Baym, 2011) are played out in relation to WhatsApp provides a vivid example of the meanings and emotions through which children navigate the tensions between the affordances of smartphone apps—namely, the potential "perpetual contact" that keeps children tethered to the app—converging peer pressures and, at the opposite side, the expectations of the adults' world. Especially since the app introduced check marks to notify reception and reading of messages, children have expressed anxiety and fear of missing out (FOMO) (Mascheroni & Vincent, 2016). Distress and practices such as checking their phone frequently, even when not appropriate—for example, at school, during family meals, or when out with friends—are commonly interpreted through a medical framework as symptoms of "addiction." However, the full-time access to peers enabled by the communicative affordances[2] of smartphones, platforms, and apps does not drive and determine children's behavior on its own; rather, it is through the incorporation and naturalization of communicative affordances within peer cultures that it acquires a normative character and is turned into the obligation to always be contactable (Mascheroni & Vincent, 2016). As one of us argued in an earlier publication, "addiction and social accessibility are two sides of the same coin ... Instead of being passive victims of addictive technologies, young people are navigating their way through the conflicting demands of peer pressures, adults' regulation, and communicative affordances" (Mascheroni, 2018, p. 132).

The same interplay between the business-driven algorithmic shaping of users' practices and the social norms governing peer networks can be observed in relation to the social media logic of popularity (van Dijck & Poell, 2013) and the new regimes of algorithmic visibility (Bucher, 2018). Visibility on Facebook, as much as on other social media, comes to be constructed as a reward for high rates of engagement on the platform and as a direct outcome of popularity: "being popular enhances the probability of becoming visible, thus increasing the probability of generating even more interaction" (Bucher, 2018, p. 89), augmenting the platform's stickiness. An individual's popularity, and hence visibility, is achieved through the user's conformity with, and exploitation of, a platform's metrics that quantify and influence popularity. While this is mainly achieved through self-presentations, as we will explore in the next section, friendship ties are also used as a metric for a user's own popularity. When children form hundreds or even thousands of connections on social media, they do so in a concerted effort to construct a successful persona (Livingstone & Sefton-Green, 2016): having a thousand "friends" is a symbolic token that signals a manifest popularity. However, children are aware of the discrepancy between strong friendship ties—usually a dozen or so (Livingstone & Sefton-Green, 2016)—and "computable friends" with whom they may hang out online, but who are often just a marker of identity.

YouTubers and Influencers in Children's Identity Projects

Online, as much as offline, identity is constructed through claims about yourself, your friends, and your tastes and consumption—what music, movies, and clothes you like or dislike. Since online platforms are centered round displaying and sharing connections and media content, they seem perfectly suited to the task of presenting and performing identity on the internet. However, we should not forget that social media constitute coded spaces of identity:

> The generic template structure of Facebook's user profiles provides not so much a space for specific individuals but a space that makes the structured organization of individual's data easier and more manageable. (Bucher, 2018, p. 85)

For children, creating identities through relations with people and content on social media potentially means being exposed to a more diverse pool of role models for imitation and identification, and a wider repertoire of symbolic resources to be acted on in their project of the self. For example, girls have been found to use online platforms as identity spaces where they engage in playful experimentations of their gender and sexual identities (Bosch, 2011) and express their resistance to hegemonic models of femininity (Mazzarella, 2010). Similarly, Siibak's (2010) analysis of boys' visual self-representation practices has shown how, in their profile pictures, they also engage in experimenting with different models of masculinity. However, the opportunities to encounter a plurality of identity templates is actually narrowed down by the mechanisms of algorithmic visibility and popularity that promote and emphasize the content that receives more likes. In practice, then, children end up being socialized online to the same stereotyped cultural conventions regulating gendered self-presentation that they encounter in media industries, advertisements, as well as in offline contexts. More specifically, the dominant visual codes of femininity on social media align with the post-feminist model of sexually attractive and active young women (Siibak & Hernwall, 2011). Research based on qualitative interviews and focus groups with 9- to-16-year-old children highlighted the tensions arising from contrasting discourses of social desirability, whereby the hyper-sexualized female model represented in advertising and media industries conflicts with the sexual double standard of the peer network (Mascheroni, Vincent, & Jimenez, 2015). Girls adapt to conformist expectations on the appropriate female model by playfully engaging with the hyper-sexualized codes of visual self-representation on their Instagram and Facebook profiles. They do so in an attempt to conform to the beauty standards promoted through consumer and celebrity culture, and to achieve popularity—in its double meaning of algorithmic visibility and social acceptance, both measured and validated through a high number of likes. However, the pressures of algorithmic visibility and the codes of impression management on social media often contrast with the peer-driven moral discourse on sexy pictures: boys often blame girls in their peer group for "posing sexy" as a way to increment their online popularity, to the detriment of their offline reputation. Therefore, pushed by their desire for social validation, girls learn how to navigate these contrasting social expectations and moral standards—being sexually attractive versus being "a good girl" (Mascheroni et al., 2015). Similarly, a survey of Estonian 11- to 18-year-old students (N = 713) has shown how their visual impression management on SNSs varies according to the expectations of the reference group (Siibak, 2009). Children and young people construct and reconstruct their profile images based on the values associated with "the ideal self"—that, in the case of girls, is "built upon the self-beliefs, norms and values that are associated with the traditional female gender role" (Siibak, 2009)—or "the ought self"—conformity to the peer group's expectations through the strategic incorporation of features such as beauty, sexiness, and the "right" clothes that are believed to be conducive to online popularity (Siibak, 2009).

While the mechanisms of automated popularity favor the visibility of hegemonic representations of (gendered, sexual, ethnic) identities, the range of discourses and identity models that children can explore on social media is nonetheless more diverse than in mainstream media. And this not because of the unprecedented access to celebrity culture and consumer culture that social media as identity spaces offer. Rather, new identity models are being provided by microcelebrities whom children engage with on platforms such as YouTube and Instagram. Microcelebrity (Marwick & boyd, 2011) refers to the bottom-up practice of constructing a public persona to be consumed by others and managing popularity through constant engagement with followers—who are perceived and treated as fans. Similarly to celebrities, microcelebrities equally attempt to establish and maintain a sense of affiliation with their fans—that is, they strategically perform a connection with their audiences through language and other symbolic codes and conventions in order to create a sense of proximity and intimacy with their followers (Marwick & boyd, 2011). In a word, they construct and trigger a sense of "mediated intimacy at a distance" (Thompson, 1995, p. 219) through which their fan base is encouraged to feel that they intimately know them, and that they can relate to influencers or YouTubers as close friends. The feeling of "mediated intimacy at a distance" is not peculiar to microcelebrities and social media; Thompson theorizes a non-reciprocal intimacy between TV audiences and actors or TV presenters. However, there are some important differences in the performance of celebrity on social media and the relations it generates. First, microcelebrities perform their public identities under the structural conditions of social media, with its algorithmic measurement and manipulation of popularity (van Dijck & Poell, 2013). Indeed, influencers and YouTubers are formerly non-famous individuals who have fruitfully exploited the metrics of influence by performing acts of self-promotion (van Dijck, 2013) and monetizing their own popularity. The monetization of influence through the same metrics that measure the number of followers or viewers means that microcelebrities depend on the engagement of their audiences in order to achieve an economic remuneration for their self-branding performances. The strategic pursuit of intimate and affective relations with their audiences is not dissimilar to the self-branding techniques employed by traditional celebrities: in fact, microcelebrities generate substantial revenues by branding themselves as authentic and intimate (Abidin, 2015). Moreover, even if microcelebrities generate an impression of immediate accessibility through constant engagement with their fans, the resulting bonds of "intimacy at a distance" are still constitutively asymmetrical: while apparently democratic, microcelebrity is just the star system of connected media (van Dijck, 2013; van Dijck & Poell, 2013). In the most recent configuration of the star system, then, the boundaries between traditional celebrities and microcelebrities are actually blurred, even though children perceive YouTubers and influencers as being closer to them—their lives and their problems—contrary to the inaccessible celebrities from the movie industry and TV (Balleys et al., 2020; Marôpo, Jorge, & Tomaz, 2020).

What children and teenagers appreciate most of microcelebrities is this enhanced sense of proximity and authenticity, although authenticity is "staged" to generate the impression of an informal conversation among peers. In relation to the performance of authenticity through a non-professional, amateur style, Crystal Abidin (2017) talks about "calibrated amateurism," a practice and aesthetics crafted to simulate the aesthetics of an amateur with the intent to "give the impression of spontaneity and unfilteredness despite the contrary reality" (Abidin, 2017, p. 1). Through direct solicitation of their viewers, intimate confessional declarations, an informal and amateur communication style, personalized responses to followers' comments and questions, and emphasis on their ordinariness, microcelebrities make children "feel like active participants" in their lives (Marôpo et al., 2020, p. 33). Moreover, young YouTubers and influencers provide identity models children can identify with and imitate, based on the perceived proximity between the concerns and experiences represented in these microcelebrity performances and their own problems and experiences. Beyond a stronger sense of connection and intimacy, following young microcelebrities on social media platforms also provides children with the opportunity to interact with other followers. Although these interactions with peers with whom they share an interest in certain microcelebrities may not result in new friendship ties, they still provide important symbolic resources that are incorporated into the ongoing project of the self (Balleys et al., 2020). However, children's engagement with microcelebrities varies in intensity and meaning: Murumaa-Mengel and Siibak (2020) distinguish between fans, followers, and anti-fans. Fans are the followers who invest heavily in the subcultures surrounding a microcelebrity as part of their identity project—for example, they are eager to internalize the labels that microcelebrities append onto their fan communities: "the YouTuber Logan Paul's fans make up the 'Logang,' Tessa Brooks has the 'Brookters,' KSI's followers form the 'KSI army' and, an Estonian example from our studies, the popular YouTuber Istoprocent's fans have taken on the collective label of '#teamisto'" (Murumaa-Mengel & Siibak, 2020, p. 234). Anti-fans equally turn their relationship with a celebrity into an identity marker, yet they do so to communicate their distinction from the community of fans and what the microcelebrity represents (Murumaa-Mengel & Siibak, 2020). Followers are regularly keeping up with the microcelebrity's life, but do not include this as a central component of their own identity-making practices.

Successful microcelebrities as young as pre-teens (Marôpo et al., 2020, p. 33), and even toddlers (Abidin, 2020), also inspire children to take up vlogging and unboxing themselves, thus incorporating the practice of microcelebrity in their own project of the self. The highest paid YouTuber in 2020, and for the third consecutive year, was Ryan, a now nine-year-old boy who started his Ryan's World channel[3] back in 2015, and who earned nearly US$30 million from "unboxing" and reviewing games and toys. Indeed, unboxing—the unwrapping of toys from their boxes, and their later construction and play—is highly popular with younger children (Marsh, 2016), many of whom also engage in "unboxing" themselves. Analysis of less popular and non-professional unboxing channels (Nicoll & Nansen, 2018) revealed that the majority of unboxers were primary school-aged. The study frames children's engagement with the unboxing and toy assembling genre as a form of "mimetic participation" (Nicoll & Nansen, 2018) characterized by mutual shaping and reciprocal influences: non-professional unboxers imitate the codes of professional video production and self-branding, while most popular unboxers try to professionally re-enact the amateur and vernacular aspect of their imitators, through a form of "calibrated authenticity" (Abidin, 2017). However, despite the rhetoric of participation and transparency that dominates social media (van Dijck, 2013) and encourages users' participation by representing other social media users as content producers (Bucher, 2018), the path towards popularity and profit is not available to many—indeed, the rhetoric of participation serves the interests of data capitalism by encouraging users to disclose as much as possible of their personal lives as profitable resources for corporations. Therefore, although many children engage in aspirational work (Duffy, 2017), and some even base their self-projects on pursuing a career as a full-time microcelebrity, only a few children succeed. However, the inspiration they get from YouTube stars is seen as beneficial in terms of the acquisition of digital literacy—not only content creation skills, but also critical skills—namely, the awareness of sponsored content and the "affective literacy" (Nicoll & Nansen, 2018) related to the manufacturing of intimacy and affinity through staged authenticity.

The incorporation of children's creativity and of the unboxing peer culture into the entertainment industry and the social media star system has also raised numerous concerns. First, thinking of the young audiences of young

YouTubers' videos, it has been noted how the algorithmic selection and organization of content on YouTube traps children into an endless loop of repetitive content (Lafrance, 2017), thus creating "addiction" and exposure to a hyper-commodification of the self (Smith & Shade, 2018). Moreover, the commercial exploitation of microcelebrity children has become a matter of public concern after some parents have been charged of committing abuses on their children to force them into performing in videos (Durkin, 2019) or of profiting from their children's emotional distress to make pranks (Levin, 2017). While these are extreme cases, child microcelebrities can nonetheless be interpreted through the lens of child labor, and the associated ethical and privacy concerns (Abidin, 2015, 2020; Leaver, 2020).

Constructing children's biographies as commodities to be virally consumed on YouTube can be exploitative as children are represented with the intention of cultivating an audience and, therefore, maximizing revenues: indeed "social-media-famous children [are children] whose public visibility in digital space is not only intentionally prolific but deliberately commercial" (Abidin, 2020, p.226). However, the commercial exploitation of children by their parents varies in intensity, as the children's own engagement and representation in these popular YouTube genres differs. Abidin identifies three different types of child microcelebrity. First, there are children in family influencer units who are exposed as part of the parents' productions (Abidin, 2017; see also Chapter 4, this book); then there are the micro-microcelebrities, children born to already famous microcelebrities who derive their visibility and fame from their influencer mothers and who are raised to become commodities (Abidin, 2015); and finally, there are children who stumble into popularity by accident and who are later cultivated into microcelebrity by their parent managers (Abidin, 2020). The relationships between children and their parents implied by these microcelebrity assemblages are asymmetrical, even when there is no intentional monetization of children's lives. Indeed, as Leaver points out, younger children, including babies, toddlers, and pre-schoolers, have no "self-representational agency" (Leaver, 2017, p. 2). This is also documented by a recent survey of a nationally representative sample of 1000 Italian parents of children aged eight and younger, collected in September 2020 as part of the DataChildFutures project by one of the authors (see also Chapter 5, this book), which shows that children's representational agency in parents' sharenting practices is limited: parents are generally not used to asking for their children's permission before posting pictures or videos of them online, mostly because they think their child is too young to be involved in such decisions (see Mascheroni et al., 2021; on sharenting, see also Chapter 4, this book).

To conclude, while children's engagement in producing their own content on YouTube or Instagram is an opportunity in terms of self-expression, learning, and interactions, it is a form of commercial exploitation, whether consciously orchestrated by their parents, as in the case of microcelebrity children, or engineered by the platform logic of popularity. The relationship between children, their parents, and the social media platforms can thus be defined as a form of "playbor" (Archer, 2019)—a portmanteau of play and labor—which indicates the commercial exploitation of creativity, play, and relations of care under the regimes of data colonialism (Couldry & Mejias, 2019).

Mediatized Play, Between Creativity and Datafication

Although adults often overlook, trivialize, or struggle to understand play, play not only constitutes a central part of children's everyday lives; it also provides them with significant opportunities for socialization, socio-emotional development, learning, self-expression, health, and wellbeing (Cowan, 2020). If the relation between play, child's development, and learning has been at the heart of pedagogy—of early childhood education in particular—the relationship between play and peer culture has also been explored, especially within the new sociology of childhood, interested in recognizing children's agency and theorizing the process of socialization as co-participated by children. Indeed, play is a key site for interpretive reproduction (Corsaro, 2017), the process through which children learn about the social world while making their own social world. In this light, play—not understood as a set of discrete activities, but rather, as a playful disposition towards life—is simultaneously shaped by culture and generative of (peer) culture, a universal feature of children's lives (Corsaro, 1993), as well as a socially and culturally situated enactment. In her literature review on play, Cowan (2020) also emphasizes how children's inability to play threatens their health, wellbeing, and development. Since these are fundamental rights for children, we can conclude that play itself is a right: "the right to play essentially reflects the child's right to be a child" (Cowan, 2020, p. 28). Play as a right has been formally recognized under Article 31 of the United Nations' Convention on the Rights of the

Child. General Comment 17, Article 31, further clarifies the dimensions that constitute play as a right:

> Play and recreation are important to children's health and wellbeing. They promote the development of creativity, imagination, self-confidence, self-efficacy and physical, cognitive and emotional strength and skills. They are also a form of participation in everyday life, and are of intrinsic value to the child, purely in terms of the enjoyment and pleasure they afford. (UN, 2013, p. 2)

Yet, the recognition of play as a children's right has been absent from the debate around children's digital play. This is not surprising since, as happened with the technologization of children's learning, sociality, and identity, the mediatization of play has equally been the focus of both hopes and anxieties around the role of technologies in children's development as well as, ultimately, childhood itself. While assuming the unequivocal yet generalizable effects of digital play, these opposite positions converge in the idea that digital play has marked a fundamental shift in the nature, practice, meaning, and outcomes of play for children. In so doing, they implicitly endorse a position of technological determinism, whereby it is technology that determines social change—in this case, digital games and toys are assumed to enhance or, at the opposite end, corrupt and threaten children's play. As outlined in Chapter 2, and throughout this book, we have distanced ourselves from a media-centric explanation of the changes in children's lives to focus on how changing media and changing childhood co-determine each other in situated contexts and practices. However, in what follows we will review the main loci of attention around which the debate is polarized, first, because we will contrast these ideological claims against empirical evidence; and second, because these discourses actually shape social imaginaries and the very design of digital play artifacts and spaces. As Grimes writes in relation to gaming websites such as Club Penguin (Disney) and BarbieGirls (Mattel),

> ... children's virtual worlds are fundamentally negotiated spaces in which broader aspirations and anxieties about children's relationships with play, technology, consumer culture, and the public sphere resurface as 'configurations' of an imagined, ideal child player. (Grimes, 2015, p. 127)

Research on children's digital play—now encompassing not only gaming websites and videogames, but also a variety of mobile and social media apps, and the Internet of Toys (IoToys)[4] (Mascheroni & Holloway, 2019)—agrees that central to contemporary play practices is their increasing complexity.

This complexity has often been addressed through the notion of "connected play" (Marsh, 2017) to suggest the new relationships between traditional play and digital play or between children and play objects, and the social connections that children make through this play (Marsh, 2017). In other words, connected play emphasizes the multimodal practices that crisscross the boundaries between digital and non-digital domains and make connections across various axes: online/offline, material/immaterial, physical materiality/ digital materiality, private/public, global/local, owned/non-owned, self-/other-controlled (Marsh, 2017).

One of the main criticisms directed at digital play points to a narrowing down of children's creativity as opposed to children's free play.[5] The argument is that, by providing and prescribing a set of pre-programmed activities and finite options, digital play promotes a highly normative experience of play that actually embodies adults' visions of play and of what an appropriate online space for children should be. For example, in her analysis of commercial virtual worlds for children, Grimes reveals how the interfaces and architecture of such spaces embody a narrow, homogenous consumerist ideal of the child player, in which "children's requirements as players are configured as few and finite, effectively met through the provision of a handful of highly generic options" (2015, p. 136). In prior work on this topic (Berriman & Mascheroni, 2019), we have also examined how the affordances of smart "care toys" like the Tamagotchi and Furby are actually enacted by children in their play practices. Drawing on science and technology studies (STS) approaches to affordances as situated and relational, we have highlighted how "care toys" share some affordances of traditional toys—in the way they invite imaginative play, practices of care, and affection—but also remediated traditional play through a new set of affordances that lead to a shift in the child–toy interaction insofar as specific play practices are now "demanded" rather than "requested" (Davis & Chouinard, 2016)[6] in children's interactions. Such affordances "bear closer resemblance to mobile media (portability, affective stickiness) and robot technologies (liveliness)" (Berriman & Mascheroni, 2019, p. 810). While the new augmented affordances of digital play reconfigure the parameters of children's agency in relation to their toys, affordances are always relationally enacted and actualized, and smart toys never fully pre-determine children's play. Even smart toys' more pressing demands—such as Furby's insisting solicitation through various sounds to impose constant attention on users—remain only potential if they are not taken up by children. So, affordances "take shape only through interaction, but resisting and rebuffing such demands implies ending, at least temporarily, the interaction" (Berriman & Mascheroni, 2019, p. 807).

Despite the apparently more constraining nature of digital play, research has documented its numerous opportunities for learning and creativity. Having conducted a survey of 2000 parents of children aged five and under, and ethnographic case studies in six families in the UK, Marsh and colleagues (2018) examined how mobile apps contributed to children's play and creativity. The findings showed that play with the tablet is fully integrated into children's everyday play practices, and it enables a wide range of play types, including symbolic, communication, deep, exploratory, imaginative, mastery, and object play. They also identify the experience of linking digital and non-digital, online, and offline domains—such as when playing with app-enabled soft toys and robots—as a salient feature of children's home use of apps, and one that promotes imaginative play in particular. Apps also fostered children's creativity—especially in the creation of visual content and texts—and playful communication with family members and friends. Based on analysis of qualitative data and of the apps, the authors concluded that all three areas of creative thinking (exploration, involvement, and enjoyment) were cultivated in apps-enabled play activities (Marsh et al., 2018). Among the opportunities of digital play, child–toy interaction on a one-to-one basis has also been recognized as beneficial for children's learning and cognitive development, and social robotic toys in particular—that is, robots that mimic the affective dimensions of human interactions (Zhao, 2006)—can minimize children's embarrassment in learning a foreign language, thus promoting the acquisition of foreign language skills (Brunick et al., 2016). Beyond specific learning outcomes such as literacy and language skills, the introduction of social robots in preschool settings has been associated with various physical, cognitive, and social-emotional learning experiences for children (Crompton, Gregory, & Burke, 2018). A longitudinal study on computer assisted learning has also shown that when children were interacting with a social robot, rather than a purely computer-based system, the human-like interaction with the robot fostered a more positive learning mindset in children (Davison et al., 2021). Moreover, instead of replacing offline playful activities, research has shown how children's "digital activities support their 'offline' interests" as children use digital media as an expansion and enhancement of their activities (Chaudron et al., 2015, p. 16). The findings of Siibak and Nevski's (2019) ethnographic case study of two sisters—four-year-old Lily and two-year-old Mia—equally reveal the integration of digital and non-digital media in the young girls' play. For example, their "joint book-reading sessions often turned into mixed-media experiences" (Siibak & Nevski, 2019, p. 129), with the girls searching for Frozen clips on YouTube, playing them on TV and dancing and singing before resuming reading.

In addition to the perceived detrimental effect on children's creativity and free play, digital play is also associated with further limitations, namely, commodification and datafication. Indeed, "digital playgrounds" (Grimes, 2018) have been blamed for pushing children's commodification further, immersing children in an advertising and hyper-branded environment. In fact, the most popular commercial virtual worlds designed for children incorporate branded content and configure child players first and foremost as consumers (Grimes, 2015). The more recent extension of commercialized digital playgrounds (Smith & Shade, 2018), to include social media apps, mobile apps, and internet-connected toys (IoToys), has further amplified the commodification of children's play: children's personal and play data are now turned into profitable commodities, exchanged with third parties and used for personalized advertising hidden in the form of the toy–child relationship. Indeed, "the implications of advertising, based on data and information collected from children's use of digital playgrounds, remain a major consideration" (Smith & Shade, 2018, p. 9), and have been at the core of some scandals involving the IoToys. For example, the campaign launched by the Norwegian Consumer Council in November 2016 against two toys manufactured by Genesis Toys— the talking doll My Friend Cayla and the i-Que Intelligent Robot—exposed not only their security and safety failures, but also their violation of consumer laws through hidden advertising, in the form of sponsored brands and products included in the scripted interactions (Mascheroni & Holloway, 2017; see also Chapter 5, this book). Beyond opaque, or even deceitful, Terms and Conditions—which place the burden of managing children's privacy on parents and "make clear that the parent typically acts as the *data proxy* for their child" (Smith & Shade, 2018, p. 8)—that are common to other Internet of Things (IoTs) that populate the domestic environment (see Chapter 5, this book), the IoToys poses peculiar safety and security vulnerabilities (Chaudron et al., 2019), also due to the fact that most toy manufacturers have just entered the market of digital products.

The datafication of children's play is particularly problematic due to the great beneficial outcomes of play for children, as explained above. Indeed, datafication challenges not only children's right to privacy, protection, and provision of appropriate, safe and private-by-design online spaces; the commodification of children's play also threatens children's right to participation, learning, and social relations. The recent restrictive measures adopted by many countries facing the COVID-19 pandemic provide further evidence of play as a central component, and as a fundamental right of children's lives. With COVID-19 restrictions impacting heavily on children's lives, including learning, sociality, and the very experience of play, many children have turned to forms of digital play not only to compensate for lack of outdoor physical play, but also for lack of social play with peers—this is especially true of single-child families. Indeed, *The Guardian* article on children's experiences of a year at home (Godwin, 2021) include the account of Luis, a 17-year-old boy from London, who describes the disruption of daily routines and points to playing video games with his friends as a coping strategy to deal with the uncertainties and extra-ordinariness of the situation:

> When the first lockdown started I didn't really mind, to be honest. I'm at home. My friends are at home. We're all on PS4 together having fun. We'd play Fifa until about three in the morning and then we'd jump on Monopoly and it would get hectic. That's when Disney + was really hyped up, too. I watched all the Star Wars movies, all the Marvel again. Then there was Netflix on top of that.

Luis's experience is not dissimilar to that of many teenagers and children worldwide, who went online to keep in touch, play games, and even watch movies[7] with their friends; as often remarked throughout this book, the pandemic has deepened our implication in "data relations" (Couldry & Mejias, 2019) to sustain social relations, play, and entertainment.

A deeper investigation of the meaning and nature of digital play during the recent periods of lockdown has just begun. In the special issue of the *Journal of Children and Media* dedicated to COVID-19, Navarro (2021) recounts how during lockdown she eventually relented and let her son join his friends on Fortnite. Her son's experience of an "online sleepover"—during which his group "adopted" a younger solitary player—inspired her reflections on the inextricable relationship between game play and peer interaction, and its relevant role in children's development. "Given the current pandemic and that our children and adolescents are spending increasing amounts of time socializing and playing in digital spaces"—Navarro concludes—"research on the role of gaming is central in understanding development of this generation" (2021, p. 15). Yet, what is already clear is that, while we are all affected by datafication, those who are more exposed to its detrimental consequences are also less likely to benefit from the opportunities of datafied practices (see also Chapter 8, this book). Indeed, in a roundtable on the future of play organized by the 5Rights Foundation, Professor Phoenix pointed out,

> Those children who are technology-rich have had many more opportunities for social play as they Zoom or Skype with their friends. This contrasts with the experience of those who live in technological poverty, and those who do not see themselves represented in games and online, [who will] have a different emotional resonance from those who take inclusion for granted. (quoted in Mik, 2021)

In the digital and mediatized world, issues of privacy, commodification, and inequalities need a solid response, to avoid compromising children's right to play and turning it into a form of "playbor" (Archer, 2019).

Notes

1 Indeed, according to the "social compensation hypothesis" (see Mesch, 2013), introverts feel more comfortable in online self-disclosure and forming ties on the internet. However, evidence in support of this hypothesis is mixed, and other studies have shown that those who struggle to develop and maintain friendships offline also struggle to form online networks of support (Livingstone & Sefton-Green, 2016).

2 The notion of affordances is a contested one, especially due to its overuse and misuse as a synonym of functionalities. Here, we refer to the original concept of affordances as both functional and relational—that is, enabling or hindering agency depending on context and social norms (Hutchby, 2014). Therefore, we define communicative affordances as socially constructed opportunities for agency and communication that are technologically enabled but also, and fundamentally, socially legitimized (Mascheroni & Vincent, 2016).

3 Formerly Ryan's ToysReview. His popularity has been enormous since the start of the channel. Indeed, "Kaji's most popular video, Huge Eggs Surprise Toys Challenge [dated April 2016], has more than 2bn views, making it one of the 60 most-viewed videos ever on YouTube" (Neate, 2020).

4 The Internet of Toys (IoToys) comprises a set of software-enabled toys that: (1) are connected to online platforms through Wi-Fi and Bluetooth, but also, potentially, to other toys; (2) are equipped with sensors; (3) are controlled and/or programmable via apps; and (4) relate one-on-one to children, including toys-to-life figurines connected to video games (actually the first example of connected toys); dolls or soft toys based on voice and/or image recognition (Hello Barbie and the like); app-enabled mechanical toys, such as drones, toy cars, and robots; puzzles and building games; and health-tracking toys or wearables (Holloway & Green, 2016; Mascheroni & Holloway, 2019).

5 For a definition of free play, see Cowan (2020).

6 The notion of digital toys as requesting, demanding, but also encouraging, discouraging, or refusing particular play practices refers to Davis and Chouinard's (2016) work that distinguishes two main mechanisms through which affordances guide users' engagement with the

artifact towards particular outcomes, with *demands* being the most prescriptive and binding, while *requests* leave more room for users' negotiations. The authors also identify the mechanisms—namely, *encourage, discourage, refuse*—through which affordances respond to users' negotiations of the possibilities for agency opened up by a particular object.

7 There are several platform-specific or multi-platform apps that enable distant viewers to watch a movie together: for example, the Teleparty app (formerly Netflixparty) has been extended to include Hulu, Disney + and HBO. By contrast, Watchgroup is a Disney + specific app for group watching.

References

Abidin, C. (2015). Micro-microcelebrity: Branding babies on the internet. *M/C Journal, 18*(5). https://doi.org/10.5204/mcj.1022

Abidin, C. (2017). #familygoals: Family influencers, calibrated amateurism, and justifying young digital labor. *Social Media + Society.* https://doi.org/10.1177/2056305117707191

Abidin, C. (2020). Pre-school stars on YouTube. Child micro-celebrities, commercially viable biographies, and interactions with technology. In L. Green, D. Holloway, K. Stevenson, T. Leaver, & L. Haddon (Eds.), *The Routledge companion to children and digital media* (pp. 226–234). Routledge.

Archer, K. (2019). Social media influencers, post-feminism and neoliberalism: How mumbloggers' "playbour" is reshaping public relations. *Public Relations Inquiry, 8*(2) 149–166. https://doi.org/10.1177/2046147X19846530

Balleys, C., Millerand, F., Thoër, C., & Duque, N. (2020). Searching for oneself on YouTube: Teenage peer socialization and social recognition processes. *Social Media + Society.* https://doi.org/10.1177/2056305120909474

Berriman, L., & Mascheroni, G. (2019). Exploring the affordances of smart toys and connected play in practice. *New Media & Society, 21*(4), 797–814. https://doi.org/10.1177/1461444818807119

Bond, E. (2014). *Childhood, mobile technologies and everyday experiences.* Palgrave Macmillan.

Bosch, T. (2011). Young women and 'technologies of the self': Social networking and sexualities. *Agenda, 25*(4), 75–86. https://doi.org/10.1080/10130950.2011.630579

boyd, D. (2014). *It's complicated: The social lives of networked teens.* Yale University Press.

Brunick, K. L., Putnam, M. M., McGarry, L. E., Richards, M. N., & Calvert, S. L. (2016). Children's future parasocial relationships with media characters: The age of intelligent characters. *Journal of Children and Media, 10*(2), 181–190. https://doi.org/10.1080/17482798.2015.1127839

Bucher, T. (2018). *If . . . then: Algorithmic power and politics.* Oxford University Press.

Buckingham, D. (2008). Introducing identity. In D. Buckingham (Ed.), *Youth, identity and digital media* (pp. 1–24). The MIT Press.

Chaudron, S., Beutel, M. E., Černikova, M., Donoso Navarette, V., Dreier, M., & Fletcher-Watson, B. (2015). *Young children (0–8) and digital technology. A qualitative exploratory study across seven countries.* Joint Research Centre. European Commission. http://publications. jrc.ec.europa.eu/repository/handle/JRC93239

Chaudron, S., Geneiatakis, D., Kounelis, I., & Di Gioia, R. (2019). Testing Internet of Toys designs to improve privacy and security. In G. Mascheroni & D. Holloway (Eds.), *The Internet of Toys: Practices, affordances and the political economy of children's smart play* (pp. 223–240). Palgrave.

Clark, L. S. (2013). *The parent app: Understanding families in the digital age.* Oxford University Press.

Corsaro, W. A. (1993). Interpretive reproduction in children's role play. *Childhood, 1*(2), 64–74. https://doi.org/10.1177/090756829300100202

Corsaro, W. A. (2017). *The sociology of childhood* (5th ed.). SAGE Publications Ltd.

Corsaro, W. A., & Eder, D. (1990). Children's peer cultures. *Annual Review of Sociology, 16*, 197–220. http://dx.doi.org/10.1146/annurev.so.16.080190.001213

Couldry, N., & Hepp, A. (2017). *The mediated construction of reality.* Polity.

Couldry, N., & Mejias, U. (2019). *The costs of connection: How data is colonizing human life and appropriating it for capitalism.* Stanford University Press.

Cowan, K. (2020). *A panorama of play—A literature review.* Digital Futures Commission. 5Rights Foundation. https://digitalfuturescommission.org.uk/wp-content/uploads/2020/10/A-Panorama-of-Play-A-Literature-Review.pdf

Crompton, H., Gregory, K., & Burke, D. (2018). Humanoid robots supporting children's learning in an early childhood setting. *British Journal of Educational Technology, 49*(5), 911–927. https://doi.org/10.1111/bjet.12654

Davis, J. L., & Chouinard, J. B. (2016). Theorizing affordances: From request to refuse. *Bulletin of Science, Technology & Society, 36*(4), 241–248. https://doi.org/10.1177/0270467617714944

Davison, D. P., Wijnen, F. M., Charisi, V., et al. (2021) Words of encouragement: How praise delivered by a social robot changes children's mindset for learning. *Journal of Multimodal User Interfaces, 15*, 61–76. https://doi.org/10.1007/s12193-020-00353-9

Duffy, B. E. (2017). *(Not) getting paid to do what you love: Gender, social media, and aspirational work.* Yale University Press.

Durkin, E. (2019). YouTube child stars allegedly abused and forced to perform by adoptive mother. *The Guardian*, March 20. www.theguardian.com/us-news/2019/mar/20/youtube-fantastic-adventures-machelle-hackney-arrested-abuse-adopted-children

Godwin, R. (2021). The lockdown generation: 16 young people on spending a year at home. *The Guardian*, March 7. www.theguardian.com/society/2021/mar/07/the-lockdown-generation-16-young-people-on-spending-a-year-at-home

Grimes, S. M. (2015). Configuring the child player. *Science, Technology, & Human Values, 40*(1), 126–148. https://doi.org/10.1177/0162243914550253

Grimes, S. M. (2018). Penguins, hype, and MMOGs for kids: A critical reexamination of the 2008 "boom" in children's virtual worlds development. *Games and Culture, 13*(6), 624–644. https://doi.org/10.1177/1555412016638755

Haddon, L., & Silverstone, R. (2000). Information and communication technologies and everyday life: Individual and social dimensions. In K. Ducatel, J. Webster, & W. Herrman (Eds.), *The Information Society in Europe: Work and life in an age of globalization* (pp. 233–258). Rowman & Littlefield.

Hall, J. A., & Baym, N. K. (2011). Calling and texting (too much): Mobile maintenance expectations (over) dependence, entrapment, and friendship satisfaction. *New Media & Society*, 14(2), 316–331. https://doi.org/10.1177/1461444811415047

Hamel, G. (2009). The Facebook generation vs. the Fortune 500. *The Wall Street Journal*, March 24. www.wsj.com/articles/BL-GHMB-59

Holloway, D., & Green, L. (2016). The Internet of Toys. *Communication Research and Practice*, 2(4), 506–519. https://doi.org/10.1080/22041451.2016.1266124

Hutchby, I. (2014). Communicative affordances and participation frameworks in mediated interaction. *Journal of Pragmatics*, 72, 86–89. https://doi.org/10.1016/j.pragma.2014.08.012

James, A. (2013). *Socialising children*. Palgrave Macmillan.

Katz, J. E., & Aakhus, M. (Eds.). (2002). *Perpetual contact: Mobile communication, private talk, public performance*. Cambridge University Press.

Lafrance, A. (2017). The algorithm that makes preschoolers obsessed with YouTube kids. *The Atlantic*, July 25. www.theatlantic.com/technology/archive/2017/07/what-youtube-reveals-about-the-toddler-mind/534765/

Leaver, T. (2017). Intimate surveillance: Normalizing parental monitoring and mediation of infants online. *Social Media + Society*. https://doi.org/10.1177/2056305117707192

Leaver, T. (2020). Balancing privacy: Sharenting, intimate surveillance and the right to be forgotten. In L. Green, D. Holloway, K. Stevenson, T. Leaver, & L. Haddon (Eds.), *The Routledge companion to children and digital media* (pp. 235–244). Routledge.

Levin, S. (2017). Couple who screamed at their kids in YouTube "prank" sentenced to probation. *The Guardian*, September 12. www.theguardian.com/us-news/2017/sep/12/youtube-parents-children-heather-mike-martin

Ling, R. (2004). *The mobile connection. The cell phone's impact on society*. Morgan Kaufmann.

Ling, R. (2008). *New tech, new ties. How mobile communication is reshaping social cohesion*. The MIT Press.

Ling, R. (2012). *Taken for grantedness. The embedding of mobile communication into society*. The MIT Press.

Livingstone, S. (2008). Taking risky opportunities in youthful content creation: Teenagers' use of social networking sites for intimacy, privacy and self-expression. *New Media & Society*, 10(3), 393–411. https://doi.org/10.1177/1461444808089415

Livingstone, S. (2009). *Children and the internet*. Polity.

Livingstone, S. (2013). Children's internet culture: Power, change and vulnerability in twenty-first century childhood. In D. Lemish (Ed.), *The Routledge international handbook of children, adolescents and media* (pp. 111–119). Routledge.

Livingstone, S., & Sefton-Green, J. (2016). *The class: Living and learning in the digital age*. New York University Press.

Marôpo, L., Jorge, A., & Tomaz, R. (2020). "I felt like I was really talking to you!" Intimacy and trust among teen vloggers and followers in Portugal and Brazil. *Journal of Children and Media*, 14(1), 22–37. https://doi.org/10.1080/17482798.2019.1699589

Marsh, J. (2016). 'Unboxing' videos: Co-construction of the child as cyberflaneur. *Discourse: Studies in the Cultural Politics of Education*, 37, 369–380. https://doi.org/10.1080/01596306.2015.1041457

Marsh, J. (2017). The Internet of Toys: A posthuman and multimodal analysis of connected play. *Teachers College Record, 119*(15). www.tcrecord.org/Content.asp?ContentID=22073

Marsh, J., Plowman, L., Yamada-Rice, D., Bishop, J., Lahmar, J., & Scott, F. (2018). Play and creativity in young children's use of apps. *British Journal of Educational Technology, 49*(5), 870–882. https://doi.org/10.1111/bjet.12622

Marwick, A., & boyd, D. (2011). To see and be seen: Celebrity practice on Twitter. *Convergence, 17*(2), 139–158. https://doi.org/10.1177/1354856510394539

Mascheroni, G. (2018). Addiction or emancipation? Children's attachment to smartphones as a cultural practice. In J. Vincent & L. Haddon (Eds.), *Smartphone cultures* (pp. 121–134). Routledge.

Mascheroni, G. (2020). Datafied childhoods: Contextualising datafication in everyday life. *Current Sociology, 68*(6), 798–813. https://doi.org/10.1177/0011392118807534

Mascheroni, G., Cino, D., Zaffaroni, L. G., & Amadori, G. (2021). (Non-)sharenting as a form of maternal care? The dilemmas of mothers of 0- to-8-year-old children. In *71st Annual ICA Conference Engaging the Essential Work of Care: Communication, Connectedness and Social Justice.* May 27–31.

Mascheroni, G., & Holloway, D. (Eds.). (2017). *The Internet of Toys: A report on media and social discourses around young children and IoToys.* DigiLitEY. http://digilitey.eu/wp-content/uploads/2017/01/IoToys-June-2017-reduced.pdf

Mascheroni, G., & Holloway, D. (Eds.). (2019). *The Internet of Toys: Practices, affordances and the political economy of children's smart play.* Palgrave.

Mascheroni, G., & Vincent, J. (2016). Perpetual contact as a communicative affordance: Opportunities, constraints, and emotions. *Mobile Media & Communication, 4*(3), 310–326. https://doi.org/10.1177/2050157916639347

Mascheroni, G., Vincent, J., & Jimenez, E. (2015). "Girls are addicted to likes so they post semi-naked selfies": Peer mediation, normativity and the construction of identity online. *Cyberpsychology: Journal of Psychosocial Research on Cyberspace, 9*(1). http://cyberpsychology.eu/view.php?cisloclanku=2015051401&article=5

Mazzarella, S. R. (Ed.). (2010). *Girl wide web 2.0: Revisiting girls, the internet, and the negotiation of identity.* Peter Lang.

Mesch, G. (2013). Internet media and peer sociability. In D. Lemish (Ed.), *The Routledge international handbook of children, adolescents and media* (pp. 287–294). Routledge.

Mik, A. (2021). Is the gaming world getting more diverse? *Digital Future Commission.* https://digitalfuturescommission.org.uk/blog/is-the-gaming-world-getting-more-diverse

Murumaa-Mengel, M., & Siibak, A. (2020). From fans to followers to anti-fans: Young online audiences of microcelebrities. In M. Filimowicz & V. Tzankova (Eds.), *Reimagining communication: Meaning* (pp. 228–245). Routledge.

Navarro, J. (2021). Fortnite: A context for child development during COVID-19 (and beyond). *Journal of Children and Media, 15*(1), 13–16. https://doi.org/10.1080/17482798.2020.1858435

Neate, R. (2020). Ryan Kaji, 9, earns $29.5m as this year's highest-paid YouTuber. *The Guardian,* December 18. www.theguardian.com/technology/2020/dec/18/ryan-kaji-9-earns-30m-as-this-years-highest-paid-youtuber

Nicoll, B., & Nansen, B. (2018). Mimetic production in YouTube toy unboxing videos. *Social Media + Society*. https://doi.org/10.1177/2056305118790761

Paus-Hasebrink, I. (2019). The role of media within young people's socialization: A theoretical approach. *Communications, 44*(4), 407–426. https://doi.org/10.1515/commun-2018-2016

Pugh, A. J. (2009). *Longing and belonging. Parents, children and consumer culture*. University of California Press.

Ruppert, E., Isin, E., & Bigo, D. (2017). Data politics. *Big Data & Society, 4*(2), 1–7. https://doi.org/10.1177/2053951717717749

Siibak, A. (2009). Constructing the self through the photo selection—Visual impression management on social networking websites. *Cyberpsychology: Journal of Psychosocial Research on Cyberspace, 3*(1), Article 1. https://cyberpsychology.eu/article/view/4218/3260

Siibak, A. (2010). Constructing masculinity on a social networking website. The case-study of visual self-presentations of young men on the profile images of SNS Rate.ee. *Young, 18*(4), 403-425. https://doi.org/10.1177/110330881001800403

Siibak, A., & Hernwall, P. (2011). "Looking like my favourite Barbie"—Online gender construction of tween girls in Estonia and in Sweden. *Studies of Transition States and Societies, 3*(2), 57-68. http://publications.tlu.ee/index.php/stss/article/view/79

Siibak, A., & Nevski, E. (2019). Older siblings as mediators of infants' and toddlers' (digital) media use. In O. Erstad, R. Flewitt, B. Kümmerling-Meibauer, & I. S. Pires Pereira (Eds.), *The Routledge handbook of digital literacies in early childhood* (pp. 123–133). Routledge.

Smith, K. L., & Shade, L. R. (2018). Children's digital playgrounds as data assemblages: Problematics of privacy, personalization, and promotional culture. *Big Data & Society*. https://doi.org/10.1177/2053951718805214

Stoilova, M., Livingstone, S., & Mascheroni, G. (2020). Digital childhood? In R. Ling, L. Fortunati, G. Goggin, S. S. Lim, & Y. Li (Eds.), *The Oxford handbook of mobile communication and society* (pp. 129–143). Oxford University Press.

Tett, G. (2020). Generation TikTok could soon be calling the political tune. *Financial Times*, August 12. www.ft.com/content/2f730396-d41d-4256-9041-36ce2e1ba047

Thompson, J. B. (1995). *The media and modernity: A social theory of the media*. Stanford University Press.

UN (United Nations) (2013). *General Comment No. 17 on the right of the child to rest, leisure, play, recreational activities, cultural life and the arts (Article 31)*. Committee on the Rights of the Child. www.refworld.org/docid/51ef9bcc4.html

Valkenburg, P. M., & Peter, J. (2009). Social consequences of the internet for adolescents: A decade of research. *Current Directions in Psychological Science, 18*(1), 1–5. https://doi.org/10.1111/j.1467-8721.2009.01595.x

van Dijck, J. (2013). *The culture of connectivity: A critical history of social media*. Oxford University Press.

van Dijck, J., & Poell, T. (2013). Understanding social media logic. *Media and Communication, 1*(1), 2–14. https://doi.org/10.12924/mac2013.01010002

Vanden Abeele, M. M. P. (2016). Mobile youth culture: A conceptual development. *Mobile Media & Communication, 4*(1), 85–101. https://doi.org/10.1177/2050157915601455

Zhao, S. (2006). Humanoid social robots as a medium of communication. *New Media & Society, 8*(3), 401–419.

· 7 ·

THE MEDIATIZED SCHOOL AND
THE DATAFICATION OF EDUCATION

The Brave New School: Living in Dys/ Utopia?

Mike hastily dressed in his school uniform, took another anxious look on the app to see if the school bus was already nearing his stop, shouted "I'm off!" to his mother, and sped off. He reached the bus stop just in time, and after hopping onto the bus, swiped his RFID chip card through the machine that registered his arrival. As soon as Mike entered the school premises and walked through the metal detectors that had been installed ages ago in the hope of preventing school shootings, the microchip embedded in his school uniform recorded the time of arrival and sent a short confirmation video to his mother's mobile phone to assure her that her son had arrived safely at school. Mike opened the classroom door just in time to witness a football smashing into the window. The sound of glass breaking and kids screaming was immediately registered by the microphones installed in the classroom for detecting "aggressive" voices, and some seconds later, two security guards stormed into the room. After an initial fuss, the teacher was finally able to start the math lesson where they studied fractions, which were clearly not Mike's favorite topic. His facial expressions, categorized as "confused," "upset," and "angry" by the facial recognition system that was scanning students' faces every 30 seconds, evidently captured his dislike. In the civics class that followed, Mike's group soon found common ground in the discussion, so the sensor that was measuring students' electrodermal activity detected shared levels of arousal, signaling the existence of collaboration. Before his physical education class, Mike checked his Fitbit tracker, provided by the school, to see if he had done enough steps during the previous week to receive additional points for the class. After the class Mike went to the library to borrow a new English literature textbook. He pressed his index finger firmly onto the fingerprint reader, thanked the librarian, and rushed towards the canteen. He was happy to see that he was one of the first students in line, and after the iris recognition software scan confirmed that his mother had not forgotten to pay for his monthly lunches, he proceeded to pick up his lunch. While still choosing between pasta and a stew, he almost forgot to take the mandometer, which was supposed to measure the speed at which he ate his lunch as well as how he chewed, not to mention how many calories he consumed. Before Mike finished his lunch, an app on his phone alerted him that his next class would take place in room 221, not 224, as originally scheduled. Considering that the next class was biology, where they were supposed to have a test, he automatically knew that the change in the rooms meant that they were going to be taking the test online. When reaching room 221, Mike noticed that some computers were still vacant, so he chose the one by the window, logged in, and showed his student ID to the proctoring software. The test was relatively easy; only on one occasion did Mike forget that the algorithm was monitoring him, and he looked outside of the window for seconds too long. The alert from the system, however, woke him from his daydream. When the bell rang, he was quite satisfied with himself and typed a message on Facebook, "Let's get blasted tonight!" Little did he think that Mrs Simmons, his math teacher, who was among his Facebook friends, would notice the post, and who made a mental note to herself to have a longer chat with Mike the next day.

This story is only partially fictional. All the various technological solutions mentioned are already in use in a variety of educational institutions all around the world. In the 21st-century school the identities of students are constructed based on the variety of data traces they leave behind when accessing school libraries and canteens, logging into the proctoring systems, learning analytics platforms or video-conferencing sites, when walking past surveillance cameras, or using fingerprint scanners (Williamson, 2019). Thus, it is not just Mike and his friends at school who are continuously affected by dataveillance, but the datafication of education is also increasingly affecting millions of children on a daily basis.

Watching, monitoring, and controlling have obviously always been part of the education system and should thus not be viewed as a result of the edtech cult. In fact, as noted by Couldry and Mejias (2019, p. 175), "the links between continuous surveillance and the education of children are so deeply naturalized here that the panoptic notion of teachers using continuous real-time monitoring is presented as neither chilling nor threatening." At the same time, as posed by Foucault (1995), schools are mechanisms of social control where children are classified, monitored, and disciplined in terms of their knowledge, progress, and personal data. This disciplinary power is often exercised through hierarchized surveillance (teachers vs. students) as well as the techniques of normalization and standardization, all of which become crucial for forming the minds of future citizens (Foucault, 1991). So, according to Foucault, schools are places where technologies of governance and bodies traverse, representing the "small-scale models of power" (Foucault, 1995, p. 136). Thus, on the one hand, we can talk about the "subjectification" of students as their bodies are constantly measured and watched, their activities and behaviors monitored by "the government of others" (Hamann, 2009, p. 38). Such biopolitical governance functions both through continuous monitoring as well as through the application of normalizing judgments directed against a wide range of faulty behaviors (for instance, disobedience, lateness, lack of team spirit or loyalty, insolence, etc.), used with the aim of "training" the individual through discipline (Foucault, 1999, p. 97). On the other hand, schools encourage students to engage in "the government of one's self (subjectivation)," that is, students are both encouraged and required to govern and fashion themselves in order to become "certain kinds of subjects" (Hamann, 2009, p. 38). Present-day schools have increasingly adopted the idea that neoliberal subjects should constantly strive for self-improvement that can only be made visible, comparable, and assessable through numbers. Due to their mission to act as "pedagogical machines" (Foucault, 1995), the "governance by numbers" logic has become the dominant mode of governance in the education sector (Neumann, 2019), turning it into "one of the most noticeable domains affected by datafication" (Jarke & Breiter, 2019, p. 1).

Considering that surveillance is so deep-rooted and naturalized within the field (Teräs et al., 2020), it is not surprising that all the different educational institutions, from early years to higher education alike, have become accustomed to making use of data-driven educational technologies in a variety of ways—for predicting outcomes and preventing risks, for providing insights into the processes of learning, or for personalizing the education system around every student's personal needs (Williamson, 2019). In fact, as argued by Couldry and Mejias (2019, p. 176), "in the brave new world of datafied education, surveillance becomes not the enemy, but paradoxically the guarantor, of educational freedom." At the same time, these processes of datafication treat students as "data objects" (Koopman, 2019) rather than "data owners" (Broughan & Prinsloo, 2019), who could either opt out from the increasing dataveillance, or at least exercise their agency by acting as partners in discussions about what data is collected, for whom, and for what purposes.

The COVID-19 pandemic has accelerated and intensified the student data drain even further. At the height of the pandemic, almost 1.6 billion children all over the world were out of school due to lockdown measures (UNESCO, 2020), coerced into using a variety of data-intensive educational online platforms for remote learning. The edtech industry was quick to adopt the narrative of techno-solutionism—promising a solution for the schools, students, and teachers in need. At the same time, the pandemic provided the sector with a remarkable opportunity for profit-making, a chance to expand to new markets and to embed the idea of "the platformisation of schooling" (Hillman, Bergviken Rensfeldt, & Ivarsson, 2020). In fact, as argued by Williamson, Eynon, and Potter (2020, p. 108), the edtech industry saw the pandemic as a "business opportunity with potentially long-term consequences for how public education is perceived and practiced long after the coronavirus has been brought under control." In fact, a survey of students aged 10–18 in 11 European countries, coordinated by the Joint Research Centre (JRC) (Vuorikari et al., 2020), has shown that the majority of respondents reported having used video-conferencing tools (such as Zoom, Microsoft Teams, Google Hangouts, and Skype) for remote learning—the numbers varying from 60% in Germany to 94% in Slovenia. Similarly, many also reported having used a digital learning platform provided by their school (ranging from 53% in France to 92% in Norway; see Vuorikari et al., 2020). Furthermore, the datafication of the education sector is not only transforming the ways in which teaching, and learning, are organized, but is also creating a profound effect on young people's experiences of growing up (Pangrazio & Selwyn, 2020).

The Grand Narrative of the Datafication of Education

The application of new technologies has always triggered inspiring visions of hope as well as gloomy horror. Aldous Huxley's *Brave New World* (1932) most famously emphasized that the lines between utopia and dystopia are not as clearly marked as many of us would like. Discussions about the revolutionary powers of technology (cf. Selwyn, 2010), that are often blended with enthusiastic techno-optimism promising to "'reimagine' education", as noted by Williamson (2021), have been ongoing for decades, way before the COVID-19 pandemic struck the world.

The grand narrative of the datafication of education generally focuses on philanthropic goals such as promoting student engagement and personalized learning. In this regard, the developments of the datafication of education are based on the neoliberal logic urging individuals and institutions to succumb to datafication in the name of better education (Couldry & Yu, 2018). A plethora of new technological solutions has been brought to the market since 2010 in the hope of providing quick fixes to a variety of problems, from student engagement and learning motivation, to behavior and physical fitness. Advocates of datafication, as claimed by boyd and Crawford (2012), often envision that the datasets collected not only produce objective and insightful new knowledge about a complex phenomenon, but that through using edtech a variety of complex, structural societal problems can also be solved (Teräs et al., 2020). The assumptions tend to ignore the fact that data is always socially situated and framed by socially located viewpoints (Williamson, 2019), and therefore inherently political. In short, these problems cannot vanish simply because "there is an app for that." Furthermore, as argued by Selwyn (2019), this big data approach also often underestimates the complexity of student lives. Thus, rather than offering quick technological solutions, datafication happening in the educational sector not only reinforces social problems, but may also "exacerbate discriminatory decision-making in favor of those social groups most represented in the systems' datasets" (Selwyn, 2019, p. 13), leading to considerable data harm (Lupton, 2020; see also Chapter 8, this book).

One of the most recent and vivid examples of creating data harm comes from the UK, where in spring 2020, due to the ongoing COVID-19 pandemic, students were unable to take their A-Level exams that are necessary for being admitted to university. Considering that the option to award students' grades based on teacher assessment was rejected by the Office of Qualifications and

Examinations Regulation (Ofqual) due to the potential unfairness between schools, incomparability across generations, and devaluing of results because of grade inflation (Roger, 2020), a new and more objective assessment criteria had to be found. Ofqual decided to solve this problem by building an algorithm, a seemingly more objective and more accurate alternative in comparison to the supposedly subjective judgment of teachers (the center-assessed grade, CAG). Such a decision vividly portrays "the perceived *mistrust* of policy-makers of teachers' capacity for professional judgement" (Kelly, 2021, p. 14; original emphasis), framing this assumption in the typical mechanical objectivity and impartiality narrative so often associated with datafication. Due to this data-based objectivity discourse, however, concerns about potential data harm, data bias, or reproduction of social inequalities tended to be silenced. As the components of the exam grade algorithm were not announced before the grades were revealed, algorithmic discrimination remained black-boxed and hidden from public view. After it became apparent that the exam regulator's algorithm had downgraded nearly 36% of the grades lower than their teachers' original A-Level assessment would have been (Kelly, 2021), Ofqual's decision to base the algorithm on the historical grade distribution of schools from the three previous years (2017–19), the rank of each student within their own school for a particular subject, based on a teacher's evaluation of their likely grade had the A-Levels gone ahead as planned, and the previous exam results for a student per subject led to a huge "algorithmic grading fiasco" (Kolkman, 2020; see also Chapter 8, this book).

Even though a record proportion of school-leavers had received a top A* grade and there was also a considerable increase in the proportion of As awarded, improvement in A* and A grades was most significant for students attending independent schools (up by 4.7%), while the grades of students from state comprehensive schools and sixth form colleges showed very small improvement (0.3%) (Ofqual, 2020, p. 136). In fact, a survey among the sixth form college heads in England reported that many school leaders considered the results the worst in their college's history (Sixth Form Colleges Association, 2020). Comparison of the grades between 2020 and 2017–19 revealed that on average students' grades were 20% lower in 2020 than similarly qualified students three years prior to the algorithmic assessment, and there was not a single subject where the performance of the students from sixth form colleges was above the three-year average in 2020 (Allen, 2020). Analysis thus suggests that the students from smaller schools (which often means small fee-paying private schools) were more likely to benefit from the algorithm because it put more weight on the CAGs in case there were less than 15 students in a particular subject per school (Allen, 2020). The application of the algorithm, in this respect, can hence be seen as a case of "digital redlining," that is, "a set of education policies, investment decisions, and IT practices that actively create and maintain class boundaries through strictures that discriminate against specific groups" (Gilliard & Culik, 2016), as the students from lower socioeconomic backgrounds were most likely to suffer from the consequences of this experiment. Faced with public outcry that was focused on the unfairness of the results and the resulting legal action, the UK government retracted the grades provided by the algorithm and enabled the students to receive the grade based on their teacher's estimate of what their grade might have been. This meant that about 15,000 students who had been rejected by their first-choice university due to the lower algorithm-generated grades were able to reapply using their teacher's estimate (Kelly, 2021). This is a vivid illustration that we only start to notice, acknowledge, and make sense of dataveillance "when apparently immaterial data begin to have material effects/affects" (Lupton, 2020, p. 120).

Much of the students' data that is currently collected and processed should be seen as an algorithmic mediation of their activities and embodiments, preferences and habits, their bodily capacities or behavioral characteristics, all of which become quantified and repurposed back to the digital economy (Lupton, 2020). In fact, as argued by Williamson (2021), it is important to acknowledge that the neoliberal business logic of edtech companies is primarily aimed at making a profit rather than improving learning. Before the COVID-19 pandemic, big tech companies like Google, Microsoft, and Apple, had already gained an extensive presence in educational institutions around the world, with scholars becoming increasingly concerned about the "commercialization in schooling" (Lingard et al., 2017, p. 7). However, due to the disruptive school year in 2020, which was met by vocal concerns about "broken education" (Teräs et al., 2020), this provided the edtech sector with an opportunity to popularize more widely their services and platforms built on the "Netflix-inspired" commercial model (Kucirkova, 2021, p. 11), leading them towards exponential growth. For instance, according to a report by CB Insights, venture and equity financing for edtech start-ups more than doubled in 2020, surging to US$12.58 billion worldwide, from US$4.81 billion in 2019 (Singer & Browning, 2021). US educational technology start-ups alone raised more than US$2.2 billion in venture and private capital, 30% more than in 2019 (Wan, 2021). These numbers illustrate that the COVID-19 pandemic strengthened and accelerated previous developments in the realm of the datafication of education, turning edtech companies into strong social actors who have been granted the power to shape and influence class learning activities, and thereby they are able to "make considerable inroads into 'privatizing' schooling" (Williamson & Hogan, 2020, p. 59). In fact, Teräs et al. (2020, p. 873) refer to the ongoing trend as "edtech's pedagogical colonialism," arguing that the tools put into use during the pandemic could become eternally rooted in the practices of teaching and learning going forward.

At the same time, one should not be blindsided by the philanthropist mission of the edtech sector that is earning huge profits thanks to collecting and using ever-increasing amounts of student data (Teräs et al., 2020). The latter is most evident in the case of consumer tech giants Google and Zoom, that have enlarged their market share and reaped considerable benefits despite the fact that they are offering their services for free to all the K-12 primary and secondary schools around the world—Google Classroom is now used by 150 million students and educators in comparison to 40 million users pre-pandemic (Lazare, 2021), while more than 125,000 Zoom domains have been created for schools in 25 countries (Yuan, 2021). Such growth in the market share suggests that the business model of the edtech industry is firmly built on the marketing logic of surveillance capitalism—owning and assetizing personal data that can be monetized in the future is more valuable than the product or service itself (Teräs et al., 2020). The predominant business model for such services is thus "barter" (van Dijck, 2014, p. 2000), where customers agree to disclose their personal data in return for the service. At the same time, as argued by Williamson and Hogan (2020, p. 60), "the long-term 'cost' of free access needs to be tracked into the future to understand whether schools were the short term beneficiaries of edtech social responsibility, or whether the edtech industry was able to capitalise on the dramatic growth of paid subscriptions."

Edtech's efforts to datafy the student experience of education during the pandemic were obviously rife with threats to student privacy (Williamson et al., 2020). Recent analysis by an internet research firm, Top10VPN, of the government-recommended remote learning edtech platforms indicates that 58% of the platforms (N = 57) studied posed a high risk to children's digital privacy, 43 platforms contained ad tracking, and 19 had alarming security issues (Migliano & Woodhams, 2020). In April 2020 both Zoom and Google were sued in the U.S.—the former for allegedly sharing users' data with third parties such as Facebook without properly notifying its users first (Asher Hamilton, 2020), the latter for collecting children's biometric data, in particular, facial scans and "voiceprints," through its educational services (Samsel,

2020; Stoller, 2020). Similar concerns have also been voiced in the EU. In fact, a study of various remote learning platforms used during the COVID-19 pandemic revealed that in relation to the General Data Protection Regulation (GDPR) in Europe, G Suite for Education by Google performed the worst, followed by Zoom (Ducato et al., 2020).

Research in Australia (Lupton, 2021; Rennie et al., 2019) and in the UK (Stoilova, Livingstone, & Nandagiri, 2019) reveals that teachers are not very knowledgeable about personal data privacy and security issues, and feel quite powerless to exercise their agency. Recent semi-structured individual interviews, where lecturers from 11 different higher education institutions in Estonia (N = 29) were asked to reflect on their experiences with remote teaching during COVID-19 lockdown in spring 2020, indicate similar stands. The interviews revealed that most of the interviewees did not contemplate privacy issues when frantically trying to move their lectures online. Rather, the lecturers in the sample tended to brush the topic of privacy off as totally irrelevant, something that they were not at all concerned about because they believed that neither they nor their students had anything to hide. Although some of the interviewees stated that their university's IT department recommended avoiding Zoom due to potential privacy problems, the lecturers themselves believed that privacy was quite a small price to pay for the affordances (for instance, ease of use, convenience) that such platforms provide.

Although scholars have argued for the need for schools to take more of a role in thinking about which platforms to use and how best to preserve their students' privacy (Lupton, 2020, p. 11), a recent report by the World Privacy Forum (Dixon, 2020) reveals instances of "coronawashing" (Williamson & Hogan, 2020, p. 61) as student privacy and security principles were waived during the pandemic. For example, many schools within the U.S. failed to obtain informed consent when signing their students onto the edtech platforms (Dixon, 2020). Such instances could potentially lead to long-term consequences, the impact of which on the learners, teachers, and the education institutions is unprecedented.

Dominant Modes of Dataveillance and the Formation of Student Data Assemblages

In today's "post-panoptical" world (Bauman, 2000, p. 11), surveillance has become so fluid that it is almost liquified, working from afar, without the "watchers" needing to be present (Bauman & Lyon, 2013).

The biopolitical management of students (Hope, 2016), especially through the use of various biometric technologies, all of which utilize physical and/or behavioral "characteristics" unique to an individual, provide a striking example of such liquid biopower in action (Foucault, 1995). Biometric technologies, such as fingerprint readers, facial recognition software, palm vein scanners, iris scanning devices, heart rhythm detectors, typing metrics, voice biometrics, and other types of "creepy analytics" (Beattie, Woodley, & Souter, 2014) that are applied in educational institutions all over the world, serve as an illustration of how students' personal information is vigorously harvested for a multitude of reasons. Regardless of the fact that due to the unique and permanent character of biometric data such data should only be used with due care and that it requires special protection in the light of fundamental rights and freedoms, the variety of biometric technologies currently in use in schools is not only vast, but also constantly growing.

One of the main reasons such technologies have been applied in schools is for better student safety (Andrejevic & Selwyn, 2019). During the COVID-19 pandemic, for example, many educational institutions invested in temperature scanning stations, contact tracing tokens, symptom scanners, symptom checking apps, and wearable heart rate monitors that could enable the tracking of potential exposure to the virus, thereby helping to keep the students healthy and safe by fighting the spread of COVID-19 in schools (Singer & Browning, 2021). More than a decade ago, schools around the world had also started to implement CCTV cameras in the hope of combating school crime and violence (Birnhack & Perry-Hazan, 2021; Fisher, Higgins, & Homer, 2019). More recently, however, radio frequency identification tags, metal detectors, and facial recognition software have been put into use to eliminate external security threats (Deakin, Taylor, & Kupchik, 2018), and to gain a greater level of control over the school grounds. For example, even though the efficiency of these technologies has not yet been proven, many school districts across the U.S., as well as in many other countries (for example, Australia, the UK, and India), have adopted facial recognition cameras in the hope of preventing school violence, malicious events, and shootings by detecting potentially dangerous people (such as students who have previously brought a weapon to school, or who have been expelled or "flagged" by the system) entering the school property (Heilweil, 2019). In doing so, the facial recognition software aims to "discipline the young," thus fitting nicely with the historical disciplinary role of schools (Foucault, 1995). However, students' actions will only be measured against "the acceptable student" (Galligan et al., 2020, p. 10), or the imaginary algorithmic visions of what Willson (2018) has referred to as the "'ideal' child." Studies such as those by Galligan et al. (2020) reveal that on many occasions facial recognition software is thus likely to exclude students from marginalized communities (for instance, gender non-conforming students, immigrant students, low-income students, students of color, etc.). Hence, it is evident that biometrics does not provide an objective, value-free, scientific mode of identification. Rather, in addition to involving substantial intrusion and being a major privacy risk, the use of facial recognition software in schools is likely to "amplify, institutionalize, and potentially weaponize existing racial biases, resulting in disproportionate surveillance and humiliation of marginalized students" (Galligan et al., 2020, p. 9). Also, considering that the technology is often sold to entire school districts rather than single schools, the data collected through the apps could follow the child from kindergarten to college (cf. Ng, 2020), locking the young in a certain "records prison" (Igo, 2018), not to mention normalizing the experience of being constantly surveilled. For these reasons, the use of facial recognition technologies for identification purposes within the EU is only allowed if someone has given explicit consent, although a recent court case in France (Pascu, 2020) indicates that even after gaining consent from students and parents, such invasive surveillance could still be considered neither necessary nor proportionate, and thus in violation of the GDPR.

Various biometric technologies are also used for assessing student attendance—data thus being used as evidence for disciplining students. In China, for instance, students in a south west province of Guizhou wear school uniforms with embedded microchips that enable their time and date of arrival to the school premises to be recorded, and a short video confirmation sent to their parents' mobile phones (Tai, 2019). Furthermore, as this is used together with facial recognition technology, it ensures that each uniform is worn by its rightful owner, and in case the student wants to leave the school premises without permission, a voice alarm is activated, which serves as a vivid reminder of the saying "discipline 'makes' individuals" (Foucault, 1999, p. 97). Schools within the EU (for instance, in Sweden) have also been tempted to use facial recognition software, regardless of the fact that such usage is in violation of different articles in the GDPR (EDPB, 2019).

Attendance tracking technologies are not only popular in secondary schools (Ervasti, Kinnula, & Isomursu, 2010), but also in universities. Some of these tracking apps (for example, SpotterEDU) offer the opportunity to monitor both student attendance in classes (or sports practice) as well as students' academic performance or even their mental health. Such intrusive technology, which operates through short-range phone sensors and campus-wide Wi-Fi networks, is able to collect up to 6000 data points per student per day (Harwell, 2019). According to Harwell (2019), who conducted interviews with dozens of students and faculty members, the students feel coerced to make use of the apps and feel they are unable to escape from the watchful tech-gaze of the institution, enabling the adults to produce "docile" bodies (Foucault, 1995). According to Harwell (2019), student athletes, especially those on a scholarship, are one of the groups who might be monitored the closest as they are supposed to live up to the disciplined patterns of behavior. Playing truant or being late for a class or a training session may thus not only result in being scolded by a professor or coach, but also end with their scholarship being taken away (Harwell, 2019). As argued by Harwell (2019), educational institutions see the value in such monitoring mainly because the "personal risks scores" (based on the factors such as whether the student is going to the library) the apps provide for each student give the schools enough information to intervene before real problems arise. Here, again, we can see how data is used to manage and transform the students. There is a chance, however, that some students under such heightened educational vigilance might decide against pursuing their hobbies or other interests for fear of failing the system and not living up to the measurements of the "'ideal' child" (Willson, 2018).

Beyond tracking student bodies in physical environments, facial recognition is also being used in various virtual learning contexts, for example, as a means for authenticating learners (Valera, Valera, & Gelogo, 2015), controlling their access to learning environments, or for controlling student integrity during online tests and exams—studies indicate that the use of online proctoring services, for example, surged during the COVID-19 pandemic. The findings of a poll among EDUCAUSE community institutions (N = 312; 294 from the U.S.) carried out in April 2020 suggests that at the time of the study, 54% of the surveyed educational institutions were using online proctoring software and another 23% were considering using them (Grajek, 2020), regardless of the fact that no remote proctoring software had a stellar privacy record (Faherty, 2020). This demonstrates that many students from secondary schools to universities have been coerced into taking online exams and tests under the watchful eyes (both human and automated) of third-party programs without the real option to opt out from such surveillance. Some of the proctor software companies depend on facial recognition, eye tracking, and other AI and machine learning components to detect suspicious examinee behaviors, while others (for example, ProctorU), make use of human proctors who are required to watch students' faces, demand that the students show them their rooms and desktops to find evidence of their dishonesty, and listen in through a student's microphone during the test to ensure the test taker is not asking for advice from someone else (Harwell, 2020). Proctors also often have access to the test-taker's computer, so that they receive alerts when the system detects the student doing something unacceptable such as opening a new browser window or copy-pasting from another file. Activities like looking off-screen for too long during the exam could raise a test-taker's "suspicion" score, and potentially even lead to failing the exam (Harwell, 2020).

The use of such proctoring systems has already triggered considerable public coverage, resulting in student petitions and legal actions in the U.S., but also in the EU—in January 2021 61 digital and human rights organizations called on the European Commission to include limits of the harmful uses of AI in legislation, including student surveillance technology (EDRi, 2021). In fact, although some purveyors claim to be compliant with legal protections, for example, the GDPR, and ensure that they have no access to encrypted data (Coghlan, Miller, & Paterson, 2020), others retain the rights for all the data collected through students' computers and scans. According to Harwell (2020), ProctorU's privacy policy for test-takers in California, for example, reveals that a plethora of sensitive student data (such as their home address, medical records, including any physical condition or mental disability), as well as students' biometric data (for example, fingerprints, facial images, voice recording and iris or retina scans) is shared by both the proctors and the schools.

Such virtual monitoring of students' virtual selves, however, is not only happening on various online learning platforms or through edtech, but also takes place in various social media platforms. In fact, studies (Räim & Siibak, 2014; Siibak & Otsus, 2018) indicate that due to the "context collapse" (Marwick & boyd, 2010), students and teachers have gained access to each other's information, which was previously considered private, thus blurring boundaries and (un)written rules related to privacy–publicity, authority–friendship, or availability–responsibility (Asterhan & Rosenberg, 2015) that have otherwise existed in student–teacher relationships. The blurring of such boundaries has not only led to various professional, ethical, and legal dilemmas among teachers (Russo, Squelch, & Varnham, 2010), but has also led to an unspoken tension "between whether, how, when and with whom to engage using social media and on what basis these connections and interactions are being made—whether as an individual (personally) or as a teacher (profes-sionally)" (Fox & Bird, 2015, p. 22). Although different social media guide-lines for teachers strongly advise against "friending" students through personal accounts (Graham et al., 2018), focus group interviews with Estonian primary school students (N = 25, grades 7–9) and secondary school students (N = 20, grades 10–12) indicate that communicating through personal social media accounts was still the most common way for teacher–student interactions to develop (Siibak & Otsus, 2018). In fact, in contrast to previous research that has claimed that the initiation of such "friendships" on social media should come from students rather than from teachers (Teclehaimanot & Hickman, 2011), Estonian focus groups with students revealed that teachers were often the initiators of these online friendships. The students in our sample had no objections to "friending" teachers if their relationship with the teacher was positive and supportive, but if the teacher–student relationship in class was not positive and encouraging, the teacher's "friend requests" were a cause of discomfort (Siibak & Otsus, 2018). At the same time, the students believed that interacting with their teachers on social media provided them with a unique opportunity to see teachers as "real" human beings, with hobbies, likes and dislikes, and family, rather than mere professionals standing in front of the class, thus enabling more positive teacher–student relationships to emerge.

Analysis of focus group interviews with Estonian secondary school teach-ers (N = 21), however, suggests that accessing each other's social media pro-files and familiarizing themselves with the content shared works both ways (Murumaa-Mengel & Siibak, 2014; Räime & Siibak, 2014). In fact, our find-ings indicate that teachers have become "nightmare readers" (Marwick & boyd, 2010), who acknowledge that students' social media posts were often inappropriate. Teachers condemned students for sharing party photos where they were consuming alcohol, or where they were wearing clothing that was too revealing, and when coming across such content, the teachers in our sample claimed that they felt a need to intervene and address the issue. On those occasions, usually either a private message was sent to the student or a private chat was called at school; at times, however, teachers sent their com-ments publicly, underneath the student's original post (Räim & Siibak, 2014). Taking an active stand and compiling such a response was viewed as an oppor-tunity to stay true to their role as a teacher and to take up the role of a "moral agent" who feels morally responsible for their students' actions (Thunman & Persson, 2018). Focus groups with primary and secondary school students, however, suggest that such telling off is deeply frowned on by the students, and interpreted as inappropriate attention that teachers should avoid (Siibak & Otsus, 2018).

Data-Driven Personalization of Learning

Research suggests that present-day schools are not only interested in disciplining student bodies but also minds, harvesting a multitude of students' behavioral data via surveillance capitalism (Zuboff, 2019). Following the Taylorist ideas of efficiency, productivity, and achievement, the neoliberal education system has thus been fast to borrow and adopt a variety of ideas and technologies from other fields, for instance, business intelligence, to improve student achievement and motivation. Growing interest in "affective computing" (Williamson, 2017a) relies on the development of edtech systems, in particular biometric technologies, which can monitor and collect physiological data from the students so as to surveil their "engagement" in learning (Andrejevic & Selwyn, 2019). The techniques of affective computing could include speech analysis applications that are able to detect emotion from the human voice, as well as textual sentiment analysis that can be performed through natural language processing, tone, or linguistic analysis (Williamson, 2017a). Most commonly, however, facial analysis and machine vision algorithms are used for detecting "facial microexpression states" (Chiu et al., 2014), that is, facial states lasting less than half a second. The information gained through such scanning is believed to provide insights into what the learners are thinking, as well as being used as indicators of students' (non)engagement—acting as evidence of frustration, surprise, delight, confusion, or boredom (Dewan, Murshed, & Lin, 2019). As reported by *The Wall Street Journal*, some schools in China also make students wear headbands that track brain waves, enabling students' level of engagement and concentration levels to be monitored (Tai, 2019). Such technologies could thus be seen as an example of "engagement pedometers" (Williamson, 2017a) that aim to measure student engagement in class through applying electrodermal skin response sensors. All these technological advancements aim to make student "engagement" observable and measurable, and provide "no option for the students to self-curate and restrict what data they 'share'" (Andrejevic & Selwyn, 2019, p. 8). Such technologies thus also act as responsibilization machines, nudging students towards certain patterns of favorable behavior, or at least producing favorable data. The data collected through such means, however, as argued by Williamson

(2017a, p. 284), is most valuable not for the students, but for those academic, commercial, philanthropic, and political actors who "seek to gain from their possession of psycho-informatic power."

The uptake of these data-infused technological developments, as well as the growing popularity of learning analytics, that is, the measurement, collection, analysis, and reporting of information about learners and their contexts for the purposes of understanding and optimizing learning, is built on the idea that the "factory model" (Couldry & Mejias, 2019, p. 175), a one-size-fits-all education, is outdated and needs to be revolutionized. Since the education sector has become a venture where data technologies pervade all levels of the system, present-day students have the opportunity to profit from an individualized approach with personally tailored educational pathways, where data relations become enablers of a supposed new autonomy (Couldry & Mejias, 2019). Thus, drawing on the "technologies of the self" (Foucault, 1988), the increasing dataveillance of students is not only presented as control, but also as an opportunity to transform their own subjectivities (Hope, 2016). However, rather than developing autonomous, self-directed learners, Knox, Williamson, and Bayne (2020, p. 35) argue that learning analytics becomes just another form of data governance, where data is positioned as the "authoritative source for educational action," where learners are "recast as the product of consumerist analytic technologies." In short, tracking students' moods and affective capacities can also exploit students' unpaid labor by making them "instrumental as value generating data points" (Nemorin, 2017, p. 17). In the context of the continuing development of edtech and increasing uptake of such technologies there is thus a need for a "transparency paradox" (Nissenbaum, 2011). The students and their parents, but also teachers and educational institutions, need a brief and clear overview of what types of data are being collected about them, with whom the data is being shared, and for which purposes. Only then is there hope that they will be able to give meaningful and genuinely informed consent.

Learning analytics and other big data technologies not only enable the data to be harvested in real time, providing high-speed automated analysis of learners' progress, but also enable students to compare themselves against the aggregated norms, as well as their classmates. ClassDojo, a cloud-based game-like educational software and classroom management platform that is used in more than 180 countries around the world (Sherman, 2020), for monitoring, identifying, and reporting students' behavior, serves as an example of such technology. The gamified behavior-shaping function built around behaviorist principles is central to the app (Manolev, Sullivan, & Slee, 2018), as each student is assigned a child-friendly colorful monster avatar, to whom teachers start to award points based on their behavior. Similar to many other edtech platforms, ClassDojo employs a new data-based version of behaviorism, also referred to as "machine behaviorism" (Knox et al., 2020), where students are nudged towards conforming to the certain patterns of behavior that have been determined by algorithms to be effective and efficient. ClassDojo is built so as to harvest data about students' non-cognitive social-emotional learning, with the aim of helping the students "to conform to the behavioral ideals" (Williamson, 2018) of growth mindset, grit, perseverance, wellbeing, self-control, and character that are viewed as normalized culturally produced ideals. The latter is achieved through "hypernudging" (Yeung, 2017), that is, psychological data about students is used together with "persuasive computing" techniques with the aim of predicting, targeting, and changing their emotions and behaviors. In this respect, the popularity of ClassDojo and similar "big-data driven guidance-technologies" (Yeung, 2017, p.122) is a vivid illustration of the wider and ongoing "affective turn" (Ecclestone & Hayes, 2009) in education systems happening around the world, and the adoption of what Williamson (2016) has referred to as "psychopedagogy," that is, a method to approach students through the lens of positive psychology. Although such hypernudging "entails the use of 'soft power'" (Yeung, 2017, p. 123), its spread and magnitude in the edtech context is immense and should not be underestimated.

On the ClassDojo app, the acquired points can be shared with parents in real time and also displayed in the classroom so that students can see how their personal score matches up with their peers, thus helping to promote a worldview where success is grounded in neoliberal notions of competitive individualism (Williamson, 2017b). Such a stance, as argued by several scholars (cf. Manolev et al., 2018; Williamson, 2016), however, completely ignores the contextual, cultural, socioeconomic, and political factors, all of which shape students' behaviors and their identities. The app also has a TrendSpotter feature that gives an overview of the acquired points over time, so that the points can also follow children from one class to the next, entrapping them in the loop of the "records prison" (Igo, 2018).

Furthermore, due to this vastly expanding regime of measurement, various scholars (Knox et al., 2020; Williamson et al., 2020) have also started to criticize edtech for redefining, simplifying, and reducing the concept of learning. In fact, critics of the datafication of education have also emphasized that in the era of learning analytics, only the information that shows up in the data, that is, only the learning that the data makes visible, is considered learning, and all the information that cannot be quantified, measured, and compared is not considered learning and is thus marginalized. Through these technologies the work of teachers also becomes data managed, subject to normative processes of algorithmic exposure and measurement (Ross & Macleod, 2018, p. 235). Not only is there a need to make changes in the curricula and pedagogies to ensure that students develop and grow in the measured categories, but also, as argued by Roberts-Mahoney, Means, and Garrison (2016, p. 414), the autonomy and expertise of the teacher is seriously minimized as they no longer have to make pedagogical decisions but rather manage technology that is making the decision for them (see the UK A-Level exam algorithm fiasco referred to earlier).

In addition to the growing uptake of "biopedagogies," that is, the use of health tracking devices for encouraging the data-based bodily optimization of children, "psychopedagogies" that are based on students' affective and psychological data, and "neuropedagogies" that rely on students' data collected and processed through neurocomputational devices (Williamson, 2016, p. 402), the sociotechnical imaginaries for the use of students' data just keep on expanding. For example, Williamson (2018) has noted a growing interest among scientists working in the field of "educational genomics," making use of human genome data and educational neuroscience, to work towards the development of personalized "precision education." The latter, according to Williamson (2018), entails an understanding that "the sciences of genes, neurology, behaviour and psychology can be combined in order to provide insights into learning processes, and to define how learning inputs and materials can be organized in ways best suited to each individual student." Advancements in these fields could thus potentially lead to a day when educational institutions are creating tailor-made curriculum programs based on the students' DNA profile (Gaysina, 2016). While it is for everyone to decide whether such developments are illustrations of utopian or dystopian imaginaries of education futures, it is evident, however, that present-day education systems are undergoing "radical 'reimagining' and prototyping" (Williamson & Hogan, 2020, p. 57).

References

Allen, N. (2020). *Summer 2020 results: Analysis of performance in 2020 compared to 2017–2019.* Sixth Form Colleges Association. www.sixthformcolleges.org/382/sfca-publications

Andrejevic, M., & Selwyn, N. (2019). Facial recognition technology in schools: Critical questions and concerns. *Learning, Media and Technology*, 45(2), 115–128. doi: https://doi.org/10.1080/17439884.2020.1686014

Asher Hamilton, I. (2020). Zoom is being sued for allegedly handing over data Facebook. *Business Insider*, March 31. www.businessinsider.com/zoom-sued-allegedly-sharing-data-with-facebook-2020-3

Asterhan, S. C., & Rosenberg, H. (2015). The promise, reality and dilemmas of secondary school teacher–student interactions in Facebook: The teacher perspective. *Computers & Education*, 85, 134–148.

Bauman, Z. (2000). *Liquid modernity*. Polity.

Bauman, Z., & Lyon, D. (2013). *Liquid surveillance: A conversation*. Polity.

Beattie, S., Woodley, C., & Souter, K. (2014). Creepy analytics and learner data rights. In B. Hegarty, J. McDonald, & S.-K. Loke (Eds.), *Rhetoric and reality: Critical perspectives and educational technology* (pp. 421–425). Ascilite.

Birnhack, M., & Perry-Hazan, L. (2021). Differential rights consciousness: Teachers' perceptions of privacy in the surveillance school. *Teaching and Teacher Education*, 101, 1–12.

boyd, D., & Crawford, K. (2012). Critical questions for big data: Provocations for a cultural, technological, and scholarly phenomenon. *Information, Communication & Society*, 15(5), 662–679.

Broughan, C., & Prinsloo, P. (2019). (Re)centring students in learning analytics: In conversation with Paulo Freire. *Assessment & Evaluation in Higher Education*, 45(SI1), 617–628. www.tandfonline.com/doi/full/10.1080/02602938.2019.1679716%40caeh20.2020.45.issue-SI1

Chiu, M.-H., Chou, C.-C., Wu, W.-L., & Liaw, H. (2014). The role of facial microexpression state (FMES) change in the process of conceptual conflict. *British Journal of Educational Technology*, 45(3), 471–486. https://doi.org/10.1111/bjet.12126

Coghlan, S., Miller, T., & Paterson, J. (2020). Good proctor or "big brother"? AI ethics and online exam supervision technologies. November. https://ui.adsabs.harvard.edu/abs/2020arXiv201107647C/abstract

Couldry, N., & Mejias, U. A. (2019). *The costs of connection. How data is colonizing human life and appropriating it for capitalism*. Stanford University Press.

Couldry, N., & Yu, J. (2018). Deconstructing datafication's brave new world. *New Media & Society*, 20(12), 4473–4491.

Deakin, J., Taylor, E., & Kupchik, A. (Eds.). (2018). *The Palgrave international handbook of school discipline, surveillance, and social control*. Palgrave Macmillan.

Dewan, M. A. A., Murshed, M., & Lin, F. (2019). Engagement detection in online learning: A review. *Smart Learning Environments*, 6, 1. https://doi.org/10.1186/s40561-018-0080-z

Dixon, P. (2020). *Without consent: An analysis of student directory information practices in US schools, and impacts on privacy*. World Privacy Forum. www.worldprivacyforum.org/2020/04/without-consent/

Ducato, R., Priora, G., Angiolini, C., et al. (2020). Emergency remote learning: A study of copyright and data protection policies of popular online services. *Kluwer Copyright Blog*, June 4. http://copyrightblog.kluweriplaw.com/2020/06/04/emergency-remote-teaching-a-study-of-copyright-and-data-protection-policies-of-popular-online-services-part-ii/?doing_wp_cron=1591282019.5066540241241455078125

Ecclestone, K., & Hayes, D. (2009). *The dangerous rise of therapeutic education*. Routledge.

EDPB (European Data Protection Board) (2019). Facial recognition in school renders Sweden's first GDPR fine. August 22. https://edpb.europa.eu/news/national-news/2019/facial-recognition-school-renders-swedens-first-gdpr-fine_en

EDRi (European Digital Rights) (2021). Civil society call for AI red lines in the European Union's Artificial Intelligence proposal. January 12. https://edri.org/our-work/civil-society-call-for-ai-red-lines-in-the-european-unions-artificial-intelligence-proposal/

Ervasti, M., Kinnula, M., & Isomursu, M. (2010). User experiences with mobile supervision of school attendance. *International Journal on Advances in Life Sciences, 2*(1 & 2), 29–41.

Faherty, C. (2020). Big Proctor. *Inside HigerEd*, May 11. www.insidehighered.com/news/2020/05/11/online-proctoring-surging-during-covid-19

Fisher, B. W., Higgins, E. M., & Homer, E. M. (2019). School crime and punishment and the implementation of security cameras: Findings from a national longitudinal study. *Justice Quarterly, 38*(1), 22–46. https://doi.org/10.1080/07418825.2018.1518476

Foucault, M. (1988). Technologies of the self. In L. H. Martin, H. Gutman, & P. H. Hutton (Eds.), *Technologies of the self* (pp. 16–49). University of Massachusetts Press.

Foucault, M. (1991). Governmentality. In G. Burchell, C. Gordon, & P. Miller (Eds.), *The Foucault effect: Studies in governmentality* (pp. 87–104). University of Chicago Press.

Foucault, M. (1995). *Discipline and punish: The birth of the prison*. Vintage Books.

Foucault, M. (1999). The means of correct training. In A. Elliott (Ed.), *Blackwell reader in contemporary social theory*. Blackwell.

Fox, A., & Bird, T. (2015). The challenge to professionals of using social media: Teachers in England negotiating personal–professional identities. *Education and Information Technologies, 22*(2), 647–675.

Galligan, C., Rosenfeld, H., Kleinman, M., & Parthasarathy, S. (2020). *Cameras in the classroom: Facial recognition technology in schools*. Gerald R. Ford School of Public Policy, University of Michigan. http://stpp.fordschool.umich.edu/technology-assessment

Gaysina, D. (2016). How genetics could help future learners to unlock hidden potential. *The Conversation*, November 15. https://theconversation.com/how-genetics-could-help-future-learners-unlock-hidden-potential-68254

Gilliard, C., & Culik, H. (2016). Filtering content is often done with good intent, but filtering can also create equity and privacy issues. Common Sense Education, May 24. www.commonsense.org/education/articles/digital-redlining-access-and-privacy

Graham, A., Bahr, N., Truscott, J., & Powell, M. A. (2018). *Teacher's professional boundary transgressions: A literature review*. Centre for Children and Young People, Southern Cross University. https://az659834.vo.msecnd.net/eventsairseasiaprod/production-tcc-public/9f96bd9883844186a7d62fe220866b96

Grajek, S. (2020). EDUCAUSE COVID-19 QuickPoll results: Grading and proctoring. https://er.educause.edu/blogs/2020/4/educause-covid-19-quickpoll-results-grading-and-proctoring

Hamann, T. H. (2009). Neoliberalism, governmentality, and ethics. *Foucault Studies, 6*, 37–59.

Harwell, D. (2019). Colleges are turning students' phones into surveillance machines, tracking the locations of hundreds of thousands. *The Washington Post*, December 24. www.washingtonpost.com/technology/2019/12/24/colleges-are-turning-students-phones-into-surveillance-machines-tracking-locations-hundreds-thousands/

Harwell, D. (2020). Mass school closures in the wake of the coronavirus are driving a new wave of student surveillance. *The Washington Post*, April 1. www.washingtonpost.com/technology/2020/04/01/online-proctoring-college-exams-coronavirus

Heilweil, R. (2019). Schools are using facial recognition to try to stop shootings. Here's why they should think twice. *Vox*, December 20. www.vox.com/recode/2019/12/20/21028124/schools-facial-recognition-mass-shootings#:~:text=Facial%20recognition%20technology%20compares%20images,admitting%20someone%20into%20an%20area

Hillman, T., Bergviken Rensfeldt, A., & Ivarsson, J. (2020). Brave new platforms: A possible platform future for highly decentralised schooling. *Learning, Media & Technology*, 45(1), 7–16.

Hope, A. (2016). Biopower and school surveillance technologies 2.0. *British Journal of Sociology of Education*, 37(7), 885–904.

Igo, S. E. (2018). *The known citizen. A history of privacy in modern America*. Harvard University Press.

Jarke, J., & Breiter, A. (2019). Editorial: The datafication of education. *Learning, Media and Technology*, 44(1), 1–6.

Kelly, A. (2021). A tale of two algorithms: The appeal and repeal of calculated grades systems in England and Ireland in 2020. *British Educational Research Journal*, 47(3), 1–15.

Knox, J., Williamson, B., & Bayne, S. (2020). Machine behaviourism: Future visions of "learnification" and "datafication" across humans and digital technologies. *Learning, Media and Technology*, 45(1), 31–45.

Kolkman, D. (2020). "F**k the algorithm?" What the world can learn from the UK's A-Level grade fiasco. LSE Blog, August 26. https://blogs.lse.ac.uk/impactofsocialsciences/2020/08/26/fk-the-algorithm-what-the-world-can-learn-from-the-uks-a-level-grading-fiasco

Koopman, C. (2019). *How we become our data: The genealogy of the informational person*. University of Chicago Press.

Kucirkova, N. (2021). *The future of the self. Understanding personalisation in childhood and beyond*. Emerald.

Lazare, M. (2021). A peek at what's next for Google Classroom. February 17. https://blog.google/outreach-initiatives/education/classroom-roadmap/#:~:text=Today%2C%20Google%20Classroom%20helps%20more,and%20improve%20teaching%20and%20learning

Lingard, B., Hogan, S., Hogan, A., & Thompson, G. (2017). *Commercialisation in public schooling: An Australian study*. New South Wales Teachers Federation. www.nswtf.org.au/files/17251_cips_international_edition_finalv02.pdf

Lupton, D. (2020). *Data selves: More-than-human perspectives*. Polity.

Lupton, D. (2021). "Honestly no, I've never looked at it": Teachers' understandings and practices related to students' personal data in digitised health and physical education. *Learning, Media and Technology*. https://doi.org/10.1080/17439884.2021.1896541

Manolev, J., Sullivan, A., & Slee, R. (2018). The datafication of discipline: ClassDojo, surveillance and a performative classroom culture. *Learning, Media and Technology*, 44(1), 36–51. doi: https://doi.org/10.1080/17439884.2018.1558237

Marwick, A. E., & boyd, d. (2010). I tweet honestly, I tweet passionately: Twitter users, context collapse, and the imagined audience. *New Media & Society*, 13(1), 114–133.

Migliano, S., & Woodhams, S. (2020). Privacy risks of remote learning. TOP10VPN, September 2. www.top10vpn.com/research/investigations/remote-learning-privacy/

Murumaa-Mengel, M., & Siibak, A. (2014). Teachers as nightmare readers: Estonian high-school teachers' experiences and opinions about student–teacher interaction on Facebook. *International Review of Information Ethics, 21*, 35–44.

Nemorin, S. (2017). Affective capture in digital school spaces and the modulation of student subjectivities. *Emotion, Space and Society, 24*, 11–18.

Neumann, E. (2019). Setting by numbers: Datafication processes and ability grouping in an English secondary school. *Journal of Education Policy, 36*(1), 1–23.

Ng, A. (2020). How schools may use kid's phones to track and surveil them. CNET, February 25. www.cnet.com/news/how-schools-may-use-kids-phones-to-track-and-surveil-them/

Nissenbaum, H. (2011). A contextual approach to privacy online. *Daedalus: Journal of the American Academy of Arts & Sciences, 140*(4), 32–48.

Ofqual (2020). *Awarding GCSE, AS and A levels, in summer 2020: Interim report.* www.gov.uk/government/publications/awarding-gcse-as-a-levels-in-summer-2020-interim-report

Pangrazio, L., & Selwyn, N. (2020). Towards a school-based "critical data education". *Pedagogy, Culture & Society.* doi: https://doi.org/10.1080/14681366.2020.1747527

Pascu, L. (2020). French high court rules against biometric facial recognition use in high schools. *Biometrics News*, February 28. www.biometricupdate.com/202002/french-high-court-rules-against-biometric-facial-recognition-use-in-high-schools

Räim, S., & Siibak, A. (2014). Õpetajate-õpilaste interaktsioon ja sisuloome suhtlusportaalides: õpetajate arvamused ja kogemused. [Teacher–student interaction and content creation on social networking sites: Teacher's opinions and experiences.] *Estonian Journal of Education, 2*(2), 176–199.

Rennie, E., Schmieder, K., Thomas, J., Howard, S. K., Ma, J., & Yang, J. (2019). Privacy and app use in Australian primary schools: Insights into school-based internet governance. *Media International Australia, 170*(1), 78–89.

Roberts-Mahoney, H., Means, A. J., & Garrison, M. J. (2016). Netflixing human capital development: Personalized learning technology and the corporatization of K-12 education. *Journal of Education Policy, 31*(4), 405–420.

Roger, T. (2020). The fairest possible way to recognise students' achievements this year. www.gov.uk/government/news/the-fairest-possible-way-to-recognise-students-achievements-this-year-by-roger-taylor-chair

Ross, J., & Macleod, H. (2018). Surveillance, (dis)trust and teaching with plagiarism detection technology. In M. Bajić, N. B. Dohn, M. de Laat, P. Jandrić, & T. Ryberg (Eds.), *11th International Conference on Networked Learning* (pp. 235–242).

Russo, C. J., Squelch, J., & Varnham, S. E. A. (2010). Teachers and social networking sites: Think before you post. *Public Space: The Journal of Law and Social Justice, 5*, 1–15. https://doi.org/10.5130/psjlsj.v5i0.1493

Samsel, H. (2020). Google facing lawsuit over collection of facial scans, personal data from children. *Security Today*, April 7. https://securitytoday.com/articles/2020/04/07/google-facing-lawsuit-over-collection-of-facial-scans-personal-data-from-children.aspx

Selwyn, N. (2010). Looking beyond learning: Notes towards the critical study of educational technology. *Journal of Computer Assisted Learning, 26*(1), 65–73.

Selwyn, N. (2019). "There's so much data": Exploring the realities of data-based school governance. *European Educational Research Journal, 15*(1), 54–68.

Sherman, R. (2020). Education monitoring tech soars as a result of COVID-19. www.codastory.com/authoritarian-tech/class-dojo-app-surveillance/

Siibak, A., & Otsus, M. (2018). "Mingid bikiinided pildid ei ole OK!" Õpetajate enesepresentatsioon ja interaktsioon sotsiaalmeedias: õpilaste arvamused ja kogemused. ["Bikini photos are not OK!" Teachers' self-presentation and interaction on social media: Students' opinions and experiences.] *Ariadne Lõng*, 91–106.

Singer, N., & Browning, K. (2021). Colleges that require virus-screening tech struggle to say whether it works. *The New York Times*, March 2. www.nytimes.com/2021/03/02/technology/college-coronavirus-tests.html

Sixth Form Colleges Association (2020). *Summer 2020 results: Survey report.* www.sixthformcolleges.org/382/sfca-publications

Stoilova, M., Livingstone, S., & Nandagiri, R. (2019). *Children's data and privacy online: Growing up in a digital age. Research findings.* London School of Economics and Political Science.

Stoller, D. (2020). "Explosion" in distance-learning tech sparks privacy worries. *Bloomberg Law*, April 6. https://news.bloomberglaw.com/privacy-and-data-security/explosion-in-distance-learning-tech-use-sparks-privacy-worries

Tai, C. (2019). How China is using artificial intelligence in the classrooms. *Wall Street Journal*, October 1. www.youtube.com/watch?v=JMLsHI8aV0g

Teclehaimanot, B., & Hickman, T. (2011). Student–teacher interaction on Facebook: What students find appropriate. *TechTrends, 55*(3), 19–30. doi: https://doi.org/10.1007/s11528-011-0494-8

Teräs, M., Suoranta, J., Teräs, H., & Curcher, M. (2020). Post-Covid-19 education and education technology "solutionism": A seller's market. *Postdigital Science and Education, 2*, 863–878. https://doi.org/10.1007/s42438-020-00164-x

Thunman, E., & Persson, M. (2018). Ethical dilemmas on social media: Swedish secondary teachers' boundary management on Facebook. *Teacher Development, 22*(2), 175–190.

UNESCO (2020). UN Secretary-General warns of education catastrophe, pointing to UNESCO estimate of 24 million learners at risk of dropping out. August 6. https://en.unesco.org/news/secretary-general-warns-education-catastrophe-pointing-unesco-estimate-24-million-learners-0

Valera, J. P., Valera, J., & Gelogo, Y. E. (2015). A review on facial recognition for online learning authentication. *2015 8th International Conference on Bio-Science and Bio-Technology (BSBT)*, 16–19.

van Dijck, J. (2014). Datafication, dataism and dataveillance: Big data between scientific paradigm and ideology. *Surveillance & Society, 12*(2), 199–208. https://doi.org/10.24908/ss.v12i2.4776

Vuorikari, R., Velicu, A., Chaudron, S., Cachia, R., & Di Gioia, R. (2020). *How families handled emergency remote schooling during the time of Covid lockdown in spring 2020: Summary of key findings from families with children in 11 European countries.* Publications Office of the European Union. https://doi.org/10.2760/31977

Wan, T. (2021). A record year amid a pandemic: US edtech raises $2.2 billion in 2020. *EdSurge*, January 13. www.edsurge.com/news/2021-01-13-a-record-year-amid-a-pandemic-us-edtech-raises-2-2-billion-in-2020

Williamson, B. (2016). Coding the biodigital child: The biopolitics and pedagogic strategies of educational data science. *Pedagogy, Culture & Society, 24*(3), 401–416.

Williamson, B. (2017a). Moulding student emotions through computational psychology: Affective learning technologies and algorithmic governance. *Educational Media International, 54*(4), 267–288.

Williamson, B. (2017b). Decoding ClassDojo: Psycho-policy, socio-emotional learning and persuasive educational technologies. *Learning, Media and Technology, 42*(4), 440–453.

Williamson, B. (2018). Personalized precision education and intimate data analytics. https://codeactsineducation.wordpress.com/2018/04/16/personalized-precision-education/

Williamson, B. (2019). Datafication of education: A critical approach to emerging analytics technologies and practices. In H. Beetham & R. Sharpe (Eds.), *Rethinking pedagogy for a digital age* (pp. 212–226). Routledge.

Williamson, B. (2021). Education technology seizes a pandemic opening. *Current History, 120*, 15–20.

Williamson, B., Eynon, R., & Potter, N. (2020). Pandemic politics, pedagogies and practices: Digital technologies and distance education during the coronavirus emergency. *Learning, Media and Technology, 45*(2), 107–114.

Williamson, B., & Hogan, A. (2020). *Commercialisation and privatisation in/of education in the context of Covid-19.* Education International Research. https://go.ei-ie.org/GRCovid19

Willson, M. (2018). Raising the ideal child? Algorithms, quantification and prediction. *Media, Culture & Society, 41*(5), 620–636.

Yeung, K. (2017). "Hypernudge": Big data as a mode of regulation by design. *Information, Communication & Society, 20*(1), 118–136.

Yuan, E. S. (2021). A year later: Reflecting and looking ahead. March 17. https://blog.zoom.us/reflecting-looking-ahead/

Zuboff, S. (2019). *The age of surveillance capitalism. The fight for a human future at the new frontier of power.* Profile Books.

· 8 ·

DATAFIED CHILDHOODS, DATAFIED FUTURES?

The Promise and Perils of Algorithmic Governance

Throughout this book we have documented how children are increasingly dataveilled and datafied at home, at school, in the context of peers or parent–child relationships. Whether in the form of digital traces children themselves leave behind when interacting with digital media or the IoTs, or via aggregated data generated by their parents' online activities—including parental mediation practices—children's data are extracted, abstracted, processed by algorithmic predictive analyses, and responded to through automated outputs. Data practices in children's lives raise questions about their future consequences and even their legitimacy. In this final chapter, we argue that the datafication of childhood involves more than a threat to children's privacy: what is at stake is the future of human agency—and ultimately, of society and culture—in the context of the material practices and infrastructures of automation and algorithmic governance. Children are key in understanding this sociotechnical transformation because they experience datafication from before they are born (Barassi, 2020). Before asking, then, what the consequences of datafication are for children, both in the short and long term, we should take a step back and examine further the processes of algorithmic classification and automated decision-making—both its implications and its consequences.

Datafication and automation have profound consequences on the shape and nature of our societies. However, in order to fully understand such consequences, we first need to understand how datafication is reconfiguring social knowledge itself: that is, how data—and their sociotechnical infrastructure—generate a form of "knowledge through automation" (Couldry & Hepp, 2017, p. 142) that is "actionable" (Andrejevic, 2020) and put to use in the creation of a new social order.

As already explained in Chapter 2, datafication and algorithmic-based automation would not have become so pervasive, so taken for granted, if it weren't accompanied by a legitimizing ideology called "dataism" (van Dijck, 2014). Dataism is an emergent epistemological paradigm premised on the extraction of each and every human practice, relation, opinion, and emotion, which is then abstracted into digital data. More specifically, dataism rests on the assumption that once converted into data, everything can be measured, quantified, predicted, and ultimately pre-empted through algorithmic calculations and automated processes. In the abstraction from the physical-material world to the digital-material world of datafication, data are socially constructed as intrinsically objective, impartial, and accurate means of knowledge—that is, dataism is characterized by a blind faith that numbers speak for themselves and, as such, they can effectively supplement or dispense with human judgment, which, conversely, is by nature subjective, inaccurate, and partial. A further ideological ground on which such unconditional trust in data lies is the postulation of "a self-evident relationship between people and data" (van Dijck, 2014, p. 199). In other words, only to the extent that we acknowledge data as authentic representations of individuals and social life—and that we trust the (corporate or institutional) agents that collect, store, and process data—can we legitimize both the extension of data-driven processes of governance to increasingly more domains of social life as well as the pervasive colonization and profitable annexation of our everyday life through data extraction.

Datafication, then, brings along automation, insofar as the reach and speed of data circulation now requires automated processing. In fact, the ideology of dataism supports and presupposes the ideology of robotification: both originate in the context of surveillance capitalism (Zuboff, 2015) but extend beyond such a framework to permeate every social sphere with the value of efficiency and productivity: "automation in the field of media and information is driven by the attempt to generate value from data—whether for economic, political social or security purposes" (Andrejevic, 2020, p. 28). Yet, despite the fact that these ideologies construct data "as natural traces," and the platforms or sensors through which they are extracted "as neutral facilitators" (van Dijck, 2014, p. 199), the discourses and systems of data harvesting and algorithmic processing carry a number of built-in systemic biases. In his latest book, Marc Andrejevic (2020) identifies three interrelated biases that characterize contemporary automated systems and automated processes and involve a profound shift in the production, distribution, and consumption of culture—a shift that reconfigures knowledge, social interactions, and practices, and ultimately, governance. The biases of automation discussed by Andrejevic, then, do not refer to what is normally conceived of as algorithmic bias—namely, the discriminatory outputs of algorithmic governance that we will address later. However, this does not mean neglecting the biases produced by automated decision-making systems, such as those exposed by Virginia Eubanks (2018), Cathy O'Neil (2016) and Safiya Umoja Noble (2018). Rather, Andrejevic's latest works point to the tendencies of automation that render algorithmic bias possible, normalized, and even desirable. The biases of automation "include the displacement of comprehension by correlation, of explanation by prediction and pre-emption, the triumph of efficiency over other social values, and the imperative of total information collection" (2020, p. 30).

The first bias is the "imperative of total information collection," that is, the compulsion to quantify as much of social life as possible, and translate it into data, as raw material for the monetization strategies of data colonialism (Couldry & Mejias, 2019) as well as for the correlational patterns that underpin pre-emptive logics (Andrejevic, 2020). The impulse towards the "datafication of everything" (as we entitled Chapter 2) is associated with the emergence of a new form of knowledge that Andrejevic calls "automated correlational knowledge" (2020, p. 32), which thrives on the continuous generation and flow of data. In fact, developments such as the IoTs (see Chapter 5), face and voice recognition software, emotion detection, or "empathic" media (McStay, 2018) respond to the imperative of datafication by rendering individuals, their practices, material objects, and the environment into their "data doubles" (Lyon, 2003), which ultimately enable the identification and documentation of correlational patterns amidst huge volumes of data. Algorithms are pattern extractors that identify any potential association surfacing from a dataset. However, correlational findings are not aimed at providing explanations— indeed, "the 'why?' question only slows things down" (Andrejevic, 2020,

p. 31). Rather, correlations provide "the basis for actionable information" (Andrejevic, 2020, p. 32): that is, for real-time interventions aimed at predicting future behavior, in order to anticipate, shape, and even pre-empt it. As danah boyd and Kate Crawford already pointed out in 2012, "Big Data enables the practice of apophenia" (p. 668), that is, introducing as many data points as possible into the mix allows for strong but spurious correlations to emerge. Whether such patterns offer a sensible interpretation is less relevant, provided that they persist over time and predict the future incidence of certain phenomena. The practice of predictive policing offers an exemplary model of the displacement of causality and prevention policies with correlations and pre-emption. In the context of predictive policing, understanding the causes that explain higher crime rates in certain neighborhoods, and addressing them through long-term prevention programs (for example, by providing job opportunities, better education and healthcare, etc.), is no longer required or desirable. Indeed, prevention demands for a huge investment in time, financial, and human resources. Instead, if the data showed a correlation between crime rates and weather conditions, holidays and days of the week (see, for example, Towers et al., 2018), the police could employ more officers under those climate and temporal conditions in order to pre-empt potential offenders from committing a robbery or a burglary.

Pre-emption, the second bias of automation, dispenses with explanations, replacing questions of causality with effective but opaque insights provided by AI—as the example of predictive policing above well illustrates. This is a major epistemological shift: datafication not only redefines the very boundaries of social knowledge (Couldry & Hepp, 2017)—what we are able to know—but, more significantly, what is worth knowing about our social world is what can be abstracted into and represented through data. Conversely, what eludes the conversion into quantifiable data and its algorithmic classification is not relevant and, ultimately, does not exist. A new form of knowledge is also valued, one that substitutes narrative explanations with correlational patterns that cannot be fully explained but support pre-emptive actions. In this sense, dataism as an emergent epistemological paradigm asks us to accept "on faith" unexplained or inexplicable proclamations of databases, thus reversing "one of the core principles of the Enlightenment: that knowledge is sharable because explicable" (Andrejevic, 2020, pp. 31–32).

Finally, the new epistemology enabled by datafication results in a third bias of automation that relates to the new modes of governance and surveillance that Andrejevic, drawing on Foucault, calls "environmentality."

Environmentality presupposes a shift from selective to environmental surveillance; from disciplinary power to pre-emptive power; from deterrence to "operational surveillance" (Andrejevic, 2020, p. 74) and immediate pre-emptive interventions. In other words, the focus of surveillance is no longer a particular individual who is deemed likely to commit a crime, but the environment and population as a whole. Moreover, in transforming the environment in sensing networks of internet-connected things, environmentality is post-disciplinary in the sense that it does not require the interiorization of discipline by individual subjects: it replaces it with the anticipation and pre-emption of objectionable behavior.

Combined, the three biases configure automation as fundamentally post-social: that is, aimed at displacing social processes with AI and automated processes (Andrejevic, 2020). The promise of data and automation is to replace our subjective, partial, finite, and therefore flawed and inefficient knowledge of the world, with the all-encompassing, fine-grained, objective, impartial knowledge of sensors and algorithms. Insofar as it conflates knowledge with action, automation aims to pre-empt agency. The trend towards infallible automation displacing flawed human judgment is discursively constructed as inevitable and a change for the good. The inevitability discourse is an important part of how datafication and automation are being legitimized and socially accepted (Couldry & Mejias, 2019) to the point that they become invisible:

> We don't often think of AI when we scroll or search online, and that is a sign of its commercial success. Firms have so much data about our viewing habits, our digital journeys across the web, our emails and texts and location, that they are building compelling, even addictive, infotainment machines. The less we think about how we are being influenced, the more powerful influencers can become. (Pasquale, 2020, p. 113)

Yet, despite such presumed inevitability, critical data scholars agree that, while the expansion in and further normalization of datafication, automated decision-making, and pre-emptive interventions is predictable, it is all but inevitable (Andrejevic, 2020; Couldry & Mejias, 2019).

The choice to implement massive data extraction and automation in the infrastructure and processes of governance has important social, political, and cultural consequences. The biases of automation identified by Andrejevic (2020) translate into the more familiar experience of algorithmic bias and systemic discrimination that characterize data-driven governance—automated systems of classification based on algorithmic correlational patterns and used to regulate access to resources and services and predict future behavior. The effect of the biases embedded in automated social sorting is what is usually referred to as "predictive privacy harms," that is, harms that "emerge from the inappropriate inclusion and predictive analysis of an individual's personal data without their knowledge or express consent" (Crawford & Schultz, 2014, p. 94), and can manifest in the form of discriminatory practices and "allocative harms"—namely, when they are used to legitimize the unequal allocation of resources. Predictive privacy harms, however, can also manifest in the form of "representational harms" (Burkell & Bailey, 2018), which affect how we are represented, how we perceive the world, and ultimately, how we act within it.

Algorithmic Governance, Allocative Harms, and Children's Rights

February 2021: a young boy is sitting at home in front of his laptop. His school was closed last year for a couple of months, at the height of the COVID-19 outbreak. Now schools have reopened, but his own school has already implemented the government's new plan to introduce regular remote learning days for secondary schools in an attempt to promote digital skills. After attending his online classes and completing all his school assignments, Ryan looks for emotional support to help him cope with the anxiety and challenges of the global pandemic. Ten years later, Ryan, now a successful graduate from a business school, struggles to find work as he is systematically excluded from job interviews. Eventually, he finds out that the AI recruitment software sorts his résumé out based on the online search for mental health information done during the COVID-19 pandemic. As futuristic as this scenario may sound, it is actually already present. Amidst school closures during the COVID-19 pandemic, and in order to ensure that all students had access to computers, the Singapore government provided secondary school students with laptops equipped with monitoring software. Students using their own devices have to download the software, which "would capture data such as students' search history to restrict 'objectionable material'" (Lin, 2021). Moreover, while résumé-sorting software has long been employed in large companies, AI recruitment systems, which assess an applicant's personality through voice and image recognition software, are already being used by multinational companies worldwide (Hymas, 2019; Murad, 2021). Whether it is AI recruitment software or AI emotion-recognition software in schools (Chan, 2021), the promise of dataveillance technologies of this kind is to make the process more efficient and customized, helping recruiters find the candidate who is the best fit for the position and the company, or helping teachers design individualized, emotion-maximizing learning schemes.

The COVID-19 pandemic has further exacerbated the trend towards datafication and automation, often serving as the pretext for the introduction of new intrusive monitoring systems into the very fabric of everyday life. Indeed, the exploitation of fear in times of uncertainty has always provided a fertile terrain for the experimentation and later normalization of new surveillance technologies (Lyon, 2018). A combination of facial recognition and other forms of digital identification such as digital health passports are currently being anticipated as a solution to resume air travel in the months ahead (Adams, 2021). Lockdown and other restrictive measures have already made adults and children alike even more dependent on data relations—defined as "the new types of human relations that data as a potential commodity enables" (Couldry & Mejias, 2019, p. 27)—and through which data extraction gets stabilized and normalized. Learning, working, shopping, entertainment, play, creativity, fitness, health, and social interactions have fully or partly moved online, feeding more data and turning more areas of human life into resources for data capitalism. The algorithmic classifications fueled by such data are not merely used to construct accurate profiles of consumers and deliver personalized advertising, services, and content; they are also employed in automated decision-making processes, which generate "new and opaque regimes of population management, control, discrimination and exclusion" (Kennedy, Poell, & van Dijck, 2015, p. 1).

Data and metrics have always been a constitutive part of how modern nation-states exercised power—indeed, legal rational authority for Weber (1978) is premised on bureaucracy and domination through knowledge: "Historically, the state performs sovereignty with control over and dependence on especially education, fiscal, and cultural data regimes" (Ruppert, Isin, & Bigo, 2017, p. 3). However, while it is important to historicize surveillance as the central organizing feature and mode of governance of modern societies (Lyon, 2003, 2018), we have yet to acknowledge "that the digital era represents a moment of rapid expansion of monitoring abilities, aligned with shifts in power relations and expanded forms of justifications and normalization" (Hintz, Dencik, & Wahl-Jorgensen, 2018, p. 15). Not only has the state's monopoly over the generation, collection, analysis, and use of data been challenged by pervasive commercial data extraction, with governments' increasing reliance on global corporations (Lyon, 2018), it is the unprecedented scale of data extraction and algorithmic social sorting in the allocation of both opportunities and risks that marks a shift from a surveillance state to a surveillance culture (Lyon, 2018).

Algorithmic social scoring systems, such as the infamous Chinese social credit system, embody the "total information capture" bias (Andrejevic, 2020) discussed above, in the sense that they aim to be "comprehensive" (Pasquale, 2020, p. 137) and include as many data points as possible from various sources—combining credit card records with driving behavior, posts on social media, health data, home life data, etc. A second feature of such systems is to have a "*rippling* impact well beyond the original source of violation" (Pasquale, 2020, p. 137; original emphasis), so that unjustified absence from the workplace could affect one's access to credit, if correlational knowledge (Andrejevic, 2020; see also above) showed that work conduct is related to financial credibility. Finally, an individual's credit score would have "*networked consequences*" (Pasquale, 2020, p. 137; original emphasis), affecting the reputation of friends and family. As Frank Pasquale (2020) notes, the problem lies in the systemic application of automated decision-making and algorithmic classification that, based on decontextualized and repurposed data, end up reproducing discriminatory and exclusionary practices.

In fact, algorithmic classifications regulate and govern an individual's position in society by shaping the directions and futures that become available to them, thus potentially producing new forms of digital and social inequality. While everyone is datafied and subjected to the impacts of misrepresentations and distortions of algorithmic bias, we are not equally affected:

> The pervasiveness of data relations does not mean, however, that the subjects of data colonialism are all treated the same … Today, it would superficially seem as though we are all equal subjects of data colonialism, so that economic violence is diffused almost to imperceptible levels. But in fact we are still unequally positioned by our class, race, and gender in relation to the global infrastructures and categorizing practices of the Cloud Empire. (Couldry & Mejias, 2019, p. 107)

Examples of unequal experiences of the new data regimes and of discriminatory allocation of resources on the basis of algorithmic bias have already been documented. Virginia Eubanks (2018) has shown how the introduction of automated decision-making within the infrastructures of poverty management across the U.S.—with the promise of maximizing efficiency, minimizing fraud and thus, saving money—results in the further marginalization of already vulnerable populations: immigrants, African Americans, working-class peo-ple, people with physical or cognitive impairments, and those suffering from chronic diseases are not only more exposed to government, commercial, and public dataveillance (see also Marwick & boyd, 2018); they are also discour-aged from claiming life-saving public resources by the complex and opaque procedures of automated eligibility systems. In a word, the new data regimes reproduce inequalities and further "punish the poor" (Eubanks, 2018). The U.S. is, of course, not the only country where algorithmic governmentality, implemented in order to dispense with human errors and biased judgments, ended up reproducing such biases on a larger scale and more systematically. In 2019, *The Guardian* published the "Automating Poverty" series, which hosted contributions from diverse countries including, among others, the UK (Booth, 2019), where the Department for Work and Pensions has heavily invested in the automation of the welfare system, leading to rising concerns; and India (Ratcliff, 2019), where at least 13 cases of malnutrition in Jharkhand have been linked to glitches in the Aadhaar system, the world's largest biometric identification system.

How exactly can algorithms discriminate people based on gender, age, ethnicity, and socioeconomic status? Despite popular beliefs around the neu-tral and impartial nature of algorithms, algorithms and automation systems are designed by humans. For example, in discussing the experiment with wel-fare eligibility automation in Indiana, Eubanks demonstrates how the system's fallacies are grounded in "race- and class-motivated assumptions about wel-fare recipients that were encoded into performance metrics and programmed into business processes: they are lazy and must be 'prodded' into contributing their own support, they are sneaky and prone to fraudulent claims, and their burdensome use of public resources must be repeatedly discouraged" (2018, p. 81).

"Although algorithms can be biased and designed to overvalue or under-value particular data with discriminatory effect" (Burkell & Bailey, 2018, p. 219), most of the time the bias is not encoded in the software. Rather, it can be traced back to the data. In other words, bias in the training data will be learned by the algorithm, and later systematically reproduced in their classifications, leading to "the self-reinforcing character of algorithmic dis-crimination" (Burkell & Bailey, 2018, p. 221). For example, facial recognition systems are not inherently racist for failing to identify darker skin tones—Joi Buolamwini's work (2017) has shown that darker-skin females were most often misclassified by commercial facial recognition software, whereas light-skin males were more accurately identified and classified. The misclassification lies in the biased training of AI, based mostly on images of Caucasian faces. Similarly, if a recruitment software is trained on male managers, it is unlikely to assess a woman fit for a managerial position. When a cropped photo of Alexandria Ocasio-Cortez is given to an image-generation algorithm, most of the time it will be completed with the body of a woman wearing a bikini (Hao, 2021). This is because image and language generation are trained, unsupervised, on what they find online, including hate speech and misogynous content. Other times, the source of discrimination is more hidden: for example, when the historical data used to train the algorithm do not contain explicit measures of gender or race but other measures that can act as proxies for gender and race—such as neighborhood of residence, educational attainment, and income—the algorithm can still reproduce discrimination of women and minorities (Burkell & Bailey, 2018).

More generally, the inaccuracy of algorithms originates in the very process of abstraction of lively, embodied subjects and messy practices into abstract categories that we call datafication. We shall return to the problem of data doubles in the next section on representational harms. However, to further substantiate our points with an example, let's think of automated predictions of the risk of recidivism (O'Neil, 2016). In their analysis of COMPAS (Correctional Offender Management Profiling for Alternative Sanctions), Larson et al. (2016) found that the algorithm correctly predicted the risk of recidivism only 61% of the time. Moreover, black offenders were predicted to be more likely to recidivate, on the grounds that recidivism among this group is more common in the historical data used to train the algorithm. By contrast, recidivism among white defendants tended to be under-estimated. Thus, the problems with the automated prediction of recidivism are numerous, including biased historical data—which reflect the systematic discrimination and more intense surveillance of poor and racialized communities—and biased statistical generalizations based on stereotypical assumptions about groups. Furthermore, the data fed to automated predictions of recidivisms are not representative of crime itself; rather, they only represent those criminals who have been convicted and jailed, but many crimes remain unpunished (Pasquale, 2020). Labeling theory in sociology has already highlighted how "deviance" is socially constructed through a power relation between those who have the power to label certain behaviors and categories as deviant and those who are subordinated to such labels (Becker, 1963). Deviant identities are now algorithmically produced, but the technologization of the social process of labeling deepens power inequalities and discrimination through a systematic application of the multiple prejudices and subjective biases embedded in the historical data, as the example of COMPAS shows. Therefore, whenever we are tempted to "discount algorithmic biases on the ground that they represent statistically valid generalizations" (Burkell & Bailey, 2018, p. 219), we should remember that algorithmic predictions depend on the accuracy and representativity of training data. If training data are not sufficiently representative of the populations on which the algorithm will be applied, it will likely produce problematic consequences. Far from impartial and generalizable, then, correlational knowledge is irrevocably socially situated and inextricably "entangled with the data used for training" (Pasquale, 2020, p. 129).

Moreover, algorithmic judgments are opaque, "unexplained (or unexplainable)" (Pasquale, 2020, p. 129), raising issues of (in)accountability and even alienation. According to Shoshana Zuboff, surveillance capitalism is premised on "illegible mechanisms of extraction, commodification, and control" that "effectively exile persons from their own behavior" (Zuboff, 2015, p. 75). The opacity and inexplicability of the mathematical models used in automated decision-making is the rule, not the exception (O'Neil, 2016), against which citizens are powerless, having little knowledge, resources, and opportunities to challenge algorithmic predictions and inferences. Therefore, we can conclude with Barassi that:

> ... algorithms are always and inevitably fallacious for three main reasons: 1. They rely on imprecise and decontextualized data (algorithmic inaccuracy); 2. They are often un-explainable and unaccountable (algorithmic un-explicability); 3. They are biased (algorithmic bias). (Barassi, 2020, p. 151)

Insofar as they prevent access to basic resources, algorithmic allocative harms extend and exacerbate "the impact of racialized and other instances of violence" (Hoffmann, 2020, p. 4) and erode citizenship and/or human rights. Against this background, critical data scholars and data justice activists have called for efforts to mitigate algorithmic bias and systemic automated discriminations through transparency, accountability, and fairness of AI. However, calling for more inclusive and transparent AI is not without problems. As Hoffmann (2020) argues, inclusion is not a solution to algorithmic discrimination, since it does not question the legitimacy of practices of data extraction, nor of the practice of classifying individuals under socially and algorithmic-constructed categories that are assumed as natural. Inclusion is often addressed by simply "expanding the checkboxes and data input fields for identity markers like gender, race, or sexuality" (Hoffmann, 2020, p. 2) in ways that result in more accurate profiling of consumers. Inclusion also means reproducing inequalities, such as when Google's contractors scanned black homeless people's faces to improve Google's facial recognition technology (Nicas, 2019). Rather than a panacea, then, inclusion:

> ... neutralizes critical calls to not collect certain kinds of data or build and deploy certain technologies by reframing the issue as exclusively one of iteration, improvement, and doing things more inclusively. (Hoffmann, 2020, p. 10)

Attempts to mend automated decision-making, therefore, are complemented by calls for ending it altogether, on the grounds that "just and inclusive governance is not [and can never be] algorithmic" (Pasquale, 2020, p. 103).

Algorithmic Identification, Representational Harms, and Children's Wellbeing

In addition to discriminatory allocative outcomes, algorithmic biases have serious symbolic and cultural consequences that span from the epistemic gaps of algorithmic identifications—the inevitable distance between the datafied identity and the lived identity it represents—to the impact of harmful stereotypes—what legal scholars refer to as "representational harms"—to the novel social imaginary that legitimizes the social order of data colonialism.

Algorithmic identification has been the focus of attention for many scholars, encompassing both those mainly interested in accounting for the emergence of a new business logic that thrives on the pervasive expansion of data extraction and monetization and those who take a broader view of algorithmic classifications by examining issues of symbolic power and emerging epistemologies. Among the first, Zuboff (2015) talks about the "formal indifference" of algorithms to explain the conversion of lived experiences into abstract, decontextualized data that can be commercially exploited. Algorithmic classifications do not aim at providing authentic representations of individual users, but effective models that allow predictive anticipations of such users' future behavior. In her own words, "Google is 'formally indifferent' to what its users say or do, as long as they say it and do it in ways that Google can capture and convert into data" (Zuboff, 2015, p. 79). In pointing out the asymmetrical process at play, Zuboff anticipates later theorizing on data relations as new forms of power relations, by highlighting how the conversion from life to data is a unidirectional process of translation: "extraction is a one-way process, not a relationship" (Zuboff, 2015, p. 79). Every translation is always a form of betrayal, in which something gets irremediably lost.[1] Data extraction and abstraction involves a process of translation in which what is lost, ultimately, is our subjectivity, that comes to be configured as a flaw against the background of datafication. Surveillance capitalism does not allow for singularity and plurality to emerge. Rather, subjectivities need to be standardized into common patterns:

> Indeed, it is the status of such data as signals of subjectivities that makes them most valuable for advertisers. For Google and other 'big data' aggregators, however, the data are merely bits. Subjectivities are converted into objects that repurpose the subjective for commodification. Individual users' meanings are of no interest to Google or other firms in this chain. (Zuboff, 2015, p. 79)

Further theorization of algorithmic "data selves" is provided by John Cheney-Lippold, whose 2017 book investigates the power relations and epistemological shifts involved in the making of data doubles. Many points raised by Cheney-Lippold are relevant for our understanding of the symbolic consequences of datafication for children's futures: first, the observation that algorithmically produced categories are neither static nor stable constructs; rather, they are dynamic and continuously changing. As a consequence, algorithmic identifications are always ephemeral and temporary. Users are temporarily assigned to "measurable types" (Cheney-Lippold, 2017)—such as "child" or "adult," "boy" or "girl," etc.—based on the correspondence of their personal and behavioral data with pre-identified algorithmic templates. In other words, a measurable type is "a dynamic data template" that "compares streams of new data to existing datafied models" (Cheney-Lippold, 2017, p. 47) in order to generate more accurate and effective analytical models for users' profiling and consumers' behavioral predictions. Such datafied identity templates "become more important of who we *really* are or who we may choose to be" (Cheney-Lippold, 2017, p. 47; original emphasis). Yet, as with every form of representation, data doubles are inaccurate measures that reduce the complexity and diversity of lived experiences. The extraction and abstraction of data from the messiness of everyday life always involves some form of imperfection and reductionism. An epistemic gap comes to exist between the nuanced and complex offline identities and their online simplistic and absolute, although ephemeral, transcoding. While a similar partial translation is constitutive of datafication, it is ultimately irrelevant provided that quotation-marked categories fit into effective users' profiles and provide actionable knowledge—that is, "algorithmic truth" (Cheney-Lippold, 2017, p. 9) replaces authenticity with efficacy and near real-time pre-emption. As Cathy O'Neil explains:

> . . . the real world, with all its messiness, sits apart. The inclination is to replace people with data trails, turning them into more effective shoppers, voters, or workers to optimize some objectives. (O'Neil, 2016, p. 48)

Furthermore, since algorithms are proprietary and opaque, "measurable types" are also fundamentally unknowable and unexplainable: "when algorithmic pattern analyses produce the discursive contours of our identification, who we are becomes an unexplainable phenomenon" (Cheney-Lippold, 2017, p. 58). The process of algorithmic identification means that on the internet children are not what they claim they are, nor exactly the identities they perform online. Rather, "a child 'is' according to what they do" (Willson, 2018, p. 13), or, more precisely, a child "is" according to how closely his or her data stacks up to pre-existing categories of children. While question-marked categories are based on the interplay between the data that represent users' performances and their near real-time algorithmic interpretation, within the process of algorithmic transcoding subjects' agency and knowledge is null.

Compared to adults, children's ability to control their data doubles is even lower, since they are reconfigured into "algorithmic assemblages" (Lupton & Williamson, 2017, p. 787) on the basis of data often generated through adult profiles or aggregated household profiles (Barassi, 2020). Children are classified as temporary members of "measurable types" without their knowledge or expressed consent. Ultimately, datafication turns children into always present but invisible data subjects. As a result, they are not only positioned within partial and reductionist data templates; they are also represented and spoken for in ways they cannot understand or control. Within the process of datafication and algorithmic translation, then, "the embodied and subjective voices of children are displaced by the supposed impartial objectivity provided by the technological mouthpieces of data" (Lupton & Williamson, 2017, p. 790).

The process of algorithmic translation of subjects into their data doubles is a demarcation of power: we are represented, spoken for, and regulated by unknown data and opaque algorithms that set the discursive boundaries of our identities and our agency, by assigning us into transient measurable types. Algorithmic social sorting frames the conditions of possibility for our self-expression and agency. As Cheney-Lippold writes:

We are not simply well filled of data but made of data that is interpreted, conferred truth, and disseminated for motives of profit, organization and/or control. The resulting classifications become the discursive terrain from which we, and others, compose our digital selves. (Cheney-Lippold, 2017, p. 12)

In this perspective, we can conclude that datafication is first and foremost a discursive process that enables algorithmic governance and the reallocation of material resources based on the quantification of the value of individuals and their algorithmic classifications (Couldry & Mejias, 2019; Hoffmann, 2020). Algorithmic social sorting, in this respect, is a more efficient and enhanced administration of the power to bestow recognition on specific groups while excluding others. Algorithmic correlational knowledge means that what can be known about the social world is exclusively what can be digitally monitored and quantified; conversely, what is not represented by data is not only invisible, but also excluded and marginalized, as it did not belong to the social world. Furthermore, beyond the allocational harms already discussed in the previous section, the inevitable reductionism of algorithmic identifications generates representational harms. Individuals are targeted as members of social groups (Eubanks, 2018) rather than for their diverse, multiple, and complex subjectivities. Algorithmic classifications generate stereotyped identities, which influence both the impressions that others form about us as well as our own self-image. Therefore, quotation-marked datafied identities mediate and profoundly reshape our self-presentation and interactions with others—which, as Goffman (1959) well exemplified, are aimed at controlling the definition of the situation and managing the impressions we project onto others. Not only do we end up being represented by data doubles that are unexplainable and unknowable to us; the very social interactions that such data doubles allow are opaque and evade our control. Algorithmic representation is, therefore, a form of violation, a systematic symbolic violence, as we will argue below. Indeed, representational biases:

... that generalize about groups of people based on socially constructed categories like race degrade, diminish the dignity of, and marginalize individuals who are understood to occupy the categories that come to be defined by these biased generalizations. They affect not only who others believe us to be, but also who we believe ourselves to be, and thus they influence psychological well-being and behaviour. (Burkell & Bailey, 2018, p. 220)

Representational harms affect not only the redistribution of, and access to, resources and opportunities, but also one's sense of self. In fact, when algorithmic classifications are returned to us in the form of advertisements, suggestions for cultural products, identified gender of friends and acquaintances, or allocative harms, they shape, in turn, our horizons of expectations and practices (Burkell & Bailey, 2018). In so doing, they contribute to normalize arbitrary discriminations that lie behind gendered, racist, class, and other stereotypes. That is, algorithmic identifications are a form of symbolic power that consists of "the power to constitute the given by stating it, to act upon the world by acting upon the representation of the world" (Bourdieu & Wacquant, 1992, p. 148). In Bourdieu's social theory, algorithmic classifications are not dissimilar to language, in that both reproduce the power of dominant actors by imposing it as legitimate and even natural. The resulting symbolic violence, in fact, requires the recognition and legitimization by those who are subordinated and subjected to discrimination. Symbolic violence is "defined in and by a definite relation that creates belief in the legitimacy of the words and of the person who utters them, and it operates only inasmuch as those who undergo it recognize those who wield it" (Bourdieu & Wacquant, 1992, p. 148). Therefore, symbolic power is violent precisely because it is premised on misrecognition: a specific form of violence characterized by not being recognized as a form of oppression and, conversely, being taken as a given, natural condition, because it operates in the background, hidden beneath stereotypes, commonsense knowledge and social norms. In her critical examination of the discourse of inclusion as a (flawed) remedy to mitigate allocative harms, Hoffmann equally insists on the symbolic violence of algorithmic classifications, which accomplishes power relations in the form of normative discourses, deepening our implications in oppressive and discriminatory social orders:

> ... the ways data are labeled, people are classified, or systems are implemented may inflict symbolic or representational violences—that is, they may reproduce racist, sexist, and other norms and stereotypes that position some people as subordinate, inferior, or irredeemably 'other.' (Hoffmann, 2020, pp. 3–4)

Dataism and algorithmic knowledge give shape to a social imaginary in which dataveillance, algorithmic identifications, and the resulting discriminatory classifications that reproduce social inequalities and power imbalances are normalized and legitimized. Social imaginaries can be defined as "common understanding that makes possible common practices and a widely shared sense of legitimacy" (Taylor, 2004, p. 23). The contemporary algorithmic and datafied imaginary informs individuals' self-presentation, social interactions, and agency through shared expectations and norms regarding the regimes of visibility and invisibility (Lyon, 2018). A further influence of algorithmic identifications on children, therefore, relates to the colonization of the most mundane yet intimate and affective dimensions of everyday life (Couldry & Mejias, 2019) and the associated socialization to datafication as a natural condition of society. When children are coerced to participate in data relations as the normal form of mediatized connectedness—a tendency that has been further accelerated by restrictions on face-to-face interactions during the COVID-19 pandemic—their classification according to the personal, behavioral, and emotional data extracted and abstracted from the flow of their everyday lives is perceived as natural and inevitable. Yet children are not indifferent or completely inure to the privacy implications of their datafied selves. A systematic evidence review of children's understanding of privacy online (Stoilova, Nandagiri, & Livingstone, 2019) has shown that, since most research is concentrated on privacy problems in the context of interpersonal relationships online, there is little evidence on whether and how children understand the complexity of profiling and datafication in commercial relationships. Studies on children's understanding of the consequences of algorithmic identifications, however, highlight that children feel annoyed and disempowered by their inability to control the collection, analysis, and use of data about them by internet companies (Perez Vallejos et al., 2021).

The pervasive diffusion of the imaginary of dataism (van Dijck, 2014)—with its imperatives of data collection, connectivity, and transparency, and the discourses of inevitability and personalization (Couldry & Mejias, 2019; see also Chapter 2)—embeds children in ever-intensifying networks of surveillance, through which they "become 'calculable persons' who are the subject of calculations performed by others (and by other digital things)" (Lupton & Williamson, 2017, p. 787). The result is a deeper, more effective interiorization of a "quantified habitus" (Mascheroni, 2018). Since early childhood, children learn how to share mundane aspects of their daily lives as a constitutive component of their interactions with others and with the world, and in so doing, incorporate the habit of measuring and benchmarking their identities, appearance, and performance against the backdrop of standard measures and normative pressures. When the presentation of self and identity is substantially mediated by the opaque regimes of algorithmic visibility (Bucher, 2018) and the social media logic of popularity (van Dijck & Poell, 2013), tensions arise out of the conflicting pressures in social media: the pressure to conform to the socially accepted conventions and codes of self-presentation of a peer group versus the pressures of the dominant celebrity culture, and the desperate attempt to avoid the "threat of invisibility" (Bucher, 2018). Since becoming visible or invisible is, partly, at least, an algorithmic achievement that goes beyond an individual's ability to control their accessibility and popularity— except for influencers and DIY celebrities (see Chapter 6)—constructing and interacting with peers online can have harmful consequences for children's wellbeing and sense of self (Mascheroni, Vincent, & Jimenez, 2015; Perez Vallejos et al., 2021). For example, studies show how girls conform to popular feminine beauty standards in constructing their online identities and pursuing algorithmic visibility because of the social pressures to ground their self-confidence in beauty and appearance (Gill, 2003). However, when they successfully perform the normative sexualized pattern that dominates visual representations of (adult) femininity, they are blamed by boys for "posing sexy" (Mascheroni et al., 2015; see also Chapter 6, this book). Conversely, girls (and boys) who reject the visual gendered codes of advertising and popular culture, or who do not conform to binary, mono-sexual gendered representations, are equally at risk of being marginalized.

Automation and the Future of Democracy

The widespread use of automated decision-making systems, and the resulting allocative and representational harms, "impacts the quality of democracy for us all" (Eubanks, 2018, p. 12). Throughout this book we have made the argument that the consequences for children cannot be fully speculated but are likely to be serious. When their future is decided by algorithms predicting their probability of success at university, or their suitability for a job position, or their likely recidivism—and, therefore, their inclusion in re-education programs—inequalities are introduced in their very access to resources and opportunities. Moreover, when algorithms are programmed based not only on children's data but also on their parents', inequities and discriminations come to be systematically reproduced, conditioning children's entitlement to social, civic, and political rights. Social inclusion and a better future can become unattainable for many.

In addition, there's a further way in which the influence of automated algorithmic processes on democracy is played out: namely, on the remediation of our "public connection" (Couldry, Livingstone, & Markham, 2007). Public connection is the "orientation to the public world where matters of shared concern are, or at least should be addressed" (Couldry et al., 2007, p. 3): that is, a basic civic orientation to social and political issues as problems that affect every member of a given (national, local, or transnational) community. As such, it is a form of latent engagement, which can be activated and translated into attention and political participation under specific conditions, including elections, environmental, health, political, or economic crises. In contemporary societies the shared orientation to issues of common concern or interest and our civic engagement is sustained through the media—in fact, we can now speak of a "mediated public connection" (Couldry et al., 2007) to highlight how everyday practices of media use and news consumption are interwoven with public engagement. However, the media, and the process of mediatization (Couldry & Hepp, 2017), has been highly relevant to the current changes in social structures and political institutions that are reshaping public connection. Moreover, new questions arise regarding the relationship between media engagement and public engagement, since "networked publics" (boyd, 2010) emerging out of the infrastructures and logics of social media (van Dijck & Poell, 2013) provide interactional contexts where the political and non-political, the public and the private, converge and collapse. The question is, then, how news consumption in algorithmically governed online environments such as social media shape, pollute, or threaten (young) citizens' "mediated public connection."

The changes in news consumption that result from the algorithmic selection and customization of digital content have captured most of the attention in both the academic and public agendas. However, the research aimed at empirically verifying the existence, and the consequences, of algorithmic "filter bubbles" (Pariser, 2011) and "echo chambers" (Sunstein, 2009)—namely, political fragmentation and polarization—has surfaced contested results. Most recent research claims that the use of social media and online outlets is associated with incidental exposure to a more diverse range of news sources (Fletcher & Nielsen, 2018; Vaccari et al., 2016), concluding that the existence of echo chambers has been overstated due to methodological limitations (Dubois & Blank, 2018). Alternatively, the latest Pew Research Center report on US citizens' pathways to news consumption (Mitchell et al., 2021) shows that during the 2020 election campaign, one in four Democrats or Republicans chose news media outlets that aligned with their political leanings.

Whether online media outlets and social media lead to greater political homophily or, vice versa, exposure to more diverse opinions may not be the right question. In fact, as Andrejevic (2020) argues, the focus on the range and quality of contents to which internet users are exposed diverts attention from the other side of both Pariser's (2011) and Sunstein's (2009) argument—that is, the shifts in public connection towards a greater individualized orientation. In fact, while the evidence regarding the existence of filter bubbles and echo chambers is disputed, the evidence around the resulting political polarization and fragmentation is less contested. On the first side, "one of the apparent effects of the automated distribution of content is the mainstreaming of what were once considered fringe, extremist views" (Andrejevic, 2020, p. 50). The Pew Research Center report (Mitchell et al., 2021) found a strong correlation between exposure to like-minded news media outlets and reinforcement of an individual's political views. The same report also provides empirical evidence for the idea of a more fragmented public sphere by showing how Americans inhabited different and isolated information environments that led to competing views of COVID-19 and the development of the elections. Furthermore, those citizens who relied mainly on social media to get their news were generally less informed about politics and current events, and more exposed to disinformation and misinformation during the course of 2020—including the belief that the spread of the virus is related to 5G, and that daily intakes of vitamin C are an effective prevention strategy (Mitchell et al., 2021). So, even if we refuted the idea of filter bubbles altogether, political radicalization and fragmentation cannot be dismissed. Rather,

> . . . it may be that, in a context of media surfeit, people find themselves both exposed to a broader range of information and less inclined to take into consideration the larger community of which they are part and the perspectives of those unknown others who comprise it. (Andrejevic, 2020, p. 48)

Political radicalization is also exacerbated by algorithmically generated, data-driven disinformation campaigns, orchestrated through a combination of automated and human-curated social media campaigns—what Howard (2020) has defined as "computational propaganda." "Lie machines" are organized to reach three simultaneous goals: radicalizing ideological differences and mainstreaming extremist views; discrediting political opponents; and suppressing voter turnout (Howard, 2020). Cambridge Analytica's (CA) involvement in both the Vote Leave campaign in the UK and the 2016 presidential elections in the U.S. (Cadwalladr, 2017; Cadwalladr and Graham-Harrison, 2018)—in which CA first managed the campaign of Senator Ted Cruz and, from September, that of Donald Trump[2]—is the most emblematic example of a manipulative campaign strategy that exploits the networked infrastructure and advertising services offered by social media to seek out networked-specific effects, by reaching undecided voters in particular electoral districts with personalized political ads that match their personality traits. Lie machines embody the "subversive style" of data-driven, micro-targeted campaigns: that is, data and automation are employed in an attempt to demobilize turnouts for competitors and sow resentment and fear (Römmele & Gibson, 2020). In generating new conspiracy theories, subversive campaigns deepen citizens' distrust in the institutions of representative democracy. In fact, computational propaganda operations:

> ... appeal to emotions and prejudices and use our cognitive biases to bypass rational thought. They repeat big political lies to misinform some people and introduce doubt among even the most active and knowledgeable citizens. They work because we ourselves generate the data used to craft manipulative content. (Howard, 2020, p. 137)

The costs of political radicalization and fragmentation, either generated by filter bubbles or lie machines—or, most probably, a combination of the two—are both personal and social. If the consequences are already visible now, with disoriented networked publics torn between fear, anger, and distrust, what will happen to children and young people who are growing up in a time when real and counterfeit cannot be told apart? Will the continuous production of misinformed citizens and misinformed political leaders, and the displacement of public connection with individualized consumerism, eventually lead to the dissolution of any civic orientation? Shall we be resigned to the idea that "this thing we think of as 'the public' will almost fully dissolve" (Howard, 2020, p. 154)?

The (Digital) Rights of the Child

If, in spite of the examples provided throughout this chapter, you are still not fully persuaded that data collected by and about children since they are born—or even since gestation—can impact their futures through allocative and representational harms, let us provide a further example. In February 2021, *The Guardian* published the story of a South London boy who saw his dream of becoming an architect threatened by an algorithm (Lamont, 2021). Josiah is just one of the many British young people who failed their A-Level tests because of the fallacies and biases of an algorithmic rating system, which especially penalized students in disadvantaged schools. His battle was eventually won, but how many children have been left behind? It's time we asked not only how children's data will be used, by whom, and with what purposes—data and algorithmic decision-making systems could be used to inform long-term evidence-based preventive programs to ensure all children have access equal education opportunities, and to foster social inclusion and cohesion. Alternatively, as the numerous examples of automation bias suggest, data and algorithms could define pre-emptive, discriminatory practices, which would exclude children assigned to specific profiles from certain types of education, or from health insurance and loans, with the effect of exacerbating inequalities and fully pre-determining children's experiences and life course. We should also consider whether to end, rather than amend, the collection and manipulation of children's data altogether, at least when used by companies for profiling and behavioral advertising, and by institutions in ways that run the risk of exacerbating structural vulnerabilities and social injustice.

The problem is that addressing the issue of the future consequences of datafication and automation for children goes beyond the inclusion discourse, with its fallacious attempt at circumventing algorithmic bias through a more accurate profiling (Hoffmann, 2020). It also means balancing the risk and safety agenda that has dominated much research and policy-making so far with "rights-based approaches to children's digital media practices" (Livingstone & Third, 2017, p. 666) that would acknowledge the tensions between rights to protection and rights to participation.

Even though 1989 marked both the birth of the World Wide Web and the adoption of the United Nations Convention on the Rights of the Child (UNCRC), these two worlds have proceeded autonomously, with almost no intersection. So, a paradox exists whereby children make up one-third of the overall internet population, and are usually conceived of as digital pioneers, yet the internet "has been largely conceived, implicitly or explicitly, as an adult resource in terms of provision, regulation and ideology" (Livingstone & Third, 2017, p. 658). In fact, embedding children's interests in the design of the digital world has long been considered too complicated and expensive. Moreover, the regulative frameworks have either neglected children or, whenever children are taken into consideration as rights holders, focus on protection alone. Livingstone and Third attribute the failure to recognize children in regulatory frameworks of the internet to two tendencies: first, the assumption that children are implicitly included in the human rights framework; and second,

... an exceptionalist approach [which] constructs the child as precisely unlike adults in being developmentally inferior and more vulnerable, thereby denying children rights that go beyond vulnerability, notably the right to participate in society as agents, let alone citizens (Lister, 2008) or, even, recognizing their agency only to burden them with an excessive responsibility—for self-protection, for peer responsibility, for acting 'better' than the adults around them, under the banner of 'digital citizenship.' (Livingstone & Third, 2017, p. 661)

Two normative frameworks explicitly address children (although they are limited to children's rights to privacy and data protection, and ignore their rights to participation, provision, learning, and so on). The first is the U.S. federal law, the Children's Online Privacy Protection Act (COPPA), that aims at providing parents with control over their children's data, by imposing a set of requirements on digital platforms and services. "The main legislative rationale behind COPPA is that the personal data of children under 13 years of age must not be processed by an operator unless parental consent is obtained" (Milkaite & Lievens, 2019, p. 289) through a number of verification methods, including the "print-and-send" method, the "email plus" method, requiring the parent to call a toll-free telephone number, or to use a credit card. While COPPA represented a first step towards children's privacy and data protection, uncertainties persist both in relation to the verification methods and to voice assistants and smart devices that are not specifically intended for children but collect their data as part of adults' or aggregate profiles. The EU legal framework for children's right to privacy is provided by the General Data Protection Regulation (GDPR), which entered into force on May 25, 2018. If Article 38 of the GDPR identifies children as more vulnerable data subjects, Article 8 specifies the requirements regarding parental consent for the processing of personal data of children under the age of 16. The age threshold can be lowered by Member State to 15, 14, or 13 (see Milkaite & Lievens, 2018, for age limits in each EU country). As with COPPA, Article 8 raises significant challenges regarding its practical implementation and its implications for children's rights. Even if the problem of age verification is eventually solved, it remains questionable as to whether parents are, in fact, best suited to protect their children online. Many parents lack knowledge of what their children do online and feel that their children are better informed regarding online services. Additionally, parents may have little time or patience to read complex privacy policies, raising questions as to what extent consent can actually be considered informed (van der Hof, 2017). Moreover, children's rights to privacy and data protection could actually conflict with children's right to participation, as when parents fail to provide consent, so restricting a teenager's opportunity to engage with peers on social media, maintain their online identity, pursue their interests, etc.

In fact, the UNCRC provides a more complex framework for children's rights, encompassing both children's right to privacy (Article 16) and protection against economic exploitation (Article 32), but also to participation and to have their voices heard in matters of their concern (Article 12), to have their best interests respected (Article 3), the right to identity (Article 8), education (Articles 28 and 29), and play (Article 31), the rights to freedom of expression and association (Articles 13 and 15), and the right to information and media (Article 17). It is, therefore, a great achievement of children's rights advocates that on February 4, 2021 the UN Committee on the Rights of the Child adopted General Comment 25, which extends children's rights to the digital environment (Livingstone, 2021). The document includes guidelines on how states should implement the Convention. More specifically, General Comment 25:

> ... clarifies what the digital environment means for children's civil rights and freedoms, their rights to privacy, non-discrimination, protection, education, play and more. It also explains why States and other duty bearers must act and, within the limits of 10,700 words, how they should act. (Livingstone, 2021)

While its enforcement will not be without challenges, General Comment 25 represents the public recognition of an alternative discourse, one that contrasts the imperative of dataism and its supposed inevitability with the claim that children's rights apply online as well as offline. Therefore, we believe that we are at an opportune moment, given current trajectories, to call into question the continued datafication of childhood at home, at school, and in a child's peer group, and to imagine a different future in which data are repurposed for the social good and best interests of children.

Notes

1 This is what Giovanna's teacher of Ancient Greek and Latin in high school used to say, and which became so deeply stuck in Giovanna's memory as to be transposed to algorithmic transcoding (which, indeed, is a specific form of translation).
2 Alexander Nix, CEO of Cambridge Analytica, presented the company's behavioral marketing strategy and revealed their involvement in Cruz's and later Trump's campaigns—although he does not mention Trump, but only one of the candidates—at the Concordia Summit in New York (see www.youtube.com/watch?v=n8Dd5aVXLCc&t=86s).

References

Adams, D. R. (2021). Facial recognition executive talks vaccine passports, data privacy, and surveillance. TechRepublic, February 18. www.techrepublic.com/article/facial-recognition-executive-talks-vaccine-passports-data-privacy-and-surveillance/

Andrejevic, M. (2020). *Automated media*. Routledge.

Barassi, V. (2020). *Child | Data | Citizen. How tech-companies are profiling us from before birth*. The MIT Press.

Becker, H. (1963). *Outsiders: Studies in the sociology of deviance*. Free Press.

Booth, R. (2019). Benefits system automation could plunge claimants deeper into poverty. *The Guardian*, October 14. www.theguardian.com/technology/2019/oct/14/fears-rise-in-benefits-system-automation-could-plunge-claimants-deeper-into-poverty

Bourdieu, P., & Wacquant, L. J. (1992). *An invitation to reflexive sociology*. University of Chicago Press.

boyd, D. (2010). Social network sites as networked publics: Affordances, dynamics, and implications. In Z. Papacharissi (Ed.), *Networked self: Identity, community, and culture on social network sites* (pp. 39–58). Routledge.

boyd, D., & Crawford, K. (2012). Critical questions for big data: Provocations for a cultural, technological, and scholarly phenomenon. *Information, Communication & Society, 15*(5), 662–679. https://doi.org/10.1080/1369118X.2012.678878

Bucher, T. (2018). *If . . . then: Algorithmic power and politics*. Oxford University Press.

Buolamwini, J. (2017). *Gender shades: Intersectional phenotypic and demographic evaluation of face datasets and gender classifiers*. MIT Master's Thesis. www.media.mit.edu/publications/full-gender-shades-thesis-17/

Burkell, J., & Bailey, J. (2018). Unlawful distinctions? Canadian human rights law and algorithmic bias. In *2016/2018 Canadian yearbook for human rights* (pp. 217–230). Human Rights Research and Education Centre. https://cdp-hrc.uottawa.ca/sites/cdp-hrc.uottawa.ca/files/uottawa-cyhr1618-v11.pdf

Cadwalladr, C. (2017). The great British Brexit robbery: How our democracy was hijacked. *The Guardian*, May 7. www.theguardian.com/technology/2017/may/07/the-great-british-brexit-robbery-hijacked-democracy

Cadwalladr, C., & Graham-Harrison, E. (2018). Revealed: 50 million Facebook profiles harvested for Cambridge Analytica in major data breach. *The Guardian*, March 17. www.theguardian.com/news/2018/mar/17/cambridge-analytica-facebook-influence-us-election

Chan, M. (2021). This AI reads children's emotions as they learn. *CNN*, February 17. https://edition.cnn.com/2021/02/16/tech/emotion-recognition-ai-education-spc-intl-hnk/index.html

Cheney-Lippold, J. (2017). *We are data: Algorithms and the making of our digital selves*. New York University Press.

Couldry, N., & Hepp, A. (2017). *The mediated construction of reality*. Polity.

Couldry, N., Livingstone, S., & Markham, T. (2007). *Media consumption and public engagement: Beyond the presumption of attention*. Palgrave.

Couldry, N., & Mejias, U. A. (2019). *The costs of connection: How data is colonizing human life and appropriating it for capitalism.* Stanford University Press.

Crawford, K., & Schultz, J. (2014). Big data and due process: Toward a framework to redress predictive privacy harms. *Boston College Law Review, 55*(1), 93–128.

Dubois, E., & Blank, G. (2018). The echo chamber is overstated: The moderating effect of political interest and diverse media. *Information, Communication & Society, 21*(5), 729–745. https://doi.org/10.1080/1369118X.2018.1428656

Eubanks, V. (2018). *Automating inequality: How high-tech tools profile, police, and punish the poor.* St Martin's Press.

Fletcher, R., & Nielsen, R. K. (2018). Are people incidentally exposed to news on social media? A comparative analysis. *New Media & Society, 20*(7), 2450–2468. https://doi.org/10.1177/1461444817724170

Gill, R. (2003). From sexual objectification to sexual subjectification: The resexualisation of women's bodies in the media. *Feminist Media Studies, 3*(1), 100–106.

Goffman, E. (1959). *The presentation of self in everyday life.* Doubleday.

Hao, K. (2021). An AI saw a cropped photo of AOC. It autocompleted her wearing a bikini. *MIT Technology Review,* January 29. www.technologyreview.com/2021/01/29/1017065/ai-image-generation-is-racist-sexist/

Hintz, A., Dencik, L., & Wahl-Jorgensen, K. (2018). *Digital citizenship in a datafied society.* Polity.

Hoffmann, A. L. (2020). Terms of inclusion: Data, discourse, violence. *New Media & Society.* https://doi.org/10.1177/1461444820958725

Howard, P. N. (2020). *Lie machines. How to save democracies from troll armies, deceitful robots, junk news operations and political operatives.* Yale University Press.

Hymas, C. (2019). AI used for first time in job interviews in UK to find best applicants. *The Telegraph,* September 27. www.telegraph.co.uk/news/2019/09/27/ai-facial-recognition-used-first-time-job-interviews-uk-find/

Kennedy, H., Poell, T., & van Dijck, J. (2015). Data and agency. *Big Data & Society, 2*(2), 1–7. https://doi.org/10.1177/2053951715621569

Lamont, T. (2021). The student and the algorithm: How the exam results fiasco threatened one pupil's future. *The Guardian,* February 18. www.theguardian.com/education/2021/feb/18/the-student-and-the-algorithm-how-the-exam-results-fiasco-threatened-one-pupils-future?CMP=Share_iOSApp_Other

Larson, J., Mattu, S., Kirchner, L., & Angwin, J. (2016). How we analyzed the COMPAS recidivism algorithm. *ProPublica,* May 16. www.propublica.org/article/how-we-analyzed-the-compas-recidivism-algorithm

Lin, C. (2021). Singapore plan to use monitoring app on students' computers sparks privacy fears. *Reuters,* 8 February. www.reuters.com/article/us-singapore-privacy/singapore-plan-to-use-monitoring-app-on-students-computers-sparks-privacy-fears-idUSKBN2A80Q6

Lister, R. (2008). Unpacking children's citizenship. In A. Invernizzi & J. Williams (Eds.), *Children and Citizenship* (pp. 9–19). SAGE Publications Ltd.

Livingstone, S. (2021). Children's rights apply in the digital world! Media@LSE blog, February 4. https://blogs.lse.ac.uk/medialse/2021/02/04/childrens-rights-apply-in-the-digital-world/

Livingstone, S., & Third, A. (2017). Children and young people's rights in the digital age: An emerging agenda. *New Media & Society, 19*(5), 657–670. https://doi.org/10.1177/1461444816686318

Lupton, D., & Williamson, B. (2017). The datafied child: The dataveillance of children and implications for their rights. *New Media & Society, 19*(5), 780–794.

Lyon, D. (2003). Surveillance as social sorting. Computer codes and mobile bodies. In D. Lyon (Ed.), *Surveillance as social sorting: Privacy, risk, and digital discrimination* (pp. 13–30). Routledge.

Lyon, D. (2018). *The culture of surveillance: Watching as a way of life.* Polity.

Marwick, A. E., & boyd, D. (2018). Privacy at the margins | Understanding privacy at the margins—Introduction. *International Journal of Communication, 12,* 9. https://ijoc.org/index.php/ijoc/article/view/7053

Mascheroni, G. (2018). Researching datafied children as data citizens. *Journal of Children and Media, 12*(4), 517–523. https://doi.org/10.1080/17482798.2018.1521677

Mascheroni, G., Vincent, J., & Jimenez, E. (2015). "Girls are addicted to likes so they post semi-naked selfies": Peer mediation, normativity and the construction of identity online. *Cyberpsychology: Journal of Psychosocial Research on Cyberspace, 9*(1), article 5. https://doi.org/10.5817/CP2015-1-5

McStay, A. (2018). *Emotional AI: The rise of empathic media.* SAGE Publications Ltd.

Milkaite, I., & Lievens, E. (2018). GDPR is here: Mapping the GDPR age of consent across the EU. Better Internet for Kids. www.betterinternetforkids.eu/web/portal/practice/awareness/detail?articleId=3017751

Milkaite, I., & Lievens, E. (2019). The Internet of Toys: Playing games with children's data? In G. Mascheroni & D. Holloway (Eds.), *The Internet of Toys: Practices, affordances and the political economy of children's smart play* (pp. 285–305). Palgrave.

Mitchell, A., Jurkowitz, M., Oliphant, J. B., & Shearer, E. (2021). *How Americans navigated the news in 2020: A tumultuous year in review.* Pew Research Center, February 22. www.journalism.org/2021/02/22/how-americans-navigated-the-news-in-2020-a-tumultuous-year-in-review/

Murad, A. (2021). The computers rejecting your job application. BBC News, February 8. www.bbc.com/news/business-55932977

Nicas, J. (2019). Atlanta asks Google whether it targeted black homeless people. *The New York Times,* October 4. www.nytimes.com/2019/10/04/technology/google-facial-recognition-atlanta-homeless.html

Noble, S. U. (2018). *Algorithms of oppression: How search engines reinforce racism.* New York University Press.

O'Neil, C. (2016). *Weapons of math destruction: How big data increases inequality and threatens democracy.* Penguin.

Pariser, E. (2011). *The filter bubble: How the new personalized web is changing what we read and how we think.* Penguin.

Pasquale, F. (2020). *New laws of robotics: Defending human expertise in the age of AI.* Harvard University Press.

Perez Vallejos, E., Dowthwaite, L., Creswich, H., et al. (2021). The impact of algorithmic decision-making processes on young people's well-being. *Health Informatics Journal, 27*(1). https://doi.org/10.1177/1460458220972750

Ratcliff, R. (2019). How a glitch in India's biometric welfare system can be lethal. *The Guardian*, October 16. www.theguardian.com/technology/2019/oct/16/glitch-india-biometric-welfare-system-starvation

Römmele, A., & Gibson, R. (2020). Scientific and subversive: The two faces of the fourth era of political campaigning. *New Media & Society, 22*(4), 595–610. https://doi.org/10.1177/1461444819893979

Ruppert, E., Isin, E., & Bigo, D. (2017). Data politics. *Big Data & Society, 4*(2), 1–7. https://doi.org/10.1177/2053951717717749

Stoilova, M., Nandagiri, R., & Livingstone, S. (2019). Children's understanding of personal data and privacy online—A systematic evidence mapping. *Information, Communication & Society*. https://doi.org/10.1080/1369118X.2019.1657164

Sunstein, C. (2009). *Republic.com 2.0*. Princeton University Press.

Taylor, C. (2004). *Modern social imaginaries*. Duke University Press.

Towers, S., Chen, S., Malik, A., & Ebert, D. (2018). Factors influencing temporal patterns in crime in a large American city: A predictive analytics perspective. *PLoS One, 13*(10). https://doi.org/10.1371/journal.pone.0205151

Vaccari, C., Valeriani, A., Barberá, P., Jost, J. T., Nagler, J., & Tucker, J. A. (2016). Of echo chambers and contrarian clubs: Exposure to political disagreement among German and Italian users of Twitter. *Social Media + Society*. https://doi.org/10.1177/2056305116664221

van der Hof, S. (2017). I agree . . . Or do I? A rights-based analysis of the law on children's consent in the digital world. *Wisconsin International Law Journal, 34*(2), 101–136. https://repository.law.wisc.edu/s/uwlaw/item/77063

van Dijck, J. (2014). Datafication, dataism and dataveillance: Big data between scientific paradigm and ideology. *Surveillance and Society, 12*(2), 197–208.

van Dijck, J., & Poell, T. (2013). Understanding social media logic. *Media and Communication, 1*(1), 2–14. https://doi.org/10.12924/mac2013.01010002

Weber, M. (1978). *Economy and society: An outline of interpretive sociology*. University of California Press.

Willson, M. (2018). Raising the ideal child? Algorithms, quantification and prediction. *Media, Culture & Society*. https://doi.org/10.1177/0163443718798901

Zuboff, S. (2015). Big other: Surveillance capitalism and the prospects of an information civilization. *Journal of Information Technology, 30*(1), 75–89.

INDEX

General Editor: **Steve Jones**

Digital Formations is the best source for critical, well-written books about digital technologies and modern life. Books in the series break new ground by emphasizing multiple methodological and theoretical approaches to deeply probe the formation and reformation of lived experience as it is refracted through digital interaction. Each volume in **Digital Formations** pushes forward our understanding of the intersections, and corresponding implications, between digital technologies and everyday life. The series examines broad issues in realms such as digital culture, electronic commerce, law, politics and governance, gender, the Internet, race, art, health and medicine, and education. The series emphasizes critical studies in the context of emergent and existing digital technologies.

Other titles include:

Felicia Wu Song
  Virtual Communities: Bowling Alone, Online Together

Edited by Sharon Kleinman
  The Culture of Efficiency: Technology in Everyday Life

Edward Lee Lamoureux, Steven L. Baron, & Claire Stewart
  Intellectual Property Law and Interactive Media: Free for a Fee

Edited by Adrienne Russell & Nabil Echchaibi
  International Blogging: Identity, Politics and Networked Publics

Edited by Don Heider
  Living Virtually: Researching New Worlds

Edited by Judith Burnett, Peter Senker & Kathy Walker
  The Myths of Technology: Innovation and Inequality

Edited by Knut Lundby
  Digital Storytelling, Mediatized Stories: Self-representations in New Media

Theresa M. Senft
  Camgirls: Celebrity and Community in the Age of Social Networks

Edited by Chris Paterson & David Domingo
  Making Online News: The Ethnography of New Media Production

To order other books in this series please contact our Customer Service Department:

peterlang@presswarehouse.com (within the U.S.)
orders@peterlang.com (outside the U.S.)

To find out more about the series or browse a full list of titles, please visit our website:

WWW.PETERLANG.COM

www.ingramcontent.com/pod-product-compliance
Lightning Source LLC
Chambersburg PA
CBHW071413290326
41932CB00047B/2822